MAKING THE BEST OF SEMEN

FAMILIES, LAW, AND SOCIETY SERIES

General Editor: Nancy E. Dowd and Robin A. Lenhardt

Masculinities and the Law:
A Multidimensional Approach
Edited by Frank Rudy Cooper
and Ann C. McGinley

Justice for Kids: Keeping Kids Out
of the Juvenile Justice System
Edited by Nancy E. Dowd

The New Kinship: Constructing
Donor-Conceived Families
Naomi Cahn

What Is Parenthood? Contemporary
Debates about the Family
Edited by Linda C. McClain
and Daniel Cere

The Marriage Buyout: The Troubled
Trajectory of U.S. Alimony Law
Cynthia Lee Starnes

A New Juvenile Justice System:
Total Reform for a Broken System
Edited by Nancy E. Dowd

Children, Sexuality, and the Law
Edited by Sacha M. Coupet and
Ellen Marrus

Divorced from Reality: Rethinking
Family Dispute Resolution
Jane C. Murphy and Jana B. Singer

In Our Hands: The Struggle for
U.S. Child Care Policy
Elizabeth Palley and Corey S.
Shdaimah

Ending Zero Tolerance: The Crisis
of Absolute School Discipline
Derek W. Black

The Poverty Industry: The Exploitation
of America's Most Vulnerable Citizens
Daniel L. Hatcher

The Politicization of Safety: Critical
Perspectives on Domestic Violence
Responses
Edited by Jane K. Stoever

Blaming Mothers: American Law
and the Risks to Children's Health
Linda C. Fentiman

The Ecology of Childhood: How
Our Changing World Threatens
Children's Rights
Barbara Bennett Woodhouse

Living Apart Together: Legal
Protections for a New Form of Family
Cynthia Grant Bowman

Social Parenthood in Comparative
Perspective
Edited by Clare Huntington,
Courtney G. Joslin, and Christiane
von Bary

The End of Family Court: How
Abolishing the Court Brings Justice
to Children and Families
Jane M. Spinak

The Architecture of Desire: How
the Law Shapes Interracial Intimacy
and Perpetuates Inequality
Solangel Maldonado

Children's Rights and Children's
Development: An Integrated Approach
Jonathan Todres and Ursula Kilkelly

Making the Best of Semen:
Prospects for Law and Regulation
Anita Bernstein

Making the Best of Semen

Prospects for Law and Regulation

Anita Bernstein

New York University Press

New York

NEW YORK UNIVERSITY PRESS
New York www.nyupress.org
© 2025 by New York University

Library of Congress Cataloging-in-Publication Data

Names: Bernstein, Anita, author.
Title: Making the best of semen : prospects for law and regulation / Anita Bernstein.
Description: New York : New York University Press, 2025. | Series: Families,
   law, and society | Includes bibliographical references and index.
Identifiers: LCCN 2025016511 (print) | LCCN 2025016512 (ebook) | ISBN 9781479832910
   (hardback) | ISBN 9781479832927 (ebook) | ISBN 9781479832934 (ebook other)
Subjects: LCSH: 342.7308/4 23/eng/20250407 | Human reproduction—Law and
   legislation—United States. | Reproductive rights—United States. | Birth control—
   Law and legislation—United States. | Abortion—Law and legislation—United States. |
   Sexually transmitted diseases—United States—Prevention. | Semen.
Classification: LCC KF3760 .B47 2026 (print) | LCC KF3760 (ebook)
LC record available at https://lccn.loc.gov/2025016511
LC ebook record available at https://lccn.loc.gov/2025016512

This book is printed on acid-free paper, and its binding materials are chosen for strength and durability. We strive to use environmentally responsible suppliers and materials to the greatest extent possible in publishing our books.

The manufacturer's authorized representative in the EU for product safety is Mare Nostrum Group B.V., Mauritskade 21D, 1091 GC Amsterdam, The Netherlands. Email: gpsr@mare-nostrum.co.uk.

Manufactured in the United States of America

10 9 8 7 6 5 4 3 2 1

Also available as an ebook

For Mae Kuykendall

CONTENTS

Introduction

Can We Talk About Semen? Probably Not. Consequences Follow.

Countless fluids travel and circulate in the world, but only a small number of liquids that move are absolutely necessary to the existence of every human being.

Water tops the list of these fluids because every human body, no exceptions, must take in water to stay alive. Two other liquids, blood and milk, also make important journeys into bodies, but they affect fewer people: most human beings live and die without ever receiving a blood transfusion, and substitutes for milk are available for nourishment. Water, in this perspective, has only one near peer. Only one other fluid that goes into the human body has an impact on one hundred percent of the population.

Because semen resembles humanity's #1 fluid in a fundamental respect, and because plans and policy can impose some control on where and when semen travels, it deserves attention from a lawyer like me. High time for law, in the sense of regulation, to examine semen. Any substance known to endanger, disrupt, and enhance human lives when it enters from one place to another calls for management from societies and governments.

The big literature about law and policy directed to our other important fluid gives a sense of how much there is to discuss. Water as an object of intervention fills hundreds of whole books and numerous domains: geopolitics, psychology, economics, agriculture, ritual, hygiene, fire control, the production of energy, and the future of the planet. Blood also occupies hundreds of books.

Entire books about semen can also be found, but one has to look for them. The U.S. Library of Congress online catalogue lists more than twice as many books with urine than semen in the title—and urine is a quiescent substance that leaves people alone when it moves. Until now, no book has invited readers to think about claiming authority over this bodily fluid for the public good. Neither, to my knowledge, has any other published writing other than a couple of short pieces that I wrote.

In the pages that follow, I'll argue that the dearth of books about human semen and the wider scarcity of published thought on the subject in any medium are bad conditions that can and should change. But while sticking to that position I will also sympathize with any reader inclined to resist it on the ground that the topic of semen is private. Evasion, indirection, and reticence can exist for good reasons. Even I, a big fan of facts, think that T.M.I. stands for something valuable. I've taken that notion to heart by choosing to say little (but not nothing) in this book about the role of semen in my life, confident that you won't miss what I leave out. Silence can be golden. More broadly, however, silence makes trouble for groups of people.

The unmentionability of semen—an absence I'll try to document in these opening pages aware that it's tough to prove a negative—hurts human beings into whose bodies this substance lands. Semen is risky stuff. It delivers two principal dangers: sexually transmitted infection, which I presume virtually nobody wants, and pregnancy, a burdensome condition even when it's wanted and worse than just burdensome when imposed against the impregnated person's will.

Don't we all know that? you might think. No. *Do we really need a book that says semen is important because it can cause pregnancy and disease?* Yes.

"We all" includes people of many ages and life stages. Some people were literally born yesterday. As we grow, most of us get told how babies are formed and about sexually transmitted diseases, always with semen undercredited as a mover and shaker. Polite speech omits "semen" from discourse or prefers a less informative substitute. "Sperm," "sexual," and "sexually" function as more tolerated usages that sacrifice meaning. Mentionability would ease the current levels of semen-related suffering and distress—including the frustration that results from being deprived of contact with this substance, a problem I take up in chapter 6.

Law, where I come from and what I bring to this book, is all about the mentioning. Legal sources favor accessible, searchable, and durably recorded expressions that report what the law has done and can achieve. Other foundations of knowledge and civilization—theology, literature and storytelling, the visual arts, psychology sometimes—build awe and beauty and wisdom out of what's hidden or unspoken. Chiaroscuro, the art of dark-and-light contrasts in a painting or photograph, puts shadow to positive use. Law rejects concealment, both the unplanned and the artful kind. It insists on accountability to do its work of guiding and constraining the state.

This raison d'être demands clear communication. In a democracy— and in any humane version of shared social life—we the people have a right to know how state actors, meaning people who hold governmental power, can hurt us. We have a related right to receive information about the actions we can choose, or alternatively eschew, to qualify for what the law delivers as a benefit.

In the United States, the country whose laws and customs occupy this book, most actions that the state may pursue to the detriment of individuals can be looked up. Exceptions to the rule of disclosing are rare. Decisions from judges and regulators typically get published. Penal codes spell out acts or elements that constitute crimes. People are entitled to notice and other procedural protections before the state can take something away from them. Commitment to transparency means that the law commits itself to communicating.

In this book I extend this transparency-ideology to semen, working from a belief that the severity of what semen can do to people is a matter of public concern just as serious as the severity of state action. State action sometimes exploits semen's travels to make physical impacts extra forceful. Legal restrictions related to pregnancy and abortion, which receive a hard look in chapter 3, are an example of how law and units of government choose to worsen the preventable consequences of being touched by this fluid. But even when law appears at a distance from semen, clearer and more open communication about it could do a lot of good and should receive public support.

Transparency about semen will call for limits. I like chiaroscuro. I admire the art of the unsaid. I care about privacy not only as a source of legally enforced protection but also in the sense of wishing not to intrude into matters that individuals want to withhold or keep to themselves. Movements of human semen will often fall in this leave-it-alone category. In my view, semen should remain undiscussed and out of public sight to the extent that what it does is none of other people's business.

But because semen has the power to upend our lives—as I'll be repeating in this book, it's the only substance that can both make people and make people sick—it needs the rein of accountability. Any source of significant risk that can be managed should be managed. For accountability to emerge, semen must be mentionable.

Now, what to mention in public discussion? I'll emphasize semen's biggest superpower. This substance is indispensable to the formation of people. Short of their own death, the most transformative and life-changing physical consequence that human beings routinely experience is impregnation, especially impregnation that proceeds to turn them into parents. Absent illness or trauma, approximately half of us can become pregnant through the receipt of semen and the other half can impregnate somebody else by ejaculating into her. I say "can experience" mindful that although the majority of individuals in the United States and around the world form at least one embryo with their bodies and go on to be parents before they die, not everyone does. The share of the American adult population whose bodies have never generated a child is now more than 15% and appears to be growing. But even if we don't make another person with our bodies, we all live under the potential of semen to flip a person into the condition of pregnancy. Three full chapters in this book will report on the magnitude of this impact.

The other great force of semen is more trivial than baby-starting and will receive less space in the pages that follow, but "make people sick" remains an important complement to "make people" among its two superpowers. Make People Sick is important not only because sexually transmitted infection is so common—most people in the United States will acquire such an infection in their lifetimes—but as an illustration of how unmentionability leads to harm. To pursue this point, I'll push back against the phrase I just used, "sexually transmitted."

It's a euphemism that obscures and silences. "Sexually transmitted," though accurate, is also imprecise to a degree that imperils. A large share of so-called sexually transmitted infections enter the body via semen on mucosa and need the boost they get from this fluid to achieve their impact. "Semenally transmitted," if it could catch on as a substitute label, would improve public health discourse with a useful increment of scientific accuracy. In chapter 4, I'll review research on seminal fluid as protector and nourisher of inclusions that generate disease. Semen adds enhancement to pathogens, including but not limited to human immunodeficiency virus (HIV), that these disease sources don't get when located in blood, open sores, cervicovaginal fluids, or saliva.

* * *

Semen ≠ sperm. The substance that occupies this book is more powerful than the gametes in it, especially when we include Make People Sick as a power. Sperm can transmit disease only by one means, the relaying of a genetic defect to a newly formed person. Semen delivers a variety of pathologies.

Away from laboratory science, semen and sperm differ from each other in life-changing ways. Each is invisible in its own sense of that word. The one of the two that we literally can't see is sperm. With effort we can spot a human egg on a blank surface unamplified by magnification, but even the keenest human eye can't see spermatozoa except under a microscope. Semen contains color. Typically it's a pale shade of grayish white but inclusions can turn it slightly green, yellow, pink, orange, even black.[1] Its thin-jelly texture is also perceivable. Semen is more visibly conspicuous than saliva too, not just sperm.

Turn to culture and society, however, and the visibility difference flips. Try an online search for semen using the images button on your screen: if your experience is like mine, you'll draw more "swimmers" than off-white puddles or laboratory vials. You can visualize sperm as you read these words: big round head, swirly curly tail. Spermatozoa can't swim in a still photograph, but even when static there they appear to move.

They don't move much, truth be told. Popular understandings of sperm exaggerate their mobility. They're puny not only in size but in energy: they depend on uterine contractions to reach an ovum. They also need the egg to move. The egg does just that, traveling more than sperm when fertilization occurs. In the public mind, by way of contrast to inside the human body, spermatozoa enjoy ascribed dynamism and an agenda to which we can relate.

Differing from the relatively inert gametes in it, semen takes action. Semen has more physical heft and content than sperm, accomplishes more, disrupts more, and makes itself felt in ways that sperm literally and figuratively cannot imagine. I don't love the cliché "hiding in plain sight," but if that expression ever deserves to be repeated, we have an occasion here. Ostensible swimmers in semen fill a just-so story about journeying. Like travelers in a picaresque novel, spermatozoa make a difference when they reach their destination, we like to suppose. Semen is no metaphor. It's the picaresque real deal; its travels matter. What sperm appear to be doing in pop culture visual imagery, in factual life they either don't do or barely do. Semen does.

Here is another way to grok how semen has more power than sperm, about which I'll say more in chapters 1 and 2. Imagine yourself alive and conscious before the microscope was invented. That's most of the span of human existence. Would you care about the question of where babies come from? I daresay you would. What information is available for you to know the answer at a time when cells, genes, molecules, and other bioparticles too small to be seen are all beyond everyone's ken? You could know that ejaculation by a male-bodied person into the vagina of a postmenarche and premenopausal female-bodied person must happen for conception to occur. That's all. No sperm in the picture. For you, the launcher of babies would be semen.

The scarcity of book titles containing semen and the absence of writing about this fluid that I've noted didn't always exist. It turns out that semen unmentionability is a kind of luxury or privilege like clean running water. Today, should we prefer to think and talk about button-cute wriggly swimmers, we can turn away from the fluid that sustains them. Ignorance about the existence and inclusion of sperm made semen mentionable in pre-microscope writing about the generation of babies. Writers had little other factual matter to consider. So, for example, the prolific doctor-philosopher Galen (born 129 AD, died 216) speculated about babymaking in an essay whose Greek name is Περὶ σπέρματο, which means (and is translated into) both *On Semen* and *On Seed*. Galen could put semen in a book title in a way that I here in the twenty-first century barely can. Semen rather than sperm to the ancients equaled seed—an instigator, starter, or generator too significant to neglect.

Galen's conjecture about babymaking engaged with a precursor by Aristotle called On the Generation of Animals, which gets read today more by feminist critics than biologists. *On the Generation of Animals* in turn built on a foundation laid by earlier Greek philosophers that situated male and female in a larger dichotomy of opposites.[2] Right on one side of the table, left on the other. Male on the right, female on the left.

Straight and crooked. Light and darkness. Good and bad. Writing about where babies come from, Aristotle perceived the generation of animals as another instance of opposites paired together. Male and female bodies each contribute material with gendered complementary characteristics. Material from the female parent is necessary to form the animal, Aristotle wrote, but male-derived material is more interesting because it's more advanced.

"Aristotle," writes the philosopher Emily Thomas, "reasons that semen must be a residue of blood. But blood is runny and red whereas (he notes) semen is 'thick and white.' Why doesn't semen look more like blood? Aristotle's answer is that males 'concoct' blood residue, thickening and purifying it, turning it into semen. Female bodies do not concoct semen, which is why they regularly lose leftover blood—a nifty explanation for menstruation. Why do only males concoct semen? Because concoction requires heat. And, as on the Table of Opposites, Aristotle connects males-hot, females-cold."[3]

There's enough truth in Aristotle's pre-microscope, sperm-ignorant male supremacy to warrant quotation in a book that looks ahead to regulating semen today. Menstrual fluid really is cold in the metaphoric sense of lacking the power to disrupt. In a prior state, a week or two before it emerged, it had a role to play in Make People. Once emitted this fluid is just residue. With diligent effort, I suppose, menstrual fluid can Make People Sick, but it has nowhere near the level of sickness-force found in semen. To the extent that an ancient dichotomy amounts to saying Boys Rule/Girls Drool, we're free to scoff. But when our focus is on preventable danger that human action can mitigate, semen outranks not only sperm but every other fluid produced by the human body.

* * *

Mucosa is another nominee for Can We Talk, Probably Not. The term gets published and mentioned even less often than semen. A medical dictionary defines mucosa as the layer of moist tissue that lines organs of the body open to the environment,[4] receptive to landings. Despite its -a ending that might remind us of plural nouns like data or fora or media, the word is singular in the grammatical sense of that word. As we'll see in ensuing chapters, mucosa is also singular in the dictionary sense of peerless, unmatched, eminent, exceptional, extraordinary.

The word contains potential to join an alternative title for this book, Making the Best of Mucosa. Why attribute power to semen alone, a reader might say, when semen does nothing significant until it touches this membrane on someone else's body? One could blame or credit the receptor that is just as necessary for consequences as semen the initiator.

Not here. In this book, semen wins the unshared recognition I think it deserves. This fluid needs a moist receptive surface to transform lives, but its active role in the transformations it achieves makes it uniquely eligible for the attentions of law, policy, and regulation. Semen travels into other people and can also be steered or encouraged to stay away from its destinations. Mucosa remains where it is, and for the most part its receptive nature also can't change. Because intervention from law and policy can change conduct, movements, actions, and choices better than static conditions like receptivity, the regulatory effort I press for here regards semen as an agent and mucosa as a recipient of semen's initiative.

* * *

The concept of externalities confirms that the right title of this book is Making the Best of Semen rather than Making the Best of Sperm or Making the Best of Semen-Mucosa Contact. Externalities are side effects or byproducts that ensue unintended or underperceived by someone who acts. It's externalities that justify what I will push for in this book. I work from the liberal premise that people ought to be left alone to do what they like as long as the behaviors they choose harm no one. Actions that put other people in danger can call for intervention.

Unpursued consequences involving sperm, as distinct from semen, need less of the controlling or meddling that I favor. Intent and purposeful action—time, money, persistence—are present whenever sperm meets ovum at the tip of a needle in a clinic. That location is the only place where sperm and semen can get separated from each other. Sperm drawn out of semen can harm people in a couple of ways. First, they could be defective at a cellular level. Second, providers entrusted with semen and sperm in fertility clinics can misuse the sperm they extract. I'll note these problems later. They are relatively slight in a book that cares about what happens to people in daily lives filled with risks, benefits, freedoms, and constraints they can negotiate and change.

To speak accurately about semen in human lives, one ought to note more than the gloom and danger of disease and the possibility of starting an unwanted pregnancy. Externalities can be positive. Semen has pleasures, upsides, and satisfactions that need to become better known; information about the substance ought to reach more people.

* * *

"Probably not," my provisional answer to the Can We Talk question, needs a preliminary word. Here I am in these pages repeatedly mentioning what I've called unmentionable. Semen semen semen. Nobody at NYU Press censored this book. Especially in the current century when infinite verbiage on all topics, sex very much included, flows into and from our screens and keyboards, the unmentionability of anything seems quaint to the point of impossible. We moderns think unmentionability may have existed in the past but doubt that it can block any communication now.

Long-gone people, sometimes labeled Victorians, supposedly wouldn't say "legs" because, it was speculated, legs lead to crotches. Victorians substituted "limbs." Even pianos had limbs rather than legs. Tee hee. We're so over it aren't we. When *The Joy of Sex*, the soi-disant Gourmet Guide to Love Making published in the triumphant we're-so-over-it era I recall here, praised sleeping naked as "part of the recovery from puritanism,"[5] it celebrated an enlightenment from which there could be no return. Twelve million copies sold, seven editions: readers must have enjoyed the assurance from Alex Comfort that we now live cured of anxiety and shame that had in a darker time vexed our ancestors.

If confidence about progress on mentionability is unwarranted, as I am suggesting it is, then we still suffer from a problem we ascribe to a benighted past. Any extremely powerful substance escapes its rightful reckoning when strong custom or predilection discourages the mention of it. Something that can wreak preventable harm needs attention. The same goes for anything that can wreak a lot of good. Semen qualifies as both.

The presence of silence or evasion with respect to any subject is inherently hard to demonstrate. Perhaps I imagine this instance of unmentionability. Just because I think it exists doesn't make it real. I could be projecting my own anxiety or psychopathology about semen onto a discourse that is in fact robust enough. As I wondered while writing this book whether I was wrong or right about unmentionability, some evidence for it arrived.

I didn't seek this confirmation: it found me when I tried to read about semen in published research about medicine, laboratory science, and public health. For this exercise in educating myself, I'd started with journal articles that I reached online.

Compared to books and literal papers that a reader can bend, shelve, misplace, and write on with a pen, electronic technology has a lot to commend it. In the aggregate, it contains much more information than any brick-and-mortar building could hold. Keystrokes can search remote collections at any time and from any place. Storage offers room to spare and helps to save up-to-the-minute information like hyperlinked authors' biographies.

Take for example one question I faced when writing about Make People Sick: whether and how semen transmits bacterial disease, in contrast to viruses. Whenever I had a particular bacterium in mind, I eschewed the library shelf and typed its name onto a screen. No need for me to read writings published in 1973 or 1998, dates you'll see referenced here in support of a different point. Searchable PDF is a great format. Being able to reach and hold content in multiple machines is even better.

But I also wanted context, including where experts had situated semen in the summaries or taxonomies they wrote. Solitary scientific papers omit that type of background; I needed it laid out in big, heavy texts. They arrived by interlibrary loan. The first textbooks I chose to borrow were on urology and human sexual reproduction.

I'd open a borrowed book, check the table of contents, turn to the S page in the index to find semen. Blink. Did I miss the entry? I didn't. More often than I expected, the word wasn't there. I repeatedly found no semen in medical library books on subjects I'd chosen as semen-inclusive. Before this turn in my research, I'd assumed that unmentionability of semen was limited to lay discussion. Surely medical doctors and their colleagues writing about health science were different, I thought. They weren't. I started pulling out my phone to photograph the semen-less S pages.

Maybe, I next speculated, the smallish number of my interlibrary loans had provided an unrepresentative sample of semen's mentionability. So I obtained permission to visit the medical school library closest to my home where I could find textbooks and monographs on shelves, no borrowing. A nice little bike ride for which I didn't need to lug anything because all I needed was the phone. After confirming with a friendly librarian there that I could pull any books I wanted from the shelves, I roamed to texts with "reproductive medicine," "public health," "urology" (again), and "infectious diseases" in their titles. I wanted old-fashioned medical reference books in my hands.

Libraries have reasons to house these headed-to-obsolescence volumes that go beyond inertia and sentimentality. The brick-and-mortar library stays informative even when the content on the pages they shelve gets superseded by newer research. Bookshelves contain information in what they unite—the tables of contents, the order of chapters, which books repose together and which at a distance.

Inside the library, I strolled from shelf to shelf until I had covered the floor; I didn't think a systematic search was possible and so I stuck to impressions. "Immunology," "public health," "reproductive medicine," and "microbiology" in book titles caught my eye because they seemed on point, but the only field I searched intentionally in the collection of textbooks was urology. I climbed into covers whenever I thought *Here's a title that seems relevant*. I took about two dozen pictures with the phone camera. Some of the books I found with titles on point had copyright dates of more than 40 years ago; only a minority were published in the last decade.

Because hardbound textbooks that synthesize factual information play a limited role in twenty-first century education in any subject, and medicine in particular, I may need to note that my report on the absence of semen from indexes of books in a medical school library comments not on what medical students are taught but on what instructional materials reveal. Textbooks set out to tell readers what a discipline purports to cover rather than what the latest findings say. They use inclusion and exclusion to draw a boundary around a field or category. I'll add that the books I'm characterizing as dated sources of information about medicine are old but not that old. Alex Comfort celebrated "the recovery from puritanism" in 1972; every book I examined in this library was younger than that.

On to S in the indexes. Every book on the shelves whose title named "public health" had an index, but only one of these indexes contained an entry for semen. I stopped after eight or nine searches, pausing to photograph the text titled *Health Promotion and Disease Prevention in Clinical Practice* because it seemed especially pertinent to semen in this book, being sited in society rather than the laboratory or theory. According to a claim on its back cover, this book is "the only text organized by risk factors—the same as your patients present in clinical settings." That organizational choice duly followed in the table of contents. The middle part of the book, for example, contained chapters that fit the risks-factors design, among them tobacco use, nutrition, exercise, weight management, and injury prevention. Sexually transmitted diseases too. But no semen in the index. Ditto for a book called *Generations at Risk: Reproductive Health and the Environment.*

Away from the public health section of this medical library, a few other indexes showed a little more acceptance of this word. Sometimes semen the noun would be absent in an index but semen as an adjective or seminal would be present. For example, page 488 of *Reproductive Immunology* omits semen in isolation but directs readers to "Semen samples, for antibody testing of bromelin-dissolved cervical mucosa." *Ovulation Induction and In Vitro Fertilization* also has no entry for semen alone while including "semen analysis." "Seminal fluid," "seminal plasma," and even "seminal emission" turned up more frequently than bare semen. One book that includes "seminal plasma, immunosuppression by" in its index, *Immunology of Reproduction*, has no entry for semen but does have one for "shrew."

Other books with on-point sounding titles didn't come close to including semen in their indexes. Not the noun, not the adjective. *Infectious Diseases* is such a hefty single volume that if the word semen were present in its index, page 2,498 would have been its location. The index of another tome that runs more than 2,000 pages, *Encyclopedia of Immunology*, contains one inclusion of our word that seems to cancel itself out: "Semen, immunity to." Immunity to. Semen won't do anything. Nothing to see here.

Viral Molecular Machines, a book whose thesis is that "viruses offer the best opportunities to achieve" understanding of "the mechanics of an organism in atomic detail" and thus can be thought of as machines, omits "semen" from its index. (We'll see in chapter 4 that semen provides viruses with an extraordinarily supportive home.) Semen-free medical textbooks, as far as their indexes report, also include *Fundamental Immunology, In Vitro Fertilization and Embryo Transfer, Introductory Immunobiology, Retroviruses, Microenvironmental Aspects of Immunity,* and *Advances in Experimental Medicine and Biology.*

Let's go to the urology and male reproductive anatomy corner of the library. No semen in the index for tomes called *Textbook of Erective Dysfunction*, *Pathology of the Testis*, or *The Endocrine Function of the Human Testis*. In *Hormonal Regulation of Spermatogenesis*, I found no semen but one of those "seminal vesicle" entries. Turning to the page referenced, I saw a chart about testis tissue in adult male rats that contained nothing on point. The phrase "seminal vesicle" was absent and so too was any other reference to semen.

Continuing a review of substances made by the human body that can contain and spread viruses, I encountered page 614 of *Principles of Virology: Molecular Biology, Pathogenesis, and Control*. It starts with Saliva, which gets an eight-line paragraph; moves on to Feces, whose paragraph is more than twice as long; next covers Blood, in a paragraph bigger than the one for Saliva and smaller than the Feces paragraph that immediately precedes it. Where's semen? Directly below, nestled between Urine, on the one hand, and Milk and Skin Lesions, on the other, and occupying just five lines.

Principles of Virology's brief discussion of four substances allots to the first of them twice as many words as semen, apparently indifferent to the relative difficulty of delivering or acquiring a virus through contact with urine. We learn that "humans may be infected by exposure to dust that contains dried urine of infected rodents." They may indeed, but a rather larger number of humans routinely become infected by exposure to the substance of which this text seems barely aware. After three more sentences—more space than all of semen will soon be given below— *Principles of Virology* allows as how viruria, the term for viruses in urine, is actually "not important for transmission of infection."

In short, my sampling of reference texts on the shelves of a medical school library demonstrated, at least to me, that semen isn't fully mentionable even in a setting where one would expect forthright communication on matters of biology.

For what it may be worth, I'm not the only writer to notice evasion and imprecision in medical references that advert to semen. In 2014, for example, the Centers for Disease Control (CDC) agreed to stop calling sexual intercourse without a condom "unprotected sex."[6] What persuaded the CDC to switch to "condomless sex" and more precision about sources of safety was a letter from activists who united under the rubric HIV Prevention Justice Alliance. The writers noted the existence of other protections including preexposure prophylaxis, a near-miracle drug about which I'll have more to say in chapter 7; antiretroviral therapy, which lowers the presence of HIV in semen and blood to undetectable and almost untransmittable levels; and modifications to sexual practices that reduce the odds of HIV transmission. So understood, "unprotected" misleads more than it communicates.

Commentary published in the journal *Sexually Transmitted Diseases* has raised a similar challenge to public health jargon familiar from scientific literature about activities that deliver semen from one person to another—"unsafe sex," "risky sex," "risky sexual behavior," "high-risk sexual behavior," and "sexual risk behavior"—as "scientifically imprecise."[7] Labeling sexual acts risky or high-risk without saying more about the exact acts and the risks they present, the authors argue, dodges and conflates separate questions that for the sake of enhanced public health demand more careful diction.

* * *

Generative artificial intelligence, in its early days of being given away for free, also ended up supporting my claim about semen mentionability without my looking for support there. The first platform to reach casual users, a group of consumers in which I include myself, was ChatGPT. I gave free ChatGPT a whirl seeking semen information.

I broached my conversation with the bot by asking it a question:

> *What role does semen play in the transmittal of bacterial disease, in contrast to viruses?*

My desktop computer responded by doling out an updated helping of the coyness and demure evasion I'd found in the medical school library. It started by telling me something I already knew:

> When it comes to the transmission of bacterial diseases, semen can potentially serve as a medium for certain bacterial pathogens.

That is true, and props to ChatGPT for speaking the word I'd started to think wasn't too speakable. But when I repeated my expression of interest in bacteria that semen can contain, ChatGPT had had enough. The response to my follow-up prompt said I needed to think less about semen and more about politer material:

> It's important to note that the transmission of any infection, bacterial or viral, is not solely dependent on semen. Other factors, such as mucosal contact, the presence of open sores or lesions, and the overall health and immune status of individuals, also play crucial roles in transmission. Practicing safe sex, using barrier methods consistently and correctly, and getting regular screenings and tests can help reduce the risk of sexually transmitted infections. If you have specific concerns or questions about a particular infection or disease, consulting with a healthcare professional is recommended for personalized advice and guidance.

And so, having brought up semen, I soon received a change of subject. Let's talk instead about "other factors," said the machine, evading my reference to bacteria. I got dinned in the importance of "safe sex," the bot-answerer presuming that my question came from a desire for suggestions about what to do with my torso rather than a disinterested search for information. Talk to ChatGPT about semen and you must be thinking about your own flawed and vulnerable body. You must, or should, consider what you didn't broach. What you neglected to mention includes the mistakes you're likely to make in dealing with other people; your "overall health and immune status" as an individual, a mark of how okay or not you are; the never-wrong choice of "consulting with a healthcare professional," ditto "getting regular screenings and tests," same for "using barrier methods consistently and correctly." I wasn't seeking sex-lifestyle advice or guidance on how to become healthier but a point of anatomical fact about bacteria and viruses. The answer I received sounded like Don't Ask Don't Tell.

Prudishness too. ChatGPT thought my intentions were probably pervy. Can't be too careful:

> *Can you help me find popular writing about semen?*

> Certainly! When it comes to popular writing about semen, there are various topics and perspectives you might be interested in exploring. However, it's

important to note that explicit or adult content is not appropriate for this platform. So, if you're looking for more general information or discussions about semen in a scientific or educational context, I'd be happy to help. If you have a specific aspect or question in mind, please let me know, and I'll do my best to assist you.

I'm interested in scientific, medical information.

I understand. When it comes to scientific and medical information about semen, there are several key aspects you might find interesting. Here are some general topics and resources to explore:

The year was 2023, and I couldn't type the name of a bodily fluid without having to defend myself.

Machine learning behind this generative artificial intelligence obviously had hoovered up a lot more about "safe sex" than factual information about semen as a substance. Let's give ChatGPT the benefit of the doubt and do what it says: I'll heed for a moment its unsolicited advice. "Safe sex" adverts to danger and admonishes listeners to be careful. It seems to unite prudence and pleasure. That's fine: but consider how useless the admonition is to a person who wants guidance about how to obey the ChatGPT order. Which sexual acts are relatively unlikely to harm participants? What conditions or characteristics of these acts furnish the safety part along with sexual pleasure? How do we know?

For someone with a male body or an interest in touching one intimately, useful answers to these questions will include semen. Proceeding with care calls for attention to the substance whenever it will be present. The whimsical-sounding phrase "semen sex," which doesn't really exist, would have provided more information for people who ejaculate or who are getting close to ejaculators than the Safe Sex dead end.

In coining neologisms like "semen sex" and "semenally transmitted" to help mention what doesn't get mentioned, I foreground safety even though I've removed "safe" and "safer" from the phrases. Both of my neologisms refer to semen as a source of transmitted infection. Protection from the transmittable diseases that semen can carry means shelter from the costs, burdens, and pain that landings of semen on intimate mucosa can cause. The safety I seek to enlarge also protects people at a physical distance from that landing, such as babies born to parents with semenally transmitted illness and parents who wish their teenage children well. Not mentioning semen even when semen is at the center of what a speaker or writer seeks to address is more than an omission: it actively misleads and endangers vulnerable human beings.

My new coinages encourage speakers and listeners to start improving mentionability by finding semen implicitly present in familiar phrases that exclude this word. Reading about semen in public discourse gave me a chance to engage in this exercise while I wrote this book. Dozens of communications that government websites publish to inform lay readers about semen-related health crossed my path. "Sex," "sexual," and "sexually" pervade these communications. Gradually, without a conscious plan, I started to superimpose variations on semen over these words. I'd ask myself as I read if the statement would become more accurate if I replaced sex/sexual/sexually with semen/seminal/seminally. Accuracy of the statements did indeed improve.

"Safe sex" and its younger, more guarded sibling "safer sex" express a warning that is in effect a reference to semen. The threat to safety that less-than-safe sex imposes occurs when semen touches mucosa directly. "Safe semen" and "safer semen" do a better job of communicating that warning than prevailing public health jargon. They articulate in just two words the longer-winded "safe from the danger of semen by keeping semen away from the surfaces on which semen can cause pregnancy or illness if it lands."

Eschewing or blocking semen, in other words, provides safety from semen's two superpowers. When a possessor of vaginal and cervical mucosa doesn't want to become pregnant, she needs to avoid or block semen around those surfaces. When this separation succeeds, she'll be safe from semen's Make People impact. As for Make People Sick, semen deserves more blame and credit than it receives. It's a far stronger disease-deliverer than other fluids transferred in sexual contact. Uniting multiple shared substances along with even more varied behaviors under the umbrella of "sex," "sexual," or "sexually" hides the force of semen.

The word sperm contributes to the same obscuring. Consider the phrases "sperm donor" and "sperm bank." This diction steers people who seek to become parents via assisted reproduction to turn away from what they can see and touch and smell and also (when they are ejaculators) emit into a cup or (when they are recipients of semen that others ejaculate) lift out of a package, moving instead toward elite expertise that expects deference. We know that sperm are present in our lives because trustworthy authority says so. Semen becomes present for us through our sensory experience, a more direct source of knowledge. Substituting "semen bank" for sperm bank and "semen donor" for sperm donor would encourage people to remember human bodies and consider the evidence of their senses, not just abstraction and external authority, when they think about generating a child.

* * *

Keeping semen unmentionable hurts people on an unequal basis. Whenever the substance is emitted from someone else and enters your body, you're at greater risk of suffering harm than that Someone Else, the ejaculator, your partner. He's male. You too might be male—I'll be paying attention to same-sex semen contacts in this book—but most people who receive ejaculate on their mucosa in sexual acts are female. This generalization means that more awareness of, and accountability for, the risks of semen would benefit a group of people who are mostly girls and women. Boys and men at the receiving end of semen would also gain from less ignorance and more reckoning about the substance, but the benefits for them are more diffuse and less urgent.

To illustrate the asymmetry and inequality that result from unmentionability, I'll turn now to a notorious trial held in 2024. Unmentionability in it wasn't quite of semen, but a semen-adjacent source of risk. At this trial, E. Jean Carroll, plaintiff, pursued money damages from Donald J. Trump, defendant.

This mentionability story requires a trip into New York law. The jury in Carroll v. Trump ruled that Trump had injured Carroll in an encounter that took place in the mid-1990s, almost two decades before the 2024 trial. Because Carroll connected her injury to a sexual assault that she attributed to this defendant, her claim qualified for an exception to the statute of limitations written by the New York legislature to benefit individuals with a particular set of old claims. Carroll wasn't prosecuting Trump for the crime of sexual assault: she couldn't; she's not the government. Instead she was a tort plaintiff. The tort Carroll alleged was battery, the intentional infliction of harmful bodily contact.

Battery has a short statute of limitations. Unless an exception applies, New York plaintiffs have to file their claim in court within a year after the conduct that touched their bodies. Most states use an equally brief limitation period. Only a short time to file applies to the majority of claims for battery that courts will hear—for punches in the nose, gunshot wounds that follow an intentional shooting, nonsexual domestic violence.

Sexual attacks qualify for a limited legislatively furnished exception to the short life of battery as a cause of action. This category stayed alive. But to proceed under this exception to the statute of limitations, these claims had to align with what state law defines as sexual offenses. Even though Carroll, as a private citizen, couldn't bring a criminal prosecution, her tort claim for battery was controlled by New York's criminal law.

Carroll had reportedly saved the dress she'd worn on the day Trump attacked her and it contained evidence of a man's DNA, but I'm bringing up Carroll v. Trump as a source of guidance about the mentionability problem applied to another source of disruption. The Adult Survivors Act as codified by the New York legislature tells plaintiffs that to qualify for the statute of limitations exception, their claim must be for actions that constitute sexual offenses as defined by Article 130 of the New York Penal Code. At trial, Carroll had to testify about behavior by Trump that would support convicting him of these crimes. The jury accepted most but not all of her claims.

Figure 1.1 shows their verdict form, whose bottom line awarded Carroll two million dollars in damages.

To think about mentionability, let's turn to the two crimes that limited what Carroll could sue Trump for. Under New York law on the books at the time, "sexual intercourse"—I'm quoting § 130.25 and § 130.35 of the statute, both of them crimes that define rape—is necessary for a sexual assault to constitute rape. The crime of rape is severe, subject to heavy punishment. The less severe crime of sexual abuse doesn't require "sexual intercourse," only "sexual contact." Sexual contact by forcible compulsion is a felony. Sexual contact without consent is a misdemeanor. In other words, being entitled to receive damages for the harm of rape requires proof of sexual intercourse—which can include testimony about it—while being entitled to receive damages for sexual abuse doesn't.

Case 1:22-cv-10016-LAK Document 174 Filed 05/09/23 Page 1 of 4

UNITED STATES DISTRICT COURT
SOUTHERN DISTRICT OF NEW YORK
- x
E. JEAN CARROLL,

               Plaintiff,

     -against-

DONALD J. TRUMP,

               Defendant.
- x

USDC SDNY
DOCUMENT
ELECTRONICALLY FILED
DOC #:
DATE FILED: 5/9/23

22-cv-10016 (LAK)

VERDICT FORM

Battery

Did Ms. Carroll prove, by a preponderance of the evidence, that

   1.   Mr. Trump raped Ms. Carroll?

         YES _____   NO ✓

         [If you answered "Yes," skip to Question 4. If you answered "No," continue to Question 2.]

   2.   Mr. Trump sexually abused Ms. Carroll?

         YES ✓   NO _____

         [If you answered "Yes," skip to Question 4. If you answered "No," continue to Question 3.]

   3.   Mr. Trump forcibly touched Ms. Carroll?

         YES _____   NO _____

         [If you answered "Yes," continue to Question 4. If you answered "No," skip to Question 6.]

   4.   Ms. Carroll was injured as a result of Mr. Trump's conduct?

         YES ✓   NO _____

         If "Yes," insert a dollar amount that would fairly and adequately compensate her for that injury or those injuries.

         $ 2,000,000 — (2 million)

Figure 1.1

Now we need to know what constitutes sexual intercourse. The statute in its Definition of Terms in effect at the time announced unhelpfully that "'sexual intercourse' has its ordinary meaning and occurs upon any penetration, however slight."[8] Pattern instructions published for judges to use as explainers to guide jurors provide more information.

The instruction used at the time of Carroll v. Trump told judges to tell the jury that sexual intercourse "means any penetration, however slight, of the penis into the vaginal opening. In other words, any penetration of the penis into the vaginal opening, regardless of the distance of penetration, constitutes an act of sexual intercourse."[9]

This instruction tells the jury that to answer Yes to the question "Did Ms. Carroll prove, by a preponderance of the evidence, that Mr. Trump raped Ms. Carroll?" they as jurors would have to agree that Carroll proved Trump had penetrated her vagina with a penis. The jury rejected that claim about rape. After the verdict, Carroll talked to a New York Times reporter and took responsibility for the jury's No answer to the rape question:

> Ms. Carroll, in the interview, blamed herself for their decision to find Mr. Trump liable for sexually abusing her but not for rape.
>
> "I didn't make myself clear when I was testifying," Ms. Carroll said.
>
> Under New York law, according to Ms. Carroll's lawyer, Ms. Kaplan, penetration by the penis must occur for there to be a rape. Ms. Carroll had testified that after Mr. Trump led her into the Bergdorf's lingerie department and into a dressing room, he shoved her against a wall and inserted his fingers and then his penis into her vagina.
>
> "I couldn't see anything that was happening," Ms. Carroll had told the jury. "But I could certainly feel it. I could certainly feel that pain in the finger jamming up."
>
> In the interview Thursday, Ms. Carroll noted that she had twice been married, and she said, "I know what a penis feels like, and he did insert his penis."

Here Carroll said that she was to blame for what she omitted from her testimony. I'll shift blame onto unmentionability—not of semen this time but of the instrument that delivers semen to the interior of another person. Crossing the mentionability line risks provoking listeners. I personally think that the upsides of speaking about male reproductive anatomy can exceed downsides for the speaker, as I suppose you can tell from the existence of this book, but Carroll had more to lose than I do. Unmentionability resulted in two contrasting renditions of what Carroll said.

Take the latter rendition first. After a trial at which she prevailed on some but not all of her battery claims, talking to a reporter, Carroll prefaced "I know what a penis feels like, and he did insert his penis" by noting "she had twice been married." This autobiographical aside added a soupçon of respectability to Carroll's confrontation. *I have been penetrated repeatedly by this instrument and you can't say I was a slut when that penetration happened. I know the unique way it feels from the time that I spent as a man's wife.*

During the first rendition at trial, testifying about the battery that Trump committed, Carroll left out "I know what a penis feels like, and he did insert his penis" from what she told the jury. The only instrument of penetration she named there was Trump's "finger jamming up." Jurors never heard Carroll say under oath that Trump's penis did the same thing, testimony that New York law obliged her to supply as support for rape redress. Redress through tort liability rather than criminal prosecution added the demand of not alienating jurors by the diction she chose. For E. Jean Carroll—a person possessed of both the utmost courage and a powerful professional command of words, also a client represented by an extraordinarily effective lawyer—testimony as precise as what she needed must have seemed at best at the edge of mentionability. It could have forfeited her entire case if jurors took offense. Safer to soften the account by blurring it.

Similar to how public discourse chatters copiously about sex while keeping silent about semen, Carroll could and did offer testimony that she had experienced "sexual abuse," the lesser wrong that required her to describe contact with her genitals perpetrated by Trump without her consent. "Sexual" mentionable, "penis" not. The jury agreed that Trump had violated the sexual abuse provision in the statute, which criminalized "any touching of the sexual or other intimate parts of a person for the purpose of gratifying the sexual desire of either party." Carroll proceeded aware that mentionability norms permitted her to speak in a high-stakes setting about some things—her own "intimate parts," for example, and a rapist's finger—but not others, like the rapist's penis.

* * *

Lifting the mentionability veil that now shrouds semen would generate and distribute lifesaving and life-enhancing information. Steps that this book takes down that road are so preliminary that I can scarcely know what speakers and writers would say about this substance if semen became mentionable. I've shown you the omission of semen from textbooks across medical fields where you'd expect semen to be examined, including urology and immunology and reproductive health and infectious disease. That sliver of the large missing-in-action landscape could stand in for a larger whole. When even pertinent medical texts implicitly deny or minify this substance, we can infer that other fields of culture and knowledge have also been stunted by semen unmentionability. And so I hope that this book about semen in law and regulation will invite people with expertise in fields other than law to write other full-length treatments of this fluid.

Other lawyers too, as there's more to say than what I say here about the possibilities of applying regulation to semen. Regulation pursues safety as a deliverer of health, wealth, and happiness. Wealthy nation-states, like the one in which I write, take a broad view of this pursuit, enlisting the government to constrain dangerous conduct and encourage socially valuable choices. A substance with the two superpower traits I've noted, Make People and Make People Sick, has enough significance to warrant more attention from the law than what I broach in these pages.

Semen is the main character of this book. I invite you to think of it as a protagonist. Like other protagonists you've met in other books, semen has journeys to take. As a substance designed to migrate rather than remain in place, it makes impacts on people when it roams. The path of improving these impacts starts with recognizing semen's travels.

PART I

Reasons to Take Action

1

Anywhere It Wants to Go

Semen prerogative makes me think of what an acquaintance of mine came up with as her answer to "What do you do?," the standby conversation starter she thought needed a new response after she retired. What she used to say, before collecting her pension: "I'm a teacher." Her follow-up, when needed: "High school. English. Junior and senior years."

Now? "Anything I want."

Semen enjoys comparable room to roam. "Anywhere It Wants to Go" up at the top of this page refers to a view—one that has roots in religion and endures in the current secular American century—that semen must not be blocked from the destination it seeks. This perspective on semen attributes initiative to the fluid, a sense of self-propelled adventure distinct from the mechanics of sperm-on-egg insemination. Semen, in this personified understanding, wants the opportunity to make a difference. Or so I shall argue.

Because holders of political and legal power in the United States accept a consensus that semen's agenda comes from Nature and thus stands outside management by human intervention, state actors can honor this ascribed desire without overt reliance on any dogma. Leaving a semen-generated impact wherever it falls, unreversed and unregulated, seems correct in a neutral way. Understood as an application of this naturalism, one semen-meets-religion case decided in 2024—LePage v. Center for Reproductive Medicine, P.C., in which the Alabama Supreme Court ascribed personhood to embryos stored in a fertility clinic—differs from most instances of Anywhere It Wants to Go as an approach to semen in American law: one of its judge-authors made explicit rather than tacit reference to the authority of religion. Calling cryogenically preserved material on a shelf "unborn children," "extrauterine children," and "embryonic children," the diction choice in the majority opinion, stopped short of connecting those ostensible children to a divine creator.

A separate opinion in this case did make that connection. Chief Justice Tom Parker gathered authorities to support his view about mandatory deference to what semen starts, starting with quotations from the Old Testament books of Genesis, Exodus, and Jeremiah and moving to theological exegeses. It turned out that the sixteenth-century Protestant reformer John Calvin, the seventeenth-century Dutch scholar Petrus Van Mastricht, the twentieth-century American clergyman John Sutherland Bonnell, the jurist-theologian Thomas Aquinas (whose magnum opus that Parker cited, Summa Theologica, attributed original sin to a chain of semen traceable to Adam as the first ejaculator), and a source identified as "Almighty God" all agreed with Justice Parker that semen has authority to change human bodies and lives when emitted.[1] Some hostility greeted this disquisition: American judges who reason that way in print stick out. The power of Anywhere It Wants to Go that semen enjoys is for the most part unspoken.

* * *

Justice Parker quoted Genesis twice: verse 17 of Chapter 1, then verse 6 of Chapter 9. Readers who stay with this biblical book will find a character named Onan in Chapter 38. I met Onan decades ago, schooled as I was in Genesis by a community that took this text seriously.

That book occupies a prestige spot in the community's liturgical season, when synagogues read early chapters of Genesis aloud during the High Holy Days. As a girl I had to go to services on Saturday mornings and sit in a balcony assigned to daughters and sisters and wives. Due to femaleness, we balcony-sitters were forbidden to speak before the congregation or enter the main sanctuary. Overhearing my father spend almost a full year drilling my brother in a Torah portion to be recited from the podium of the sanctuary taught me both the text and the prescribed singsong intonation of Hebrew-language Genesis verses, some of which I can still chant.

Genesis introduces the Bible's first patriarch, Abraham né Abram, divinely chosen in Chapter 12 to launch what God promises him will be a great nation. The chapters of Genesis tell a plan for nationhood that rests on the continuing creation of male heirs to follow Abraham, one generation of "begats" after another. My schoolmates and I took quizzes about the sons, grandsons, and great-grandsons of this founder but learned little about the cohort of Abraham's great-great-grandsons that included Onan. The tale of Onan falls in my brother's assigned-by-birth bar mitzvah share of Genesis.

Onan turns up in the last third of the book. He is notorious today for having interrupted an act of sexual intercourse he'd commenced with his sister-in-law, a recently widowed woman named Tamar. Tamar became widowed when God slew Onan's older brother, one Er, for the offense of being "wicked in the sight of the Lord." Whoever wrote Genesis reveals nothing else about Er except that his death stirred into action Judah, one of the book's better-known patriarchs. Judah was the great-grandson of Abraham, father of Er and Onan, father-in-law of Tamar. He ordered Onan to put *zera*—a Hebrew word for semen that also means both "seed" and "heir"—into Tamar in memory of Er. Onan apparently agreed to the order but then defied Judah by withdrawing deliberately before he ejaculated, scattering his *zera* on the ground.

Bible scholars speculate that Onan chose to withhold semen from Tamar because he believed that impregnating her would jeopardize his prospects of inheriting from Judah. The Genesis text, however, doesn't say that Onan had money or property on his mind. We're told only that when "he went in onto his brother's wife," Onan spilled his *zera* at a distance from her vagina. As divine punishment for asserting his will over his emission of semen, Onan became the next son of Judah to be slain.

This man is a minor player in Genesis in that his name appears in only two verses (Tamar gets more space) and we never hear about him again, but he's also a curiously big deal. Few individuals known to religious history have the "-ism" suffix after their names and the other ones I can think of—Zoroaster, Buddha, Wahhab, papa Judah—are credited with achievements more impressive than pulling out before ejaculating. Onanism is a pejorative English word that has migrated to other languages. Mostly to mean masturbation, even though what the Genesis story recounts is unambiguously not masturbation but coitus interruptus. Dictionaries recognize both acts as definitions of onanism. Using the Onan misadventure to condemn coitus interruptus and male masturbation expresses a larger view that semen is designed to make an impact through travel, changing an environment when it arrives.

This belief functions to explain the otherwise puzzling distinction announced in Humanae Vitae, an encyclical proclaimed in 1968 by Pope

Paul VI that retains theological authority in the Roman Catholic Church today, between (forbidden) "artificial" contraception and "natural" behaviors whose contraceptive effects are acceptable. Coitus interruptus, the deed done by Onan in Genesis 38, is artificial, opines Humanae Vitae. Artificiality puts contraceptive action into the forbidden category. Contraceptive technologies that human beings manufacture—condoms, diaphragms, hormones as supplied in the birth control pill or time-delayed implantation below the skin—are to the Church also artificial and thus forbidden. Same for sterilization surgery and interventions that kill an embryo or fetus. Less direct interference with semen in the form of rhythm-method abstinence for the sake of contraception, what Humanae Vitae calls "recourse to infertile periods," is not forbidden, however. Ditto abstinence in general. Humanae Vitae decrees no obligation to engage in sexual intercourse.

The only way to distinguish artificial-and-forbidden from natural-and-permitted contraceptive methods is to focus on a purpose for this substance that outranks what individuals aspire to accomplish or avoid. On any other artificial/natural axis, Onan-style withdrawal before ejaculation is just as natural as keeping the day of the month in mind when one wishes to avoid generating a pregnancy. Maybe more so. Coitus interruptus works without drugs or machinery or surgery, the other objects of condemnation in Humanae Vitae. "Recourse to infertile periods" is inexpensive but does require at least a calendar and, as practiced today, typically also uses a thermometer and written record; coitus interruptus has zero financial cost. Withdrawal prior to ejaculation seems "natural" in the sense of reminiscent of nature in that it can occur unpredictably or on a whim. The answer to the question of what is "artificial," the Church's shorthand for theologically prohibited, about coitus interruptus as birth control must be that it acts directly to obstruct a journey that could create insemination if its trip weren't impeded by purposeful and direct human action. As one Christian teaching puts this point, "the seed ought not be wasted or scattered thoughtlessly nor sown in a way it cannot grow."[2] To render this fluid inert by steering it away from a vagina hampers its prerogative, its will to power.

A modern secular counterpart of the order not to steer semen away from a vagina "in a way it cannot grow" persists in conventional disparagement of coitus interruptus as birth control. Descriptions of this contraceptive method are more tolerant today than they've been, I grant. Whereas I distinctly remember being warned as a teen that this practice was folly and nothing more, younger generations get told that for heterosexual couples who want to avoid pregnancy, pulling out is better than doing nothing. "But let's be real for a minute," says one of my first-page search engine hits. "What if he's had a few drinks? Or you're both just totally lost in the moment? Or what if he miscalculates his, uh, excitement?"

Misgivings like these hold coitus interruptus to an exceptionally high standard given how mainstream advice recommends other approaches to birth control without equally justifiable what-ifs about their lack of perfection or tut-tut references to male incontinence. Consider for example an infographic overview of birth control published by the progressive and very secular American College of Obstetricians and Gynecologists.[3] The graphic divides what it assesses into tiers. Three birth control methods—implants, IUDs, and sterilization—rank uppermost, that is to say best: each of them is associated with less than one pregnancy per hundred women in a year. Then come the middling methods: injection, patch, pill, vaginal ring, and diaphragm. On the lowest tier on the chart, blamed for (or credited with) 18 or more pregnancies per hundred women in a year, repose the male condom, the female condom, the cervical cap, the sponge, spermicide, and "fertility awareness-based methods," the approach tolerated by Humanae Vitae. The chart in one version displays images of the methods. Another version of the chart uses words.

Withdrawal is literally off the charts, lower than the bottom. The ACOG ranks this method next to lactational amenorrhea, which is not so much birth control as hoping for temporary infertility while the female partner is breastfeeding. Look a bit closer at the numbers, however, and withdrawal scores a respectable 22: it's more effective than everything else in the lowest tier except condoms (18 pregnancies per woman per year for the male kind, 21 for the female) and, to repeat, this official medical hierarchy deems withdrawal worse than the lowest tier. With vaginal intercourse regarded as a fixed fact of nature that no one can stop, pulling out before ejaculation functions as pretty okay birth control. But coitus interruptus is also the birth control method that most overtly defies Anywhere It Wants to Go. Disapproval of this defiance, I speculate, helps to explain the opprobrium that none of the other options receives.

Yielding to wishes ascribed to this substance continues beyond Humanae Vitae, official Christianity, and modern dogma on birth control in not-entirely-gone norms and rules against masturbation that focus on the male kind. People who don't ejaculate are understood as powerless to divert semen and therefore need no orders to desist from interference. Monty Python never recorded a female counterpart to their masturbation-scold satire, "Every Sperm is Sacred," about which I'll have more to say later:

> I'm a Roman Catholic,
> And have been since before I was born,
> And the one thing they say about Catholics is
> They'll take you as soon as you're warm.

> You don't have to be a six-footer
> You don't have to have a great brain
> You don't have to have any clothes on
> You're a Catholic the moment Dad came.

> Because
> Every sperm is sacred
> Every sperm is great
> If a sperm is wasted,
> God gets quite irate.

The Orthodox Judaism of my youth sang from a different and at the same time similar lyric sheet. In eleventh grade, after being schooled for more than a decade to care about particular descendants of Abraham, I was enrolled in a girls-only class called Taharat HaMishpacha, or Purity of the Family, set up to teach religious precepts about sex and birth control. Rules covered there seemed to think that semen has a raison d'être not found in any female anatomical structure, function, or fluid. A microbiologist and expositor of Jewish law once explained that men were forbidden to masturbate "because of the biblical injunction against the wasting of seed, but women may do so as a therapeutic technique since there was no written prohibition."[4] Male peers of mine were duly instructed. I never received any religious direction on point, therapeutic or otherwise. (Not for want of opportunity: bossmen at my yeshiva routinely told us girls what we were forbidden to do, and the absence of a "written prohibition" never stopped them from prohibiting.)

Birth control dogma got spelled out more explicitly. My role ahead as a Jewish wife would combine obligations and options, I learned. I was expected to produce children but also had permission to impede the journey and presumed agenda of semen. That permission extended only to me and not my husband; any actions he and I would agree on to ward off pregnancy had to confine themselves to the functions of my body, staying away from his.

Catholic doctrine tells wives to respect a divide that follows the same disinclination to square off against this substance. A wife must eschew condoms and other mechanical barriers but may without sin expect her husband to back away during a couple of days in the middle of her menstrual cycle. This option makes the two religions look different on the surface. Humanae Vitae does not forbid sex during menstruation; Jewish law, while permitting the mechanical obstacles to insemination that Catholic doctrine forbids, discourages the rhythm method of contraception by prohibiting sexual contact (all of it, not just intercourse) between a wife and husband while the wife is menstruating and for seven "clean days" after her period ends. Combining the Taharat HaMishpacha prohibition with the rhythm method tolerated in Humanae Vitae would cut off sexual contact during almost half of every month, a burdensome constraint.

Although the two theologies give conflicting orders about sex to a couple comprised of one partner who ejaculates and one who menstruates, they agree on a key point: semen may be thwarted but thwarters must exercise the restraint of tactful indirection. Negate the impact of this substance but don't say that's your goal. Purport to be doing something else. Onan drew the death penalty for his open—I want to say splashy—refusal to defer to semen.

* * *

Secular counterparts to Catholic natural law and the tale of Onan endure today in the passivity of legal responses to aggressive and dangerous semen-deployments. The law either shrugs off these impacts, as if to say nothing can be done, or proceeds gently and tentatively in expressing disapproval, implying it's important to respect the direction of this substance. Here are three ways for semen to get delivered to an unwilling recipient that American law enables by failing to prohibit. From the force of legal punishments and discouragements aimed at other behaviors people choose, we know that the law is extending exceptional indulgence to semen.

My first example of semen-indulgence lives in the ranking of sexual assault into tiers. Within American penal codes, "aggravated" as a term of art says that some variations on a codified crime deserve extra blame. Behaviors that qualify for this modifier of sexual assault—and from there make the offender eligible for heavier punishment—vary from state to state but the lists resemble one another. Using a deadly weapon while committing the attack, causing severe physical injury or disfigurement separate from the sexual contact, combining sexual assault with another felony, and aggression against a young member of one's family are among the actions that make sexual assault "aggravated" in American jurisdictions.

The possibility of labeling variations on criminal acts aggravated could have steered legislators to acknowledge that ejaculation into one's victim adds extra danger to rape. Depositing semen on the mucosa of another person can cause, and has caused, quite a range of harms. This journey frequently accompanies violent unwanted intimate penetration, but it doesn't have to: William Kennedy Smith, for example, on trial for sexual assault many decades ago in 1991, told a Florida jury that he "did not climax the second time. I did not have an orgasm, if that's helpful."[5] Because sexual assault—vaginal rape included—can occur without movement of semen onto a mucosal surface, criminal prohibitions could make an issue of semen vel non and recognize that sexual aggression without it is in effect relatively benign.

Yet the closest American law comes to condemning rape-with-semen as extra bad is in crimes on the books in several states that punish the intentional exposure of another person to HIV or enlarge the penalty for sexual assault when it's committed by an HIV-positive assailant. HIV is, of course, far from the only danger that semen can deliver. Furthermore, numerous HIV-exposure crimes around the country are written without any mention of semen or ejaculation. Prosecutors use these crimes to punish semen-free acts like biting. While insisting that certain conditions and behaviors make sexual assaults extra hazardous to victims, in short, the law has refused to include in this roster penetrations that endanger victims by injecting them with semen.

For another example of semen encouraged to roam where it pleases, consider the nonpunishment of stealthily tampering with or removing a condom during intercourse. By the time a coparticipant has become aware that the condom was removed or damaged on purpose, the person who engaged in this act has put semen into her body against her will. Her body, *her* will: a man can do it to a man, but in both complaints and studies, female victims harmed by male perps predominate. One research team, using the acronym CUR to stand for condom use resistance, studied 501 women in their twenties to investigate their experience with this practice.[6] About 12% of the subjects reported that sexual partners had engaged in nonconsensual condom removal, the phenomenon known to researchers and lawmakers as condom stealth or condom stealthing. Twelve is a smallish percentage of one hundred, yes. But the denominator here isn't rape complainants: the CUR researchers focused on young women identified as at high risk of sexual assault, a bigger group. Penal codes routinely criminalize less common dangerous acts that do less harm.

Online forums have put into words the theme of Anywhere It Wants to Go by telling men how to accomplish condom stealth and defending the practice. Among the defenses: "It's a man's instinct to shoot his load into a woman's *****," one post declared. "As a woman, it's my duty to spread my legs and let a man shoot his load into my wet ***** whenever he wants." Another post celebrated ejaculation into another person as an unstoppable prerogative. Going ahead as one pleases, indifferent to whether one's partner wants a dose of one's semen, is "how god created this universe" and what "we are born to do," the commenter wrote.[7] Shades of *Humanae Vitae,* where a vital force travels to the interior of another person under the laissez-passer of Nature, or Genesis 38, in which God struck a man dead for taking action to block that journey.

I say nonpunishment of condom tampering and removal because that's where we are in most of the United States, but the law could take steps against this consent-defeating behavior. A few courts in Canada,

Australia, Germany, Switzerland, and New Zealand have punished it as a crime. In the summer of 2021, California became the first U.S. state to impose legal consequences for this conduct. Its statute does not classify condom stealth as a crime, but a person injured by an unexpected and unwanted deliberate delivery of semen by stealth can receive damages from the offender. Maine followed suit in 2023. At the time I write, condom stealth is a legal wrong in only two states. More than 83% of the American population lacks legal redress for interior-body contact with semen achieved by stealth.

As for my use of "stealth" and "stealthing," that's the diction we have; like "nonpunishment," this verbiage is inadequate. Legislators and policymakers made what might be the best choice from a limited menu. Calling this conduct stealth or stealthing adverts to its unseen and hidden nature; both words consist mostly of "steal," which adds an accurate flavor of something wrong. But the conduct isn't just stealthy. It does active harm in a particular way.

This aggression is dishonest; it's cheating. Its impacts are physical in addition to psychological. Calling it stealth or stealthing evades the point of the action, which is to inject a human being with semen in violation of a promise that a penis about to enter a vagina or rectum will stay on the other side of a barrier. No clear diction to describe this wrongful act shows the persistence of Anywhere It Wants to Go; the feebleness of "condom stealthing" as the best available term for a wrong testifies to semen's entrenched privilege to travel indifferent to the welfare of others.

A third category of semen-involved misbehavior that the law will rarely remedy demonstrates the same problem of scant language to challenge a harmful freedom of semen to roam. Jody Madeira has named this misbehavior "illicit insemination" and "fertility fraud." Consistent with our theme of no words for semen-caused harm, neither phrase has caught on in popular discourse. Nor has any other term. More semen silence.

Medical doctors almost always escape accountability when they use their own semen to generate embryos after representing to patients that semen necessary for this purpose would come from someone else. If a patient ends up giving birth to the genetic child of a man she'd hired for a one-off medical service, a provider whom she might find repellent in all other respects or roles, instead of the child of someone she esteems and cherishes or whom she regards as genetically superior to the inseminator-doctor, too bad for her. Fertility fraud imposes a consequence for which neither punishment of the deceiver or compensation to the deceived woman will typically follow.[8]

In one exception to this no-remedies pattern, a Colorado jury ordered physician Paul Jones to pay $8.75 million to family members after he surreptitiously used his own semen for assisted reproduction.[9] Jones told patients who sought his assistance in becoming biological mothers that he'd obtain "fresh" sperm from an anonymous donor. Probably a medical student, he implied. He didn't discard the semen of anyone in particular, didn't betray another man, breached no agreement about whom he would help make a father. I wouldn't defend him, to put it mildly. But setting up this defendant as the poster doctor for fertility fraud once again discounts the harmful potential of semen.

The conduct of Dr. Jones qualified under Colorado law for both felony liability and civil recourse. Colorado uses the term "misuse of gametes"; other states proscribe fertility fraud.[10] Most American wrongdoers still get away with this misconduct.[11] Criminal law and tort law, both of which set out to address the inflicting of harm upon another person, seem designed to create remedies that hurt persons can deploy, but courts for the most part will not apply either set of legal doctrines to this deployment of semen. Professor Madeira reported in a pre-*Emmons v. Jones* article that the number of physicians in the United States and Canada who have ever faced any type of proceeding for this deceptive use of their semen is a single digit: six. Even fewer than these six suffered any legal penalty or judgment.

"You wanted a Lamborghini," a friend said by way of sympathy for fertility-fraud victims when I told him what I learned from Jody Madeira's writings, "and you got a Yugo." I'm sure he meant well. Among bad experiences, however, receiving a worse car than one hoped for would be much gentler and more forgettable than this one.

Women injured by this action opened their bodies for intimate contact with a reasonable belief about good faith. Betrayal penetrated them permanently, altering their bodies while upending their hopes. Indifference to this wrong often expresses disregard for individual men too: fraudulent inseminators who work with infertile male-female couples know the man they harm. When these malefactors jettison or misuse semen that the couple chose, they demean and deceive human beings who provided it under conditions of trust. Children of defrauded parents also suffer from this irreversible deployment of semen; many of them, Madeira writes, "feel as if they were conceived from rape."[12]

Another instance of semen indulgence is different from these three examples in that American law and policy disapprove of it. I bet you do too. It is a belief that goes by names that include the "virgin cure," the "virgin myth," and "virgin cleansing"; its conceit is that a person can rid himself of a sexually transmitted disease by ejaculating into a particular target. During the nineteenth century, before synthetic antibiotics became available, Englishmen infected with syphilis and gonorrhea ejaculated into girls under the age of 10 and then later, accused of rape, told courts about their cure agenda as an attempt at defense.[13] European writings dating to the sixteenth century mention the possibility.

As far as I can discern, this maneuver has never been respectable or esteemed by any mainstream authority. Exponents don't defend it in writing. Because nobody will own the virgin cure, I've struggled to learn which exact acts this prescription recommends and what beliefs about health or disease account for its supposed curative mechanism. Despite its vagueness, however, the idea is familiar. It drew 11,800,000 Google hits on my machine. When I polled a subset of my friends, most (though not all) said they'd heard of it.

In American popular culture, The Book of Mormon references the virgin cure with a song called "Making Things Up Again" that, like its 1938 precursor "It Ain't Necessarily So" from Porgy and Bess, mocks teachings wrapped in religion. "The story I've been told is that the way to cure AIDS is by sleeping with a virgin," sings a Ugandan male character in response to pseudo-Christian nonsense preached by the missionary protagonist. "I'm gonna go and rape a baby!"[14] Writers of the musical must have expected the audience to get the joke. Researchers who survey the public in South Africa, a country in which the virgin cure has drawn more earnest attention, report that most people there too have heard about the purportedly restorative effect of conduct consistently called sex with a virgin.

In all versions I've found of the virgin cure written over centuries across multiple continents, "sex" means intercourse initiated by a man. The Book of Mormon's euphemism "sleeping with" never occurs in any literal way. Nobody sleeps. It's penis in vagina. As for "virgin," practitioners and observers of this purported cure use it to mean a girl too young ever to have experienced any sexual intercourse that she pursued or desired. Assailants play it safe, so to speak, by choosing a child rather than an older teen or an adult as the virgin they exploit.

Most descriptions of the virgin cure maintain the same coy silence about semen that we've observed elsewhere, but occasionally the fluid gets mentioned. In a pre-HIV study, one informant used "water" to stand for semen in his explanation to anthropologist Axel-Ivar Berglund of this pursuit. A man who worries about sickness in his water, the informant told Berglund, finds a new woman to serve as his receptacle. "Perhaps the water does not affect her because it was directed towards his wife. So he expels it in this other woman." Application of the cure leaves everyone healthy and the man can now ejaculate safely at home.[15]

This much specificity about how the virgin cure works being both rare and far from current, let's now consider whether and how much this belief matters. My other examples of semen indulgence—criminal codes that withhold "aggravated" from rape with ejaculation; condom stealth condoned; fertility fraud ditto—all thrive today in the United States. Folklore about putting semen into a virgin might be figuratively as well as literally foreign to this record.

One might start by asking if the virgin cure makes any difference in human lives. Researchers in South Africa, where both HIV rates and familiarity with the myth are high, have tried to learn whether prepubescent girls or any other people are endangered by the notion. The widely accepted convention of a null hypothesis thwarts their efforts. Anyone who wants to claim that the virgin cure motivates rape must overcome what the null hypothesis teaches, a presumption of no relationship between two independent variables. It's hard to prove a connection between action and the existence of a superstitious-at-best belief. Compounding the problem, rape is extraordinarily underreported in South Africa: one estimate of the national reporting rate is 1 in 35 attacks. Researchers can inquire into an individual's motive for action only when they know or have reason to think that the person acted.

Early in this century, the British medical journal The Lancet published an exchange on point between two authorial teams with public health research experience in South Africa. The first of these short papers denounced an uptick in infant rape that the authors attributed to rapists' agendas to change their serostatus.[16] The second contended that no actual increase had occurred, just an increase in reportage by the stirred-up South African media, and what really explains infant rape are the same conditions that explain rape of women and older girls: "sex inequalities, a culture of male sexual entitlement, and the climate of relative impunity for rape."[17]

Learned efforts to investigate the virgin cure in action struggle with the difficulty of knowing what to look for. That "virgin" has no coherent meaning causes trouble not only for researchers but people who set out to purge their HIV status or another pathology through sexual contact with a person they think qualifies for the label. For example, should these diseased individuals reason that a very young infant must fit every possible definition of virgin, they'd be wrong: their victim might have lost that status by having been raped by someone else first.

Foolishness of the path might not suffice to discourage it, however. Responding to an outreach called the Global Survey on HIV/AIDS and Disability, women with disabilities told researchers that after settling into what they'd believed were romantic as well as sexual relationships, they learned that their disability had led their partners to think they were "virgins, capable of ridding them of their infection. The men did not inform the women of their HIV status and abandoned them once these women began to show symptoms of infection with the virus."[18] Presuming that disability equals virginity suggests that a sexual strategy need not make any real sense to have consequences. What women with disabilities reported in the survey also supports a Yes answer to the question of whether belief in the virgin cure makes a difference in real life.

But while the virgin part of "sex with a virgin" is as much a dead end for researchers as it is for people who seek to dump an ailment of theirs into someone else, the other noun in the phrase needs more attention. Its opacity holds power. In obscuring what exactly the myth recommends to people who have a disease they would like to jettison, the fog around "sex" distracts observers from what the practice necessarily involves: ejaculation onto the interior mucosa of another human being. No effort to inject semen into another person means no virgin cure.

Only a fraction of persons with an unwanted health condition can attempt to heal themselves this way. A person whose reproductive anatomy is female, to name one physical state that precludes the undertaking, must either endure whatever malady she wants to lose or try something different to regain her lost health. Virginity as a condition held by, or attributed to, another person holds no reparative powers for someone who doesn't shoot semen into anyone. Acts that someone with a female body can initiate might transmit a disease to or from her partner but will never—not even in her dreams—undo a sexually acquired pathology she already has.

For everyone who lacks the ability to ejaculate into someone else, virgin cleansing isn't even a delusion: it's unthinkable. Men are abler than women in this respect but even they cannot partake of the virgin cure through acts that qualify as their having sex, at least in some understandings: cunnilingus, fellatio with them as non-ejaculating participants, and digital penetration of the other person's torso.

In other words, any behavior that keeps semen inside the person who made it lies outside the virgin cure. Like lists of what makes sexual assault "aggravated" or extra bad found in state penal codes, definitions and discussions of virgin cleansing don't name the material at the center of what they address. References to dangerous acts that involve semen treat the substance with polite restraint, as if its feelings would be hurt should somebody associate it with an exceptionally heinous kind of rape.

If a joke can be explained, then something like hurt feelings might explain what's funny about "Every Sperm is Sacred," the Monty Python sketch-song that people I meet still bring up several decades after its airing in 1983: semen's indignant huff, the hissy fit it pitches about the respect it insists it's owed. Monty Python put their slogan about deference to semen in a sketch where Michael Palin and Terry Jones play a married couple with 63 children they cannot afford to feed. Told that they've been sold into science experimentation because Dad Palin and Mum Jones have no choice, the kids wonder about the birth-control path not taken. Palin leads them (and then an entire town, Catholic clergy included) in a song-and-dance answer.

Even funnier than semen getting pissy about its entitlements, maybe, is that while "sacred" usually connotes limits and boundaries that mortals ought to observe, no constraints limit what the Palin character pumped into his wife. The film can't fit all the Palin-Jones children into one frame with their faces visible: they are that numerous. Sacredness in "Every

Sperm" is the opposite of the reverent isolation that separates people from don't-touch relics or holy geographic locations like Mecca. Being sacred means that sperm, riding in the effluvium they live in, may venture anywhere they like. They and their liquid vessel answer to nobody.

Now we move to the possibility that occupies this book: we could do something different in our dealings with semen. Here I have in mind a skeptical reader who might happen to favor some or even all the policy goals I've mentioned. This person could share my reaction to the characterization of frozen embryos as unborn children with a right to life and might nod along when I denounce the so-called virgin cure, or support legal remedies for condom stealth or fertility fraud. At the same time, my hypothetical reader doubts what I posit about an entitlement that semen enjoys to travel and make an impact when it arrives. This contention of mine might seem more unhelpful or uninteresting than provocative. Semen can be understood as a mere lower-torso fluid that exits the body, just an emission. To call it a voyager or an agent with a plan might sound grandiose and futile at the same time. The interlocutor I imagine wonders which practical, material, or even theoretical consequences follow from the thesis of this chapter. I'll speak to this reader now.

* * *

Ideas for constraints on semen that the law could impose if it wanted to can be mined from the lode of existing comparable controls. All we need are pertinent analogies. Other targets of regulation that resemble semen can guide policymakers to apply familiar constraints to a new object of regulatory attention. I have two suggestions about semen comparators that could inform this move.

First, we can focus on semen as a reproduction-related emission. Its standard counterpart, going back in Western culture at least to Aristotle, is menstrual fluid.[19] Plenty of controls rein in that substance, but a different comparator is more illustrative. Unlike the half-spoken norms and customs that keep menstrual emission in an assigned place, constraints on the other comparator are published and available for anyone to read.

I'm not being coy about the identity of the comparator: it has no agreed-on name. Legislation that controls where it may go deploys a variety of misnomers. In a bill that 19 United States Senators first introduced in 2021, what I am using as a comparator to semen is called aborted children.[20] The federal-level Dignity for Aborted Children Act might never pass the Senate, but some states limit the disposal of what they call aborted fetuses.[21] "Aborted fetuses," though more accurate than a reference to "aborted children," is wrong when applied to an abortion that occurred before the eighth week of pregnancy, the stage at which an embryo becomes a fetus. The large majority of abortions in the United States, about 92%, take place in the first third of pregnancy: when used correctly, the word "fetus" applies only to the last four weeks of that trimester.

Among U.S. jurisdictions, Indiana has generated standout contributions to both state statutory and federal decisional law on mandatory reverence for this material. Start with Box v. Planned Parenthood, a 2019 Supreme Court decision that upheld an Indiana law requiring the cremation or interment of an aborted fetus.[22] Justice Clarence Thomas wrote a separate opinion that resembles the Alabama embryos case I brought up at the start of this chapter. Here too, first a Supreme Court majority attributes something like personhood to an unborn entity and then one justice on the court writes separately to escalate the rhetoric. "Indiana law prohibits abortion providers from treating the bodies of aborted children as 'infectious waste' and incinerating them alongside used needles, laboratory-animal carcasses, and surgical byproducts," said Justice Thomas in his first sentence.[23]

Misleading at best. Before the law took effect, what Thomas called "the bodies of aborted children" were dealt with the same way that excess blood and fat that surgeries produce gets disposed of: corporations that manage medical waste (not "infectious waste") come to hospitals and clinics at regular intervals to transport this material out. Regulated businesses hold permits to do this work of disposal. Abortion providers typically do not incinerate anything.

The phrase "medical waste," which may sound unpleasant, is a fact for grown-ups to reckon with. My home state keeps track of the 250,000 tons of medical waste that 36,000 generators produce every year. We emit it. We are next to it. It seeps from our bodies indifferent to whether being reminded of it makes us queasy.

The Indiana law that the Supreme Court reviewed says that abortion providers must give patients information about their options for disposal. The options they can offer are two: cremation or burial. If patients want their providers to choose a destination that's more casual, like a plastic bag in a dumpster, or more science-minded, like a research laboratory, they're out of luck.

Troubled by this law, Planned Parenthood of Indiana and Kentucky took the state of Indiana to court. It contended that forcing providers to provide a particular disposal of aborted fetuses lacks what the law calls a rational basis. Lower courts agreed with Planned Parenthood and invalidated the statute. The Supreme Court reversed those conclusions and upheld it.

Opponents of the burial-or-cremation requirement pressed on, undaunted, bringing more litigation. Their post-*Box* challenge to the Indiana statute shifted focus to abortion patients by arguing that the requirement imposed on individuals disputable notions about personhood and the proper disposal of remains in violation of their freedom to belief and conscience. Once again this opposition prevailed at the trial level, but this time the appellate court sided with Indiana. The "mandate applies only to providers," wrote Judge Frank Easterbrook, approving the law, and "women may choose to take custody of the remains and dispose of them as they please."[24]

True: but Indiana could have left abortion providers alone just as it leaves other holders of semen-related effluvia alone. Unlike semen, which is always free to travel without papers, detritus put into the hands of abortion providers must be noted on burial-transit paperwork as if it were a human corpse. A permit is required for this material to move lawfully from one place to another. When used to comply with Indiana's cremation-or-burial law, this document must recite the date that this material left a human body and the name of the licensed funeral provider that will take possession of these remains. Every state following the Indiana approach—several others impose the same requirement—directs the material to go to a particular category of destination whenever it travels. Whenever the category of destination refuses to accept it, it may not travel anywhere at all.

Whether American governments may tell individuals how to dispose of emissions from their bodies is less clear than their power to give this order to institutions. Judge Easterbrook in the post-*Box* Seventh Circuit decision implied that liberty considerations might give formerly pregnant persons a right to refuse this order. Constitutional analysis, as we saw, asks whether the requirement has a rational basis. The Supreme Court ruled that the Indiana requirements met that condition but failed to favor its audiences by explaining what it thought that rational basis might be.[25] Until we know what's special about material that exits the human body after an abortion, American decisional law poses no barrier to constraints on all disposers. In other words, perhaps the government can require dignified disposal of anything. It becomes possible to propose an Indiana-style law to govern all semen that leaves one human body without entering another.

What I'm imagining would direct every producer of this emission to gather what he ejaculated and then turn it over to someone with authority, such as a licensed funeral director. Ceremony to follow. State actors could use exceptions, excuses, lenient enforcement, or simple caprice to lighten the burden of this demand. They could also forgo that lenity.

Odd? Maybe, but every new idea is anomalous. Repellent? Eye of the beholder. No rational basis? I'll cite Box v. Planned Parenthood. If there's any meaningful difference between semen outside of the human body and the material emitted in an abortion, the Supreme Court hasn't told us what it is. And if the Monty Python songwriters were correct about every sperm being sacred—they kidded, but whoever wrote Onan's story in Genesis and the clerics who published Humanae Vitae were serious when they said something similar—then a ritual for fallen ejaculate renders honor where honor is due.

Lawmakers too shocked or offended to codify this thought experiment might feel more open to another idea where government control over semen is less direct. My burial-or-cremation suggestion compared semen as an emission first to menstrual fluid and then to the material that abortion discharges. The comparison in my second idea moves to interior reproductive anatomy. It purports to promote health and welfare of the next generation through controls of the male body that borrow, *mutatis mutandis*, from impositions on female counterparts.

Toward that end, we could hold semen to a fitness standard. Public policy ambition would resolve to cleanse semen from controlled-substance contaminants. Demanding proof of purity in an emission from the lower torso is familiar: thousands of American workers regularly demonstrate to employers that they are free of illegal substances as a condition of being hired, or of keeping the jobs they have. Urinating into a cup, the act they engage in to comply with this demand, resembles what a semen fitness test could require.

The law can promote improved fitness by prosecuting persons who consume criminalized substances at a time that their bodies are making semen. For most men, this time stretches without pause from puberty to death. No problem with the rational basis criterion for constitutionality because this new law might well improve public health: men use illegal drugs at a higher rate than women and the illegal drugs they take have an adverse effect on their fertility.[26]

A requirement to be fit in the sense of free from controlled substances could proceed leniently by imposing this condition only on semen likely to create a risk of impregnation, or stringently by demanding fitness from all semen all the time. To guide the lenient path of semen regulation, we could learn from restrictions imposed on women who appear to be or could become pregnant. Role models here would include refusals to serve alcoholic beverages and exclusions from medical research.

When they want to follow the path of stringency, drafters of new semen regulations could learn from the extensive record of miscarriage-and-stillbirth prosecutions and imprisonments. The wide menu of crimes that formerly pregnant women have been convicted of in the United States—including manslaughter, feticide, abuse of a corpse, and concealing a dead body—offers ideas to discourage and punish emissions of semen that can be characterized as in an unhealthy state. Same for child endangerment, child abuse, drug delivery, attempted aggravated child abuse, chemical endangerment of a child, child neglect, child mistreatment, homicide, manslaughter, reckless injury to a child. Only a few light edits are needed. Semen endangerment, sperm abuse, semen neglect, chemical endangerment of spermatozoa, sperm mistreatment and the like would get the ball rolling, so to speak.

Readers of my generation and older will recall a bit of policy history that could guide fitness tests for semen: concern about so-called crack babies. Worriers of yore fretted about cocaine ingestion during pregnancy as a cause of birth defects. The ones of them with power focused on one form of this drug, the rock-like crack, while indulging with more tolerance the powder kind of cocaine that white users favored—a racist stance that aligned with understandings of Black motherhood as pathological and destructive. I remember hearing the claim about the danger of crack babies made again and again without challenge. It sounded true then, or at least plausible enough to act on. The initiatives that ensued imposed hypersurveillance and criminalization on poor Black young women with substance-use disorders.

Hostility aimed at women who use drugs while pregnant continues undaunted by the evidence. Longitudinal studies confirm that prebirth exposure to cocaine is close to harmless for a neonate. Researchers have found little impact of maternal cocaine consumption on motor development, cognitive development, language skills, and memory capacity of children. Similar evidence tends to acquit opioids—all of them, including heroin and fentanyl—along with methamphetamine.[27] A pregnant individual can consume many drugs with confidence that they won't harm her baby much.

That recreational drug use in pregnancy tends to spare, rather than harm, persons who were exposed this way supports giving my semen-control thought experiment a whirl. The scientific record of little to no harm from ingesting drugs during pregnancy provides an ideal base to go after semen producers. Current interferences presume that evidence of any degree of danger, skimpy though it may be, makes this reach of law enforcement defensible. We want to protect babies. Good: then let us hone in on a source of babies' DNA. And to the extent the maternal-ingestion record shows no harm, it frees policymakers from needing to clear an evidentiary threshold before they constrain anybody. We who regulate can write semen rules, including new crimes, that rest on the same baby-protection rationale supported by the same quantity and quality of evidence that governments deploy to regulate the female body.

Other aggressive attentions to semen at its source, the male body, are also available. Harm to sperm and semen originate in more than the recreational drugs that men choose to consume. For example, under the title of "Impact of Environmental Factors on Human Semen Quality and Male Fertility: A Narrative Review," one paper limited its focus to only a single danger, threats to fertility.[28] The authors considered air pollution as a source of weak sperm and semen. Air pollution hostile to male reproductive health comes from factories, fires, exhaust from motor vehicles, agriculture, waste treatment plants, and oil refineries, the paper found. Men lucky enough to enjoy relative shelter from these exposures face threats from household chemicals, radiation, work environments generally, and excesses of temperature. These toxins pervade the air. Threats to fertility like phthalates, dioxin, heavy metals like lead and cadmium, and agricultural pesticides and herbicides continue to poison contemporary human life decades after educated alarms about them first sounded. Substances that disrupt fertility are easy for a male-bodied person to encounter.

Feebler-than-ideal sperm and semen can join attentions from the alarm about sub-replacement birthrates that, at the time I write, is filling the discourse worldwide. In a pivot from their earlier dismay about overpopulation, spokesmen for nation-states express worry about replenishing their ranks of consumers, workforce participants, soldiers, and caregivers for vulnerable human beings at the beginning and the end of life. Concerns about birth-dearth make any woman with fewer than two children look selfish or unpatriotic or misguided . . . although this individual is also deemed within reach of appeals to the common good, as evidenced by the carrots as well as sticks aimed in her direction from numerous governments. Semen being necessary to babymaking too, persons who produce this substance inside their bodies have a comparable obligation to what we might call their fatherland.

Expectations for semen quality could enforce minimum standards of reproductive fitness. Measurements of sperm mobility and motility provide a yardstick to support these controls. Clear the threshold or suffer the consequences, the government can declare. "Reproductive fitness," a term familiar from evolutionary biology, covers not only the ability to achieve fertilization and pregnancy but also the quality of offspring produced. It's plausible to suppose that anything that impairs fertility by weakening the sperm of an individual in the struggle to impregnate may also generate adverse effects in embryos that manage to take form despite this disadvantage. In scrutinizing semen, we could pursue high-quality offspring as a social goal.

As with my burial-or-cremation rule for ejaculate, there's room for moderation in enforcement of this new legal regime. The state could recognize excuses for semen inferiority. It might pay for counseling to ease the discomfort of punishment and scrutiny. Borrowing from pronatalist intervention policies that reward giving birth to children and the "wellness" perks some employers dole out to boost productivity and morale, the state could even hand out cash subsidies to shore up weak semen. A wide array of meddlesome options to choose from, in short.

On the question of which punishments and discouragements to impose on ejaculators, the sticks half of carrots and sticks, we know from female-body precedents that it will be fine to give an order with no safe path forward to guide people who want to follow the law. Consider an enlargement of the Indiana-style dignified disposal statute noted above. The Texas legislature in 2017 imposed a demand of burial or cremation on health care facilities in general, not just abortion providers, to bury or cremate every type of fetal and embryonic remains. That statute covers all possible routes to termination—abortion, treatment for an ectopic pregnancy, miscarriage, and stillbirth—while providing zero supports for compliance. Cemeteries, funeral homes, crematoria, and medical waste businesses in Texas are all free to reject this delivery. Shades of the Atlantic magazine story called "State-Mandated Mourning for Aborted Fetuses" that reported on what happens next when a state decrees that this material must be buried or cremated. A spokeswoman for the Planned Parenthood affiliate in Indiana told the Atlantic reporter she had been turned down by numerous funeral homes and cemeteries when she asked them to help her organization comply with the law.[29] One judicial opinion reviewing the Texas law, consistent with the experience of Planned Parenthood in Indiana, found that these categories of providers also declined to say Yes when asked whether they would take on the job of disposal.[30]

Scholars who study law enforcement applied to pregnancy have documented an extraordinary absence of constraint on prosecutors' prerogatives, a backdrop that enlarges possibilities for semen law enforcement. Criminal charges that blame one person for hurting another person will typically require proof of a culpable mental state. This venerable demand on the state gets dropped or relaxed, however, to support convictions of crimes that prohibit endangerment of a fetus or embryo. Courts have upheld convictions of defendant mothers in a desperate state of drug addiction. Individuals punished by the government for pregnancy crimes might have tried as hard as they could to obtain treatment for a harm that they worked as hard as they could to avoid. The state need not prove that these defendants desired to hurt their embryo or fetus. Nor even that they knew of risk. The record of wide breadth presents an open season for the semen analogy.

* * *

If I sound bitterly satirical here, or less than serious, that's because Anywhere It Wants to Go is too firmly rooted to flinch when poked at. Semen may travel where it pleases. The lack of constraint on this substance—no scrutiny, no dignified-burial rules, no obligation like the one that employers may impose on employees' urine to be drug free—is a human-ish freedom. Lack of constraint on semen is consistent with goals and motives we take for granted. Wanting to go to a new place is familiar, "relatable," apparently rooted in nature.

Legal attentions away from reproductive anatomy overtly heed and encourage this desire in the versions of it that human wanderers feel. International law, for example, identifies three distinct particulars in the transnational right of free movement. All persons share in rights to cross a national border, to move freely within a nation, and to return to a national homeland. Speaking for the common law, William Blackstone wrote that "the personal liberty of individuals" encompasses "the power of loco-motion, of changing situation, or removing one's person to whatsoever place one's own inclination may direct."[31]

A comparable right to travel reposes in contemporary American law. Unlike the Articles of Confederation, its predecessor, which stated that "the people of each State shall have free ingress and regress to and from any other State," the U.S. Constitution states nothing about this ostensible right. The Supreme Court has found it anyway. Similar to the agenda I attribute to semen, the American constitutional right to travel extends beyond an entitlement to relocate to point B from point A, which for ambulatory persons would mean being allowed to drive or walk or pedal or be transported safe from stops or interferences by the government. The constitutional right empowers *impactful* travel, a trip that makes a difference.

Like the journey of semen from one human body into another, the journey of one person from one state to another can cause what might feel like harm at the receiving end of the trip. Taxpayers who live in a state with generous welfare benefits, for example, could resent low-income newcomers who relocate there with only financial gain in mind. The Supreme Court invoked the right to travel when it ruled that states could not discourage that move by requiring newcomers to wait a year before they could collect transfer payments.[32] A later Supreme Court decision considered the defensive move by the state of California in response, which was to give these newcomers welfare benefits but only in the amount they would have received in their original home state.

No, said the Supreme Court.[33] Lower courts agree.[34] This entitlement covers other transfer payments, not just welfare. When Alaska tried to distribute its oil-reserves giveback to residents based on duration of residency in the state, two newcomers to the state, a married couple, protested. The Supreme Court sided with them too.[35] Semen-ish power to make an impact when one arrives is apparently included in the United States Constitution.

In the perspective of Anywhere It Wants to Go that we've followed in this chapter, semen wants to move and to make a difference when it lands. Again and again, this imperative to go somewhere and achieve consequences could be stopped or discouraged or punished; it's not. Supports and encouragements for the journeying semen date back to antiquity and continue in current American law. Like a modern-day pilgrim who gets his card punched to prove that he traversed a geographic swath like the Camino de Santiago, semen receives recognition respect for migration.

Later in this book, two chapters from now, I'll show how abortion prohibitions honor the ascribed agenda of semen. Reminiscent in this respect of burial-and-cremation rules governing medical waste, laws that punish or prevent the termination of a condition that imposes life-threatening risks and severe physical pain on persons who might not have done anything to deserve punishment call for explanation. I find an explanation for abortion interferences—not a reason in the sense of anything principled, just an account—in Anywhere It Wants to Go.

Consistent with my claim about the ancient origins and deep roots of this belief, positive law in the United States restricted and withheld abortion long before the Supreme Court decided Dobbs v. Jackson Women's Health Organization in 2022. Roe v. Wade, interpreted post-Dobbs to signify liberality that protects pregnant persons, supported Anywhere It Wants to Go when it asserted that externally imposed authority has an "important and legitimate interest in protecting the potentiality of human life," an interest that lessens the entitlement to be free of unwanted pregnancy.[36] I say externally imposed authority rather than law or a state mindful that Genesis 38 reported that God, who isn't government, took the same pro-"potentiality" attitude when he smote a man. So while neither of the two big Supreme Court rulings on abortion nor the Genesis story contains the word "semen," construing "the potentiality of human life" to mean the opportunity to enter another body and make an impact there by putting a person to uses she might not want gives force to Anywhere It Wants to Go. The Dobbs decision approves of that ascribed agenda more overtly than Roe: both decisions honor a tradition.

Indulgence of semen has ensued, and to an extraordinary degree. No correlative privilege of Anywhere *We* Want to Go—a few faint nods like the unenforceable notion that the Constitution furnishes some right to travel notwithstanding—applies to us human beings. We're kept out and hemmed in by national borders, owners' entitlements to exclude us as visitors from their property for any reason or no reason, rules that set up qualifications to enter a space, physical structures in place to protect and thwart us at the same time, social norms and customs we might not be able to put into words, and other effective barriers.[37] We fence in and fence out. We live behind doors and walls and locked gates and security stations; we're headed for the tight interior of a coffin or cremation furnace. The controls I'll broach at the end this book will do nothing worse to semen than what we do to ourselves.

2

Seed, the Starter

Figuring out that seed is a force for change marked a turn for the human species. After this big insight arrived about 13,000 years ago, the seed-starting that followed went on to germinate food in quantities that can be planned, cultivated, harvested, and stored. Just like us in this respect, people in the Neolithic era ate animals and plants they created to be nourishment. Our ancestors discerned how to breed animals before they learned how to grow plants, but their knowledge of what exactly generates this production reversed this order of food-making. Progenitors of ours knew about the role of seed in the creation of grains and fruits and vegetables many years before they knew about the role of seed as a starter of new animals.

In a book called The Seeds of Life, the science writer Edward Dolnick marveled at how long it took clever Homo sapiens to learn where babies come from. Geniuses including Aristotle and Leonardo da Vinci swung at the challenge and missed. Microscopes weren't around to aid these great-mind conjectures but did get invented before Shakespeare wrote most of his plays. Until the recent year of 1875, however, when a German biologist named Oscar Hertwig dabbed the semen of a sea urchin near a sea urchin egg and watched the nuclei fuse, our species was almost clueless about fertilization.

We did have one clue. "Semen," writes Dolnick, "as the only impossible-to-miss product of sex, was plainly a crucial part of the puzzle."[1] Onan the seed-spiller of chapter 1 would not have understood gametes but he did know that ejaculating into a vagina sometimes causes pregnancy, and that sexual intercourse lacks that potential when semen doesn't travel into a woman. His story dates back at least 2,500 years and whoever wrote it into Genesis took for granted that readers would understand what Onan thought he was preventing when he pulled out. More than the unseen sperm in it, semen is humanity's quintessential starter.

Modern and biblical Hebrew alike use the word *zera* to signify semen and seed. The book of Genesis includes both meanings of the word and adds a gloss of legacy for a man, his future in the physical sense: Semen contains vitality he can expect to outlive him along with earthly force right now. God killed Onan for the affront of squandering that vitality. Galen's first-century text whose title is translatable as both On Semen and On Seed follows the same multiplicity with the word σπέρματο. Powers ascribed to *zera* continue in our time and place. Twenty-first century American semen carries forward its identity as seed, the starter.

Countless nouns of Western languages flatter people who make something new or get credit for originality. Entrepreneurs, discoverers, authors (along with arty "auteurs"), creators, inventors, innovators, disruptors, pioneers, visionaries, founders, framers, venturers, and first movers all sound heroic. Routinely we bestow awe on those who generate and beget.

Semen as generator and begetter continues undercredited and underappreciated for what it does, a myriad of accomplishments of which baby-starting is the most impressive. I'll postpone to chapter 4 the other big phenomenon in starter-land, the delivery of infection, and for now limit Seed the Starter to human sexual reproduction. We've already seen in this book that semen holds force beyond the sperm in it. Onan of the Old Testament knew nothing about sperm cells but did know that his semen had babymaking potential. Today we're prone to the opposite omission. We perceive power in our little swimmers; we find them attractive and engaging. This perspective shortchanges semen. Impacts at its receiving end are not limited to what the spermatozoa in it can do.

Part of what explains this skimpy awareness, I think, may be underappreciation of the environments where this substance does its transforming, a perspective that will occupy this chapter. At least since On the Generation of Animals, where Aristotle describes menstrual blood as a cold inert counterpart of semen that lacks life force and gets awakened by input from a man, the Western heritage we live in contains tacit disparagement of the material setting necessary for human reproduction and other creations. In a counterpart to its reverence for seed, this stance thinks less of what it perceives as nonseed receptors, some of which it seems to regard as more female than male: topsoil, pastures, containers, planter beds, storage units.

Confidence that the starter outranks the location or receptive material where it germinates can obscure a simple truth about the power
of the starter: Both the launcher of a new condition and the ambient
conditions that make that launch possible are necessary for effects. One
without the other is idle. Focus only on the catalyst or first mover and
neglect the settings or partner-conditions where it works, and you won't
only overlook those other conditions; you'll also miss much of what the
seed can cause and achieve.

In this perspective, female reproductive anatomy is a starter too.
Its contributions to the creation of a new person are more varied than
the male starter-contribution delivered in semen—even at the particle
level, before we consider gestation and labor. Of the two hundred or so
types of cells in the human body, spermatozoa are the smallest and egg
cells are the biggest, each ovum weighing literally a million times more
than a spermatozoon and visible to the naked eye. Sperm contain chromosomes and enough energy to swim for a little while, that's all; ova
contain the same number of chromosomes as sperm plus mitochondria
to generate energy and food stores of their own.

Just as the sperm is puny compared to the egg, a zygote is much
smaller than the person who provides food, shelter, and waste-hauling
to nurture it. Zygotes draw life from the body of their hosts while enlarging the environment they depend on. In all its developmental stages
before it exits this home—zygote, blastocyst, embryo, and lastly fetus—
the creature never grows anywhere near the size of its mother, its home.

Referencing the size of this woman takes note of more than her physical mass. In consciousness, memories, emotional and expressive range,
biographical experiences, and complexity of plans and projects, not just
height and weight, an impregnated human being is always bigger than
the life form inside her. She exists beyond her duration of service as
a container-nurturer: when pregnancy ends, her body usually survives
and it's not the same after the fateful landing of fluid from someone else.
When we think about seeding persons inside persons, we can proceed
as if the larger of the two individuals is important.

* * *

The arrival of semen into the interior of a person sets out to upend
her life. Recipients of this fluid might welcome their newly upended

condition. Transformation is another way to speak about a healthy and successful pregnancy. Semen once again deserves more appreciation as a starter than it receives. We've already seen sperm receive undivided attention that should be shared with the fluid that these gametes rely on to travel and thrive.

Fertilization in popular imagery follows the same pattern. Click! Triumphant little swimmer swam. Sperm touched egg; egg was touched by sperm; done. Giving this much credit to sperm for fertilization neglects not only the grueling work that female anatomy will supply later but also male-supplied nurture at the start.

Scientists have known for decades about the value of semen in support of babymaking. Observational studies confirm that exposure to semen makes a pregnancy formed by in vitro fertilization more likely to succeed and more resistant to pathologies that include preeclampsia. But how exactly semen achieves these supports has needed animal studies.

They've been done. Researchers used mice to find the source of inflammatory change in female reproductive tissues that follow insemination.[2] They manipulated semen into three varieties by performing two kinds of surgery before mating their mice. The first variety, serving as a control group, came from mice who had had no surgery and whose semen was unaltered. The second variety of semen resulted from mouse vasectomies: no sperm there but other constituents present. The third variety of semen resulted from the removal of seminal vesicle glands that produce proteins. The study found that semen—not sperm and not the presence of a conceptus—activates lymph nodes that drain the uterus.

Vasectomy had no effect on the immune responses that semen causes. Only the suppression of seminal vesicles weakened semen on this front. Semen can stimulate ovulation, and, later in its reproduction-support efforts, it sends leukocytes into the female reproductive tract that "selectively target and eliminate excess sperm," to quote a review titled "The Female Response to Seminal Fluid."[3]

Another animal study concluded that, as researcher Tracey Chapman of the University of East Anglia told a reporter, "the semen protein is a 'master regulator'—which ultimately means that males effectively have a direct and global influence on the behaviour and reproductive system of the female." Protein in semen made by males of the Drosophila melanogaster (fruit fly) species alters genes in females. Some of the genes it alters cover reproduction-related functions—egg development, early embryogenesis—but other genes manipulated by this seminal protein have non-reproduction work to engrave into the female body, the study concluded. Its authors found reason to think that these effects occur in other animal species bigger than the fruit fly.

A team of biologists from three countries who focused on the proteins in semen put the phrase "sexual conflict and seminal fluid proteins" in the title of their review. These proteins wreak consequences on the female partner of an ejaculator. Though sometimes "dismissed as simply a supportive medium for sperm," the authors write, semen and its proteins press for advantage in sexual reproduction that can cause disadvantage to the ejaculated-upon.[4] Hundreds of such proteins exist. We'll revisit them later in this book when we move to sexually transmitted infection.

A few of these proteins change the female reproductive tract to get their way. A review called "Sexual Conflict and Seminal Fluid Proteins" includes a two-column table that identifies in its left column conflicts of interest between a female and a male animal that are present when the two mate. In its other column, to the right, the table lists actions that seminal proteins take inside the female body to push for what sperm cells want to achieve when they reach this environment. Evidence for their competitiveness comes from nonhuman species like fruit flies and mosquitoes, but the agenda that seminal proteins pursue is present in us apes too. Seminal proteins fight to domineer over the environment into which they travel.

Non-sperm inclusions in semen fend off sperm from rival inseminators whom the female participant might have liked better. They can both weaken and strengthen female anatomical structures that hold sperm in storage. They influence the release of female reproductive hormones. They steer the female animal's nutrient intake to support reproduction, sometimes at her expense. They alter female sleep cycles and circadian rhythms. Above all, contact with seminal fluid lowers female immune defenses against invasion. These maneuvers and strategies all come from semen rather than sperm.

Replete with consequence-making ingredients, semen is alien when it arrives as a foreign newcomer, a kind of Not Me to the person ejaculated into. To get its way, it travels onto mucosa of the female reproductive tract prepared to fight against the immune resistance that fends off disease. Insemination also forms the placenta. There too the protagonist of this book fights to gain control of someone else from the inside.

We're taught about the placenta in neutral, apolitical terms. At least that's how I learned about it. This organ creates and manages the umbilical cord, a tube that connects a pregnant woman to the conceptus inside her to deliver nourishment and carry away excretion.

This semen-begotten function of food supply and waste management to support human life seems gently benevolent. Not so much. Tubularity of the umbilical cord, it turns out, supports not only transport but the sociopolitical function of blame for women in general and mothers in particular.

Once we know that toxic substances pass through the placenta—a point of information that, like the first observation of insemination in 1875, arrived late—it took thalidomide, the prescription-drug catastrophe that imposed severe limb injuries on embryos in the early 1960s, to teach physicians and the public that what a pregnant woman ingests can harm her offspring in formation, we're good to go on scolding and punishing pregnant individuals for doing their pregnancy wrong.[5] Controlled-substance drugs, tobacco, alcoholic beverages, and caffeine are perceived, accurately enough sometimes I guess, as venturing through the umbilical cord to impart risks from which a better mother might have protected her baby. Choruses of reproach have filled popular discourse for decades.

But the placenta doesn't just ferry materials back and forth: it asserts dominion over the body it has commandeered. Reporting in her book Mom Genes on what she calls "placenta science," Abigail Tucker quotes Harvey Kliman, a Yale research scientist. "Men can't create life," Kliman told Tucker, "so we have to create something. What men create are placentas."[6] To Tucker, the placenta is "a grappling hook swung overhead and cast into the body of the mother," committed to spreading new blood vessels that pull nutrition from her body into the conceptus.[7]

All mammals make a placenta when they reproduce, but our human version of this instrument launches more invasive cells into the impregnated person than the placenta of any other primate. It's the placenta that causes a condition unknown to most of our fellow mammals, postpartum hemorrhage. Even with medical advances well established, postpartum hemorrhage today kills 125,000 women a year.[8]

At the same time that it launches a placenta, the individual spermatozoon that used semen as a travel vehicle also start a zygote, a mammal conceptus at its earliest stage. The stage directly after zygote is embryo. (Self-identified protectors of "babies" and "unborn children," also the "extrauterine children" we met in chapter 1, remind us that accuracy about gestational stages is important. Abortion bans misuse "fetus" too, overstating the age of what most abortions terminate.) The embryo spurts out genetic material in the form of microchimeric cells.

Most of these cells depart the body of the pregnant person when she gives birth. Some remain. "If you were to look deep inside my body," writes Abigail Tucker, the placenta explainer, "beneath the dark circles and stretch marks, you would find the cells of my four children, a legacy from pregnancy living on within me for the rest of my life." Having crossed the placenta into her bloodstream, these microchimeric cells "have probably settled down and embedded in various body parts, permanently integrating with my kidneys, say, or my heart."[9] Some impacts attributable to the journey of microchimerism improve maternal health. Researchers have also linked these durable cells to diabetes, cancer, preeclampsia, and other diseases—more effects that happen only when semen travels.

Once inseminated, the human body changes and it remains in that changed state after it no longer hosts a fetus. Researchers have found differences of sensory experience among groups of women that align with whether they've been pregnant in the past or not. If you have ever been pregnant, Abigail Tucker reports, you're likely to be less disgusted by conditions and substances that your never-been-pregnant peers find strikingly revolting. Fleas on the body and dog excrement, for example. You're also likely to be calmer in the face of environmental stress. Upticks in perception and in the sorting of sensations also linger in the once-pregnant person after her fetus has moved on.

* * *

Established pregnancy, where the recipient's body grows to shelter a growing fetus, means that the female body so impacted will never be the same. Literally from head to toe. The more children a woman has given birth to, the more likely she is to have lost teeth; at the other end of her body, weight gain coupled with a pregnancy hormone called relaxin causes ligaments in the arch of her feet to loosen. This loosening in turn can cause somewhat bigger feet, up another lifelong half-size or so. Becoming pregnant can take out one's gallbladder: removal of this organ is the second most common post-pregnancy non-obstetrical surgery. Bladder dropping, stress incontinence, rectocele (a type of hernia between the rectum and the vagina), along with pelvic organ prolapse, which affects 3% of American women, permanently complicate the daily lives of some persons whose pregnancies continue to childbirth. Other effects associated with full-term pregnancy that last after a baby's birth include a wider vagina, varicose veins, and weight gain. And ptosis, the medical term for sagging breasts.

Anyone who gathers the imprints of pregnancy on a body has so many consequences to report that she needs a limiting device. Seed the Starter steers me to emphasize effects named in the last paragraph, all of which continue when a pregnancy ends. Durable consequences look like bigger achievements than transitory ones.

Painful short-term transitory consequences of insemination, however, also hurt. Student commentator Haley Ferise quotes the Mayo Clinic website, a popular source of search engine results at the time of my writing, to find a partial catalogue of what being pregnant inflicts on a person. This incomplete list has named vomiting, fatigue, cramping, constipation, congestion, weight gain, Braxton-Hicks contractions, skin changes and stretch marks, dental issues, dizziness, urinary tract infections, backaches, shortness of breath, and heartburn. To examine a part rather than the whole of this landscape, Ferise chose "increased blood circulation alone" and found that this semen-started effect creates spider veins, varicose veins, and hemorrhoids.[10] The majority of pregnancies generate pain in the lower back and pelvis.[11]

For her framing of short-term pregnancy consequences, the legal sociologist Francesca Laguardia has taken an interest in what's written off as trivial. Nausea, which occurs in most pregnancies, offers a good illustration of how the arrival of semen on mucosa is minified as benign and unimportant; it's not. Vomiting experienced at the ordinary level found in three-quarters of pregnancies routinely brings debilitation and illness bad enough to interfere with work and family life. Hyperemesis gravidarum, the severe variant of nausea, sends women to the hospital for treatment of starvation and muscle wasting. Marlena Fejzo, a researcher who has linked hyperemesis gravidarum to genes, estimated that this impact of being inseminated costs patients and insurers $3 billion per year.[12]

Under the title of "Pain That Only She Must Bear," a quote from the Supreme Court abortion decision Planned Parenthood v. Casey, the Laguardia review enlarges the list of consequences that arise between the landing of semen on mucosa and the end of pregnancy. Headaches, carpal tunnel pain, back pain, round ligament pain, heartburn, leg cramps, sciatica, and urinary leaking are among the very common discomforts of this condition. A less well-known but still common inclusion in this catalogue of bad effects is lower back and pelvic girdle pain, a condition suffered in about half of pregnancies. Laguardia reports that patients describe this experience as exhausting and constant.[13]

It's only fair, at this point of transition from the consequences of pregnancy to the consequences of giving birth, to note the presence of more than pain in this picture. Second-trimester orgasms, for example, are extra intense due to increased pelvic blood flow. While many scientific publications report that giving birth shortens or worsens women's lives, an approximately equal quantity of these works find a protective effect from childbearing.[14] More pleasures and upsides attributable to the transfer of semen will fill chapter 6.

In other words, my Seed the Starter as a label doesn't call semen a bad guy. It calls semen a *consequential* guy. I give good impacts relatively scant time in this chapter because good things call for less worry and lighter meddling from the law. But good consequences are just as consistent with Seed the Starter as bad ones. Moving from nonpregnant to pregnant in response to an injection of semen is significant.

* * *

One of five consequences must follow when pregnancy starts. Every outcome of the five that can happen will have a significant impact on the impregnated person.

The first possible outcome of pregnancy is miscarriage. A large minority fraction of known pregnancies, almost one-fifth, meet this fate. (The miscarriage percentage is much higher when one includes pregnancies unknown to the impregnated person: but for consistency's sake I presume awareness of impregnation in this review of all five possible endings and exclude pregnancies that end before anyone knows they existed.) Studies link miscarriage with distress that carries over into subsequent pregnancies, a consequence that in turn is associated with negative impacts that extend into the longer term, "including unfavorable neuroendocrine regulation and impaired neurobehavioral development in children."[15] One review of medical-literature databases that examined every paper on miscarriage consequences published since 2010 found that miscarriage is traumatic and that "as many as 50% of miscarrying women suffer psychological morbidity months after loss and symptoms could persist up to 1 year after miscarriage."[16] Postmiscarriage bleeding can persist for more weeks than the premiscarriage duration of a pregnancy.

Second, the pregnant person can choose to terminate her pregnancy with medication abortion. Of the five impacts that follow from being impregnated, this one has the lightest touch. Consequences of medication abortion can include "fatigue, cramping, bleeding, a milky discharge from [the patient's] breasts, chills, fever, nausea, vomiting, and diarrhea."[17] Gentle stuff: but an impregnated person needs access to the mifepristone-misoprostol combination to get there, and in the United States interferers stand in her way. I'll say more about these human-created burdens in the next chapter. Even the easiest, lowest-hassle end to pregnancy includes experiences made possible by semen.

The third possible result after impregnation is abortion experienced on a table with instruments, sometimes called surgical abortion. Less common than medication abortion but a route to termination that offers a couple of advantages to the patient, it takes one of two forms. The more common technique to empty the uterus is suction; the alternative, abbreviated D&E, stands for dilation and evacuation. Undoing this impact of semen by either means takes less time than the medication alternative, ten minutes or less in contrast to what can fill most of a day;[18] it also requires the inseminated person to forfeit the privacy of her home and head for a clinic. A 2023 tally counted "11 murders, 42 bombings, 200 arsons, 531 assaults, 492 clinic invasions, 375 burglaries, and thousands of other incidents of criminal activities directed at patients, providers, and volunteers" since 1977 at venues in the United States that provide abortion with medical instruments.[19]

The fourth possible end of insemination, the one of the five that has the cheeriest reputation, is the vaginal delivery of a baby. This experience rolls out in three stages, each conveying a different type of pain to the person giving birth. Uterine contractions happen first, then dilation along with delivery second, and passage of the placenta third. The large majority of first-time vaginal deliveries include trauma. Some of this trauma comes from nature rather than human intervention—grazes or small cuts, vaginal tearing—and some from providers' scalpels: obstetrics teaches and imposes multiple variations on episiotomy, a maneuver that cuts into the perineum and vaginal wall.[20] A team of research-author nurses with expertise in anesthesiology and obstetrics reports that for the majority of women, labor pain is the most severe pain they will ever experience before they die.[21]

Reaching the end of childbirth doesn't necessarily put an end to pain for the person inseminated. Postpartum pain often comes next. Categories of physical pain common enough to be considered normal after giving birth include cramps and hemorrhoids plus pain in the back, neck, joints, and perineum. Harmful impacts to the bladder and bowel are consequences of insemination that also hurt.[22]

Harms that women experience when they give birth vaginally include dignitary injury as well as physical pain. Another catalogue, this one by Elizabeth Kukura, lists unconsented-to administration of medication, physical restraints, threats of retaliation for refusal to consent to induction or cesarean, and threats to withhold pain relief for noncompliance with doctors' orders. And more, including bullying, insults, disclosure of sensitive medical information. "Researchers in a 2019 study found 17% of women reported one or more types of mistreatment, including loss of autonomy; being shouted at, scolded, or threatened; and being ignored, refused, or receiving no response to requests for help," Kukura writes. Like other mistreatments in the United States, abuses related to dignity in childbirth are worse for women of color.

Cesarean or c-section is the fifth possibility, toward which Kukura's research provides a transition. Like surgical abortion, this way for a pregnancy to end occurs on a table. Its impacts are more severe than surgical abortion. A 2022 paper cited by Kukura reported that 10% of pregnant patients experience pressure to agree to a cesarean. Here too, racism makes outcomes for patients worse: "people of color were almost two times more likely to be pressured to consent to an episiotomy or cesarean."[23] If you have been impregnated, in short, your life has changed.

While all five possible outcomes endanger the pregnant person, the last two are riskier and more physically painful than the no-baby pregnancy endings of miscarriage and abortion. "At a minimum," writes Jennifer Hendricks, "carrying a pregnancy to term entails a 100% risk of either severe uterine contractions and painful dilation of the cervix, or major abdominal surgery. Childbirth is a journey to the boundary between life and death, a place where much can go wrong."[24]

Once again, and throughout this book, I'll acknowledge the positive as well as negative nature of semen impacts. Even intense physical pain can qualify as something good. "For some, it seems, labor pain can take on a satisfying element, less like the sting of an open wound and more like the burn of running a marathon," writes Stephanie Murray, and "conceptualizing it that way can help women cope with it."[25] Most women who have given birth become pregnant again. Even when we grant that a fraction of these subsequent pregnancies must have been unwelcome to the impregnated person and that in a fraction of that fraction the impregnated person tried to obtain an abortion and failed, the pattern of re-upping rather than foreswearing another pregnancy by people who know what it will feel like next time provides some confirmation of that "satisfying element."

* * *

Maternal mortality, a topic I've delayed until now, needs mention. Any review of Seed the Starter owes attention to Seed the Terminator. What insemination starts includes the death of impregnated persons.

The risk of dying during, soon before, or soon after childbirth seems to me important but it has proved hard to measure. Since 2003, the CDC has tried to improve its counts of these deaths by adding a pregnancy checkbox to the death certificates that the National Vital Statistics System collects. When this count showed that maternal deaths increased by 144% from 1999 to 2021, researchers disagreed on how to interpret this data. Maybe some women just happened to be pregnant on the day of their death, dying with pregnancy but not *of* pregnancy.[26] For purposes of attributing responsibility to semen, I'll agree that some of the

12.6 deaths per 100,000 live births in 2021 would have happened anyway without pregnancy, i.e., without semen on mucosa.

That said, two remarks. First, the semen-generated condition I'm talking about that endangered pregnant women in past centuries—before antibiotics, before prenatal-care protocols, before doctors washed their hands—remains dangerous. Seed the Starter continues to start maternal death. Sometimes promptly, sometimes after delay. A study of more than two million women in Sweden published in 2024 found an association between five common pregnancy complications (preterm delivery, small size for gestational age, preeclampsia, other hypertensive disorders, and gestational diabetes) and increased mortality more than 40 years later.[27]

The second fact about dying from insemination is especially salient for insemination that occurs in the United States: Black women suffer maternal death at a much higher rate than white women. When a much-cited Centers for Disease Control study drew attention in 2014 by announcing that childbirth is 14 times more likely to kill a woman than abortion, this multiple looked large but it understated the difference in danger: other CDC data that Francesca Laguardia reviewed showed that, in contrast to abortion, childbirth is more than 38 times more likely to kill a Black woman (and 25 times more likely to kill a white woman).[28] This gap isn't getting narrower. I happen to think this racial disparity is a public health catastrophe of itself, but even if one takes an "all lives matter" view and seeks only to gain a sense of the impact of semen, the race gap in maternal mortality is a reason to suspect systemic discounting of that impact.

Take for example maternal sepsis, a leading cause of pregnancy-related death. Black women are twice as likely to develop it as white women. Sepsis moves fast, which means it needs to be addressed fast, which in turn means that providers need to heed patient complaints of pain and fever, its signal symptoms. An AP news story about the problem quoted Dr. Laura Riley, chief of obstetrics and gynecology at Weill Cornell Medicine and New York-Presbyterian Hospital: "The way structural racism can play out in this particular disease is not being taken seriously. We know that delay in diagnosis is what leads to these really bad outcomes."[29] Any discounting of patients' perceptions that slows or blocks the diagnosis of maternal sepsis affects wide-scale perceptions of the problem. If maternal mortality harmed white people as much as it harms Black people, this consequence of being touched by semen would receive more attention and intervention.

Black women also suffer more than a proportionate share of another adverse impact of insemination, physical harm inflicted on purpose by an assailant. Most of the people who inflict this harm are intimate partners, i.e., inseminators, and easy access to guns in the United States increases the American odds that victims of these attacks will die. Pregnant and postpartum women of all races experience intimate partner violence at a higher rate than their nonpregnant and non-postpartum counterparts. The uptick in risk of being killed by partners goes up in pregnancy by 35%, with adolescents and non-Latina Black women especially endangered by violent partners.[30] In 2020, more than half the victims of pregnancy-related homicide in the United States were Black.[31] Homicide in this country kills more pregnant women of all races than deadly obstetric conditions like sepsis or hypertension.[32]

* * *

Starting parenthood marks semen's next frontier after starting pregnancy. When the landing of semen on mucosa results in the formation of a baby, it functions to flip a person from nonparent to parent and it also starts a new parent-child relationship after the babies it generates are born. That adoption can also make people parents and start new parent-child relationships doesn't weaken the strong connection between parenthood and insemination. The large majority of children in the United States (and an even larger majority elsewhere; adoption is especially popular in this country) are their parents' bio-kids, gestated by and born to women who hold the identity of their children's mothers.

"Adoption is much more common than most people realize," says the website to which my online history points first when I search, adding that "one in 25 U.S. families with children have an adopted child."[33] Hmmm. Even if 4% signifies something "more common than most people realize"—that fraction sounds not very common to me—it bears mention that four is the percentage of families that include an adopted child rather than the percentage of children who reached their parents by adoption. A family with two or more nonadopted children and one adopted child would join the 4% even though the majority of children in that family are not adopted.

What this statistic says is that semen-on-mucosa contact that occurs within a preexisting family or sexual relationship generates more than 96% of the children in American homes. Semen of course formed all adopted children too. Like genetic parents in this respect, people who become parents by adoption needed journeying by semen to create the parental relationships they hold.

As a nonparent myself, I'll presume to speak little about the significance of this impact of semen. The status transition between nonparent and parent looks like a big deal to me but I can't know what it feels like except from hearsay. What I can say about this transition comes from my decades as a family law professor. Becoming a parent changes a person's life, I tell my students, in that it launches unique obligations, restrictions, and rights. Specialists in family law take an occupational interest in social psychology as it intersects with the doctrine we teach and read about. From there I can report on what social scientists attribute to parenthood.

The status category of parent always exists multiple in social contexts. Nobody can become a parent in isolation from other adults; what being or becoming a parent entails will vary from setting to setting. Parents are also individuals unto themselves—more than just means to an end and more than just members of societies. Seeking to engage both the singular and the social facets of parenthood, I'll focus here on parenthood as something that Seed the Starter starts for one person. (Later, in chapter 5, I'll turn to the relationships that transfers of semen onto mucosa generate.) Status classifications can override what an individual might prefer to seize or reject, and the parent-child status relationship pushes especially hard against individuals' choices.

You don't want to feed, shelter, provide health care for, or educate the young person whose parent you are? Too bad. Tough luck. Indifference or neglect toward most other people—friends and siblings and your own parents—is almost always fine in the eyes of the law and you can get away with a lot of disregard for your spouse. But as the parent of a child you have rigid obligations that last until your child reaches the age of majority. In my home state, age of majority for this purpose is an old school 21. New York also joins a few other states in permitting judges to order noncustodial parents to pay college expenses. You might lose custody of your minor child if you're deemed neglectful of parental obligations. Should you ever feel okay about losing custody, which you might in this fanciful scenario that paints you as an indifferent child-maker, know that the government can—and sometimes does, though it's rare—imprison parents deemed guilty of neglect.

From here, another consequence of insemination can be measured in dollars. Parents who wish to be deemed good enough, or not neglectful, must provision both cash money and noncash supports: time, curios-ity, conversation, proactive benevolence, and attention to their minor children. In this review of what semen starts, I'll put aside the nonmon-etary burdens on parents because these expenditures vary too much from family to family and I assume that at least some of the time they also generate satisfaction.

Obligation to shell out money, by contrast, is pure detriment. Cash that you must allot to your child's well-being is cash you could have directed to your own pleasure by hoarding it or spending it on some-thing you want. A CBS News story published in 2023 found that the price of rearing a child to majority is $237,482. That estimate is bare bones: it counts only food, clothing, housing, childcare, transportation, and health insurance starting with the child's birth and ending at age 18. It omits college and it includes the tax benefits of having children. This sum is what it costs in the United States to stay clear of neglect. On aver-age. Parents spend more in Hawai'i, the costliest state to rear children, and less in Mississippi, the cheapest state. Options that parents might favor—sports, after-school activities, music lessons, leisure travel—raise the price of this consequence.[34]

Seed the Starter becomes Seed the Extender when marriages or non-marital parental relationships end. American law treats child support obligations with rigidity in comparison to other consequences of insem-inations that create shared parenthood, the majority of which can be negotiated or mitigated. Most rules applicable to family conflicts give judges discretion. Family law is notorious for open-ended doctrines like equitable division of assets and liabilities ("equitable" rather equal in the sense of a 50-50 split) and best interests of the child, both of which tell judges to make decisions based on what they deem fair or correct. Child support that courts impose after relationships end has for many years deviated from this loosey-goosey flexibility: Congress imposed so-called "guidelines" on the states to limit judicial prerogative in 1988.[35]

Formulas written to be inflexible govern this result of insemination. In a few states, parents who aren't together as a couple must allot a fraction of their income to provide for their children. The majority of states, including the one I live in, make the burden more complicated with a model called "income shares." Here are the fractions of parental income that my home state has decided an individual parent owes as child support:

One child: 17%
Two children: 25%
Three children: 29%
Four children: 31%
More than four children: no less than 35%

How these percentages work, step by step: first, add up the income of the two parents; next, apply the child support percentage to that total. To imagine how this burden might feel for you if you live it, consider a person with two children where the income of that person, Parent 1, is $60,000 and the income of the person's coparent, Parent 2, is $40,000. (Realistic numbers: New York's median household income is somewhat lower, just under $80,000.)

The income shares approach in New York says that the amount of money allotted to overall child support is 25% of the total $100,000 parental income, or $25,000. Under the New York formula, the share of this total for Parent 1 to cover is 60% of $25,000, or $15,000, and the share of Parent 2 is 40% of $25,000, or $10,000. This distribution tells a court which parent will pay money to whom and how much. Individuals can try to argue in court that in their family the formula calls for flexibility, and a few questions about how to apply these formulae remain disputed around the United States. But this consequence of insemination is strikingly rigid.

Enforcement of child support obligations continues this pattern of rigidity in consequence of insemination. Only rarely does American federal law get involved with the parent-child relation; it gets involved with child support. Congress created an Office of Child Support and a Federal Parent Locator Service and assigned responsibility for these functions to the Department of Health and Human Services, a large unit of the national government. Withholding can grab more than wage income to cover child support obligations: federal law applies this collection method also to bonuses, workers' compensation, retirement benefits, pensions, and disability payments. Variations on willful nonpayment of child support can constitute federal felonies.

Looking at child support rules through the lens of semen might seem odd, I suppose. But this lens examines a matter of fact. Insemination creates parents. Parents who get along with their co-parents well enough to keep the law away can negotiate whatever cash division they want for the support of their children but the law will domineer over them when they can't agree. Because the shadow of legal rules influences negotiations, a statutory child-support scheme affects individuals who participate in semen-on-mucosa transfers that make a baby even when they are spared having to think directly about its percentages.

Negotiated rather than unshared power over one's adult life persists beyond child support rules for anyone who has made a baby, a consequence that can exist only after human semen took a trip. Responsibility for child welfare that comes from the status of parenthood does not give parents undivided control over choices that influence the child's life. Even people who get their way elsewhere find themselves sharing rather than decreeing decisions in this realm. As just noted, the law tends to defer to the decisions of parents who are married to each other and interferes more aggressively when a parent is not married to a living co-parent. This allocation of power means that almost any individual in the role of parent must heed someone else's views on childrearing. That's a spouse when the parent is married to a co-parent, a host of onlookers when the child's parents are not married to each other.

Babymaking thus generates more than a baby. With only two exceptions found relatively rarely in the bigger category of single motherhood—delivery of a posthumous child and motherhood achieved with semen from a donor who waived his parental rights before insemination—the creation of a new baby always creates an obligation to cooperate in childrearing. Cooperation can enlarge joy, comfort, and meaning in human lives. It can also sow dissonance.

Researchers have tried to measure the impact of parenthood on individual human happiness. One review reports that the findings are mixed: "Compared with nonparents, parents have been found to experience lower levels of well-being, higher levels of well-being, and similar levels of well-being," when compared with nonparents.[36] The answer to the question about whether becoming a parent makes a person happy seems to turn on which facets of happiness one researches. Honing in on how parents feel when they spend time with their children produces evidence for parental unhappiness; stepping back to ask parents how they feel about being parents, however, produces evidence for happiness. While at work, for example, a father "may report high life satisfaction when he recalls an idealized image of his son," even though he "may be miserable when actually caring for him at home."[37]

Although finding that "high life satisfaction" and "miserable" are correct conclusions about the same person might sound contradictory, both judgments testify to the importance of parenthood as an experience. The review I just quoted reconciles the contradiction by comparing parenthood to running from a tiger for safety effectively enough to save one's life. Unpleasant in the moment, satisfying to ponder later. If the analogy fits—again, I haven't been there—then once again Seed the Starter has launched significance. Any experience that can deliver extremes of both misery and deep satisfaction is unusually potent.

Differently situated folks get different strokes from the experience of becoming parents. Researchers report an association between happiness and being relatively old at the birth of one's first child. At the less happy end of the parental-satisfaction spectrum are mothers in contrast to fathers, unmarried parents, and parents of lower socioeconomic status. These differences suggest that the strain of being responsible for a minor child, a condition generated by semen, correlates with and may worsen the burdens of social disadvantage.[38]

One psychologist whose research focuses on happiness in marriage wrote a newspaper essay summarizing what social science has found about the impact of parenthood on a marital relationship. The picture is mostly bleak. Satisfaction with one's marriage tends to decline over time for all couples, but the downhill skid for couples who have children is almost twice as steep; this generalization extends to unmarried couples too. Unplanned pregnancy, which semen is pretty good at starting, worsens the decline in happiness that parenthood brings.

Financial strain is an obvious cause of this drop, but more than money runs low when children arrive. "Parents often become more distant and businesslike with each other as they attend to the details of parenting," says this review. "Mundane basics like keeping kids fed, bathed and clothed take energy, time and resolve." A couple of non-bleak consequences comfort parents. Couples who share children are less likely to divorce, or, as Matthew Johnson puts the point, "having children may make you miserable, but you'll be miserable together." A more serious positive impact of insemination is the consistent report of surveys that parenthood is the respondent's greatest joy. Both fathers and mothers say so.[39] Again, big consequences from semen.

Continuing this pattern of impacts near the intersection of insemination and social conditions, parenthood as a status advantages men and disadvantages women as workers who need wage income to live. In her 2001 book *The Price of Motherhood* Ann Crittenden estimated that becoming a mother costs a worker a million dollars in lifetime lost wages. More recent estimates say approximately the same thing. A 2021 article cited a dozen studies, all of them published in the current century, that show a set of dual consequences in the United States and other wealthy countries: becoming a mother "leads to a wage penalty for women" and "conversely, fatherhood is associated with a 3% to 10% pay premium."[40] Consistent with Seed the Starter as the source of durable consequences, the wage penalty attributable to being a mother worsens with the birth of another child.[41]

Researchers have explored the possibility that insemination could be innocent here. Mothers might be worse workers, goes the hypothesis. Maybe they've earned the result of earning less money by being less productive than nonmothers.

Experimental studies refute this conjecture with evidence that what explains the pay gap is prejudice rather than a track record.[42] Researchers created dossiers of fictitious work records and then instructed subjects to opine on whether the parent or nonparent in the dossier should be offered a job. They also told subjects to interpret points of information about these applicants. Some of the made-up resumes indicated that the applicant was a parent.

Asked in one study to say whether they recommended the job applicants for hire, participants answered yes for fewer than half the mothers but 84% of the (female) nonmothers. Asked about the salary they recommended employers offer these applicants, they chose a sum for the mothers that was 7.4% lower than that of the nonmothers. Participants also held mothers to higher standards than nonmothers on attendance and performance on a management exam: they tolerated fewer absences from mothers and required mothers to earn a higher minimum exam score. Parenthood had opposite impacts on men. Fathers won higher ratings for commitment than nonfathers and were offered higher starting salaries.[43] Judgments like these function to judge what semen achieves.

* * *

As a semen consequence, changes in wage income take us back to the bigger point that began this chapter: Seed the Starter never works alone. Imagine an awards ceremony like the Oscars where the winner says *I'd like to thank* and then starts a recitation. Here at my invisible microphone, I'd like to thank more than semen for the effects that I've found and reported here.

Like every starter, semen depends on helpers, partners, and ambient conditions to produce its effects, of which sexual reproduction is only one. How much we're paid, how happy we are, whether we thrive or suffer—any major effect on human lives has many antecedents. The next chapter turns to law as one antecedent of this kind. State-imposed controls on pregnant persons leverage the physical impacts of insemination to make these impacts bigger.

3

Pregnancy Restrictions Leverage Semen to Control Human Lives

Human semen travels from a urethra in a modest quantity, about one teaspoon at a time. Sometimes these few milliliters of fluid make it to female mucosa when they leave the male body. More often they don't. The usual fate of semen after emission is absorption into something inert. That's oblivion, disappearance.

A minority of trips that semen takes, however, can be leveraged. Journeys that launch pregnancy offer exceptional opportunities for control. The tiny teaspoon or two starts big things when it meets a fertile destination. Becoming pregnant means occupation by a hungry growing object that owes its existence to semen.

In the last chapter we counted five ways in which a pregnancy can end. No matter which of the five endings ensues, other people hold power over the body that experienced the disruptive touch of semen, as it's physically impossible for a pregnant person to manage the life form's exit from her uterus by herself without risking her life. An early uncomplicated miscarriage can happen but that ending isn't under her management; it just befalls her. Giving birth can't safely occur unattended. Abortion as an end to the pregnancy calls for somebody else to supply her with medication, or touch her cervix with a surgical instrument, or stay with her mindful that interventions to terminate sometimes require emergency treatment. In short, being pregnant means that control over one's body will be shared.

Enter controllers. Law and policy generate and support aggressions that withhold access to abortion. Aggressions go after contraception too, but I'll be focusing on interferences with an established pregnancy. Individual deciders can choose to thwart the person touched by semen by impeding this person's travels, schooling, employment opportunities and benefits, data privacy, communications on social media, treatments for medical perils separate from pregnancy like cancer, and ability to exit an abusive intimate relationship.

If the law were neutral enough about the landing of semen on mucosa to treat pregnancy as a condition for the impregnated person to accept or reject at her election, undoing this impact could proceed safely and easily. Abortion is much safer than remaining pregnant. (So are many other risky-looking activities. Skydiving, for example, is more than twenty times safer than giving birth.[1]) Every abortion provides rescue from danger.

When you are in a condition known to be dangerous, are certain to suffer pain if you remain in that state, and could benefit from feasible help in undoing the condition, the law has a choice about the rescue you might want: it can cooperate, as Canadian law notably does on this issue, or it can impose impediments. Most United States jurisdictions have chosen interference. At the time I write, the large majority of states restrict abortion with reference to gestational limits that make terminating a pregnancy unlawful after a number of weeks. Only nine states and the District of Columbia impose no time limit on the right not to be pregnant. Fourteen states have chosen to ban abortion outright with no reference to gestation time. Manmade, in contrast to nature-made, interferences leverage a past journey of semen into your body to command harmful control over your health and your future.

I'm saying "you" and "your" here to think and speak in personal terms about who leverages this fluid and who experiences the consequences of that leveraging. About half the human population is born with internal anatomical structures that can, during a span that runs for about 30 years, go on to nurture the formation of a new person. Some uncounted fraction of these female-bodied people are infertile but almost no girl or woman alive between menarche and menopause knows for sure that being ejaculated into can't impregnate her. That the majority of female-bodied people experience pregnancy at least once before they die makes this risk (and opportunity, if you would have it so) real as both biology and sociopsychological fact. More than half of us know, informed by our minds and what our bodies reveal, about our vulnerability to semen. Now, on to who does the leveraging of this vulnerability and what these controllers achieve.

* * *

When two professors, Daniel Bonevac and John Hatfield, went to federal court in Amarillo to complain about working conditions at the

University of Texas, they carped mostly about transgender persons whose chosen third-person pronouns they didn't want to use and whose access to bathrooms and dormitories and attire displeased them. *What are you going to do about it, big guys?* came to my mind. The answer turned out to be insult other people and grumble—but for another provocation, the two had a plan to impose consequences. Bonevac, a philosophy professor, and Hatfield, a professor of business and finance, announced in a court declaration that they intended to defy university medical privacy rules by declining to "accommodate student absences from class to obtain abortions."

The Texas professors elaborated on how they would administer the control over other people's bodies that they asserted. "I will certainly accommodate students who are seeking medically necessary abortions in response to a pregnancy that threatens the student's life or health," Bonevac wrote in his declaration. Hatfield chose the same phrasing. "But I will not accommodate a purely elective abortion that serves only to kill an unborn child that was conceived through an act of voluntary and consensual sexual intercourse."[2]

Hmmm. As someone tasked for years by her employer to take attendance in class and make principled decisions in response to proffered excuses, I can report that Bonevac and Hatfield would find their stated policy impossible to administer if a student engaged it by asking them to judge the moral nature of her abortion as a reason for her absence. Figuring out medical necessity for this path is tough enough even for experts in obstetrics; a professional philosopher like Bonevac also knows, or ought to know, that he can't easily tell which acts by other people are "voluntary and consensual" either. Drawing a line between okay and not okay abortion as the reason to absent oneself from school is a doomed, even silly, exercise in that it can't coherently be done.

The policy is the opposite of doomed or silly, however, in what it declares about who is in charge of the ejaculated-upon. A condition caused by the arrival of semen inside a vagina (which of course needn't be voluntary or consensual at the receiving end for impregnation to occur) makes the person with the vagina vulnerable to other people's decisions and choices. These controls and what they can alter vary. The restriction that Bonevac and Hatfield arrogated to themselves was announced as a plan to interfere with other people's education going forward; present, on-the-books restrictions that control pregnancy exercise domination here and now. They interfere with health. By that I mean these interferences sicken, and sometimes kill, pregnant girls and women.

Impacts on freedom that I'll review in this chapter come from customs and practices either mandated by or connected to American law that disempower an impregnated person and turn decisions about the interior of her body over to outsiders. This distribution of control has since 2022 tilted harder to favor persons who are not pregnant themselves and against the impregnated, but pregnancy restrictions leveraged insemination to control pregnant persons' lives well before the Dobbs decision overruled Roe v. Wade.

As a label, the phrase "pregnancy restrictions" describes these controls by some human beings over other human beings more accurately than calling them abortion restrictions. Whether someone is or is not pregnant is understood as a matter of fact; whether and how an intervention or a particular experience related to pregnancy qualifies as an abortion gets disputed. No clear line separates miscarriage and abortion.[3] The boundary between abortion and birth control is also hard to draw, especially since a 2014 decision of the Supreme Court that cited religious freedom to side with litigants who wanted to deny payment for hormonal contraception as an employment benefit. There the Court honored the employers' assertion—which could have been a sincerely held belief, but maybe not[4]—that hormonal contraception in their minds amounted to abortion.[5] If you work for a company that wishes to characterize its preferences as religious, your boss apparently may withhold from you what you want by calling it abortion, medical understanding be damned.

Justice Clarence Thomas of the Supreme Court gave additional support to contraception interference by writing separately in Dobbs to say that his colleagues should consider overruling the 1962 decision of Griswold v. Connecticut,[6] which had found a constitutional right to contraception. At this moment, the idea that American governments can or should ban contraception remains eccentric among judges, but the lack of any agreed-on official definition of abortion encourages interferers to slap the abortion label on any safeguard from semen that they want to ban. Post-Dobbs legislation enacted to govern birth control pills in

Mississippi and emergency contraception in Louisiana, for example, deemed these medications abortion.[7]

Should the Supreme Court declare that states have the option of banning birth control, one might suppose legislators would prefer not to use this power. Birth control scores very high in opinion polls: it's popular even among Republicans and even in support of the IUD, a contraceptive that makes the uterus a hostile environment for semen.[8] Time will tell, I suppose. American legislatures already ban abortion more aggressively than voters seem to prefer; they enact constraints on contraception even now while the Griswold decision remains alive; and their opportunities to stretch the abortion label to thwart more types of medical care for the female-bodied was enlarged by the national election outcome in 2024.

Interpreted as opportunities to make the impact of semen on other people's mucosa extra severe, prohibitions of abortion and contraception differ from each other only on their timing. Ban abortion and you thwart inseminated people from undoing what semen does after it acts; ban contraception and you thwart people from fending off the impact of semen in advance. Wherever both prohibitions are in place—that's the United States that one Supreme Court justice said he'd be fine with— individuals who don't want to be forced into pregnancy followed by childbearing and whose mucosa is vulnerable to insemination have to hope that semen will stay away from their cervix. Similarity of the two interferences favors terminology that covers both. Because every abortion restriction exerts control over persons understood to be pregnant, "pregnancy" in the label is always accurate.

* * *

Occupational groups with power to make decisions about pregnancy start with medical providers, a professional cohort that includes physicians and specialist personnel like nurse practitioners trained in obstetrics and gynecology. Abortion bans in the United States focus on this occupation by criminalizing the action that one person takes to terminate another person's pregnancy. Some of these laws criminalize other actions too, but state-level felony liability for a medical provider who terminates a pregnancy is the signature trait of an abortion ban.

Because no unit of government in the United States, federal or state, makes the *refusal* to terminate pregnancy a crime, abortion bans have an effect that goes only one way in relation to semen as a traveler. Criminal codes punish only interferences with the landing of semen onto a cervix; they don't punish the choice to worsen this consequence or let it continue. Deciders can always say no with no legal consequences to themselves when someone asks them to provide an abortion.

Professional judgment as an obstacle to termination deserves more attention in abortion policy than it receives. Consider the familiar misogynous conceit of a woman who, in the last weeks of her healthy pregnancy, decides on a whim that she's done. This hypothetical, which sometimes throws in a maximally shallow motive (versions I've heard sometimes say our blithe terminator wants to fit into a femmey garment like a bikini or a prom dress), gets trotted out to say that permitting abortion "on demand" gives inseminated persons too much prerogative. Donald Trump lobbed it at Hillary Clinton during the 2016 presidential campaign and went further in 2024 by saying Democrats favored "we'll execute the baby" *after* birth as a termination option.[9] But our hypothetical pregnant woman would need a medical provider to supply her abortion and this profession doesn't obey irrational or capricious requests from patients. Here on Earth, away from fever dreams, doctors don't rip out a healthy mature fetus and toss it in the trash for no reason.

Asked to say either yes or no to abortion as a therapeutic option, these deciders face damned-if-you-do and damned-if-you-don't dangers to themselves. The path of "if you don't," or refusing to terminate a perilous pregnancy, might violate professional standards of care and expose this doctor to a claim of malpractice should their pregnant patient suffer injury. This risk to the doctor could ripen, as I can attest from having taught medical malpractice law for a long time. But this category of personal injury claim is hard for plaintiffs to win even away from the fraught context of abortion, and I'm confident that obtaining a qualified lawyer to sue for failure to terminate would need a painful, protracted death by the patient and a chorus of one-sided expert testimony. Not so very damned if you don't, in other words.

Pregnancy termination as a professional decision has much clearer risks for the doctor than declining to provide one. The Texas ban authorizes a prison sentence of up to 99 years, sets a minimum $100,000 for a fine, and permits courts to nullify a medical license. That's plenty "damned if you do." Felony punishments run lighter in Iowa, Nebraska, and Wyoming—at least as of now: Nebraska legislators have proposed to "strip doctors who perform abortions of their medical licenses if they perform one after detecting cardiac activity on an ultrasound, or even if they fail to provide an ultrasound before an abortion."[10] A reporter for National Public Radio quoted an obstetrician-gynecologist about one-way semen leverage in her abortion-ban state. "There is no way that I would risk my personal freedom and jail time for providing medical care," the doctor said. "I would love to show my children that I am brave in the world, but our society will not allow me to be a civil-disobedient citizen. I would be imprisoned, I would be fined, I would lose my license and I very well could be assassinated for doing that work."[11]

Exceptions written into abortion bans might make an observer wonder whether physicians like the doctor NPR quoted are exaggerating or misperceiving their professional peril. Even the most hostile-to-abortion U.S. penal codes have declined to take an absolutist approach to their prohibition in the mode of Let Her Die countries like Madagascar or El Salvador. Or Honduras, which topped those two in 2021 when it engraved its absolute ban into its hard-to-amend constitution.[12] American physicians are permitted to rescue patients from danger when an exception to the state ban fits, and so the leveraging of semen that these prohibitions encourage might appear to impose only a degree of control over human lives, managed and interpreted by medical experts, rather than a total power grab.

A total power grab is indeed what these prohibitions write into law. Every exception that exists in theory leaves almost every landing of semen on mucosa undisturbed and the lives of ejaculated-upon people controlled and harmed in practice. I'll go through the leading exceptions in descending order of their popularity in state statutes that ban abortion. By the time we reach the fourth, which permits abortion when the fetus is doomed and cannot survive for more than a short time after birth, we find an exception that most bans do not include.

Life of the pregnant person is the most widely accepted exception to abortion bans. It's available in states that prohibit abortion in almost every circumstance. Arkansas, for example, bans all abortions except those that "save the life of a pregnant woman in a medical emergency." South Dakota says abortion is categorically banned "except when necessary to preserve the life of the pregnant female."[13]

Now imagine yourself practicing obstetrics in a state that recognizes only this exception to its abortion ban. An emergency strikes. Your pregnant patient's death is not guaranteed. Instead, what's gone wrong presents a significant risk of death. The emergency worsens. You and your colleagues might be able to save your patient with a blood transfusion, a sudden hysterectomy, or big doses of antibiotics. Those interventions might or might not work. To be clear that nobody has volunteered to ease your dilemma by conveniently inviting you to choose maternal death, let's further imagine that the patient, or a family member of hers if she is unconscious, pleads with you as her medical provider to save her life. Savita Halappanavar, the patient whose death from sepsis in 2012 spurred Ireland to reverse its abortion ban, begged for rescue. Most people who are alive want to stay alive.

The save-a-life exception in principle might protect you from criminal prosecution if you terminate this pregnancy. Of course, if your patient does fine after the abortion you perform, onlookers are free to suppose you overreacted and killed something or somebody in haste. Before you make your choice you know you're safe from criminal prosecution if you withhold termination, vulnerable if you act to undo the consequence of semen on mucosa. You mean well. You don't want your patient to die a pointless painful death. You also don't want to suffer. When your pregnant patient isn't yet hemorrhaging and doesn't yet show signs of an infection, you'd likely slow down rather than focus on the duty of care that you owe this person. "I believe the state's law was intended to be ambiguous and confusing, to make physicians scared to provide abortion care," wrote a Tennessee physician, reflecting on what she called "one of those 5 percent situations." Delay is safer for these doctors than taking prompt action. "We're incentivized to pause, wait, reconsider."[14]

Readers who disapprove of argument by hypothetical can read the testimony of an Oklahoma patient named Jaci Statton who told about her real-life outcome in a formal complaint. Oklahoma's abortion ban is among the strictest in the United States. Statton experienced a life-threatening nonviable molar pregnancy in 2023. Zero chance of a healthy baby, extremely high risk to the life of Stratton if she remained pregnant. Staffers at a hospital told Statton that her condition hadn't yet risen to earn Oklahoma's save-a-life entitlement. She would receive no treatment, but she could sit in the hospital parking lot hoping to graduate into the exception by "actively crashing in front of them or on the verge of a heart attack" while located helpfully near the emergency room.[15]

Formal complaints like the one filed by Jaci Statton interested the Associated Press. To learn more, a reporter submitted a Freedom of Information Act request seeking all 2022 patient complaints that claimed hospitals violated the Emergency Medical Treatment and Labor Act, a federal law obliging hospitals and emergency rooms that receive Medicare funding to treat or stabilize every patient who arrives in active labor. Active labor is a condition that can occur only when semen landed on mucosa. In response to the FOIA request, government redactors sent only a portion of the complaints and investigative documents in its files, and also withheld the names of patients and medical staff.

They did name institutions. At one of them, a Houston venue called Sacred Heart Emergency Center, a pregnant woman had arrived in September 2022 bleeding heavily. Staff refused to register her. Turned away from treatment, this woman continued her miscarriage in the ER lobby restroom while her husband phoned 911 to seek help. Transcripts recorded puzzlement at the receiving end: *You're calling about a medical emergency. We'll be there. But wait, be where? You're at a medical facility?* Drawing a lesson from this complaint about its neglect, Sacred Heart Emergency Center chose to change its policies. About helping patients? No. About taking Medicare money.[16]

ProPublica, a nonprofit journalism business, undertook to learn about deaths of inseminated persons in the United States attributable to abortion bans. Dying while pregnant often has multiple causes; ProPublica looked for the subset with a documented medical record showing that ordinary standard-of-care intervention, had it been followed, would have prevented the patient's death. The criterion that ProPublica chose resolved ambiguity by excluding uncertain cases.

That filter left in several deaths that demonstrably would not have occurred but for the combination of an abortion ban and semen on mucosa. ProPublica told its readers about one patient, Amber Thurman, who died because physicians had felt unsure whether Georgia's life-of-the-pregnant-person exception covered the intervention she needed when she arrived at a suburban Atlanta emergency room bleeding heavily and having vomited blood. These providers delayed treatment even after an obstetrician among them diagnosed what a chart notation called "acute severe sepsis." Another patient followed Thurman down the path of preventable death in November 2022 when she chose to stay home in severe pain after abortion pills had failed fully to end her pregnancy. Ten physicians signed a review that concluded Candi Miller would have sought medical help in a hospital but for the Georgia prohibition. Rather than continue to tolerate the creation of material that investigative journalists like ProPublica could find in their state, in late 2024 Georgia officials dissolved the maternal health panel that would otherwise have been able to study the next preventable deaths of successors to Amber Thurman and Candi Miller. In its research away from Georgia, ProPublica also found that Texas's abortion ban, festooned with the same unavailing life-of-the-pregnant-person exception, caused the death of two other inseminated human beings.

That's the life exception. On to the next one, which references maternal health. Apparently worried that liberal interpretation would permit the exception to swallow the rule, American abortion banners do not reference the whole of maternal health. That's how abortion-ban exceptions operate in Europe and Israel, permitting medical providers to proceed as their judgment dictates. Bans in the United States use a narrower exception that demands danger to an anatomical specific.

In Florida and a few other states, that danger must be "a serious risk of substantial and irreversible impairment of a major bodily function." Kentucky and Louisiana require the possibility of "serious, permanent impairment of a life-sustaining organ." In Utah, the exception requires "serious physical risk of substantial impairment of a major bodily function."[17] Put yourself in the role of a semen-decider doctor in a state like these.

I'll site you in Texas, where the ban-and-exception that you live under will apply only if you've identified "a life-threatening physical condition aggravated by, caused by, or arising from a pregnancy that poses a serious risk of substantial impairment of a major bodily function" before you may lawfully terminate anyone's pregnancy.[18] Your patient is Kate Cox. Genetic tests found trisomy 18, a condition that dooms 90% of infants to death before they turn one year old, in the fetus that Cox carried.

Cox and her husband looked to their near-term future. No hope of a healthy end to the pregnancy. Two young children at home. Plans for a larger family. An interviewer asked Cox's lawyer whether she thought

Cox qualified for the Texas exception. "Yes, and so did her doctor," the lawyer replied. "The problem is, no one knows what that *means*. Major bodily function? Surely fertility would count as a major bodily function. But there's no clarity about this."[19]

Somebody empowered as one of Kate Cox's semen deciders, Texas attorney general Ken Paxton, disagreed about "no clarity" and proceeded with confidence. After Cox went to court seeking assurance that the health exception applied and that an abortion would be lawful, Paxton wrote to three Texas hospitals telling them they would face legal action if they furnished Cox with an abortion.[20] Another semen decider, the Texas Supreme Court, agreed with Paxton. Back to you as a potential doctor-provider of abortion. You could still go ahead, but you've been threatened effectively. Cox traveled out of Texas for her abortion.

Uselessness of the Texas health exception continued in Zurawski v. State, a judicial decision whose name became the title of a documentary film. Twenty women who had experienced severe peril during their pregnancies asked for clarity about the situations that permit abortion to protect health of the impregnated. The state's highest court ruled against these plaintiffs, faulting doctors rather than the wording of this exception that ostensibly protects semen-impacted people in the state. Doctors should go ahead with a termination when they deem the exception applicable, said the Texas Supreme Court.[21] If they're wrong they'll find out later, the hard way.

"Major bodily function" or "life-sustaining organ" in a health exception flouts medical reality by misperceiving the nature of risk. Dangerous pregnancy frequently threatens more than one particular body part or function. Whenever remaining pregnant would lead to sepsis, suicidal ideation, the worsening of a disease that's already present, physical pain more severe than the high baseline accepted as normal, or the inability to carry another pregnancy to term after a current doomed pregnancy ends, health exceptions as worded now are unavailable because no organ is pointedly in danger.

Exceptions to abortion bans that focus on body parts thwart medical expertise in specialties other than obstetrics and gynecology. Oncologists and rheumatologists face similar interferences with their judgments about patient care. Health exceptions that insist on danger to a singular body part and make no room for holistic assessment worsen the impact of diseases that these specialists treat.

Because oncology relies on interventions that inflict collateral damage when they attack tumors and pathologies, abortion bans get in the way of cancer treatment. They do so in action, not just in theory: the record of harm to real people is extensive. After one pregnant woman in Omaha, mother of a nine-month-old baby, was diagnosed with breast cancer, her oncologist invoked Nebraska's ban to withhold chemotherapy from her. Another woman in Ohio was already receiving chemotherapy when she learned she was pregnant. Her doctors said she couldn't continue this treatment until her pregnancy ended. At eight weeks, she was too far along for a legal abortion. Elsewhere in Ohio, a 37-year-old woman with melanoma received the same news about no more treatment coupled with the same gestational-limit impossibility.[22] And when a 25-year-old cancer patient in Dayton being treated with chemotherapy learned she was eight weeks pregnant, her doctor was unwilling to provide documentation sufficient to get past the barrier of Ohio's so-called heartbeat bill. This physician told her to choose either no more chemotherapy or a trip out of Ohio for a therapeutic abortion.[23]

Near-term trends point toward an increase in the problem of incompatibility between pregnancy and therapies that address cancer. Maternal age continues to go up while the risk of cancer gets larger with age. On top of this intersection, the 26 states that ban abortion or restrict it stringently account for about 41% of the nation's births. The leveraging of semen landings by abortion restrictions thus has an extra-severe impact on a growing population of critically ill people. Unlucky individuals in this cohort will die from cancers that could have been treated effectively if not for the impact of semen inside them.

As for rheumatologists and their patients, the gold-standard drug to treat rheumatoid arthritis is a medication that might be, though rarely is, deployed to end pregnancy. Methotrexate can also cause birth defects. Patients who take methotrexate receive copious warnings and admonitions: but no matter how diligent about birth control these individuals could be, individual physicians have stopped prescribing it to patients for fear of abortion-crime liability.[24] In consequence of this decision by medical providers—doctors who likely have no abortion or contraception agenda and just want to treat rheumatoid arthritis without jeopardizing their liberty and livelihood—patient pain has increased. One woman living in Texas told a reporter from the Washington Post that a brief period off methotrexate when she was young cost her permanent vision loss and now, as a visually disabled adult needing pregnancy tests to qualify for her prescriptions, she hoped that the state of abortion control would let her keep taking the drug.[25]

"Rape and incest," shorthand for the next exception, permits providers to terminate a pregnancy that originated in sexual assault. Though popular with the public as measured by opinion polls, this exception is rarely available even in principle. Abortion bans tend to leave it out. The rare bans that include this exception nullify its effect by requiring a report to law enforcement of the attack before the provider can go ahead with termination. Most sexual assaults don't get reported to the police. Children impregnated by rape can't make their own reports; adult family members, who might prefer to protect rapists more than victims, control them.

This exception could have been written differently. It could recognize statutory rape, for example. Virtually every pregnancy experienced by a child under 14 originates in a sexual assault. Imagine yourself as a physician practicing obstetrics in a state that bans abortion and adds the rape and incest exception. You as a physician might reasonably conclude that state law permits you to provide a termination after a man raped a nine-year-old girl and impregnated her—especially when the child's family promptly reported the rape, the perp went on to plead guilty, and a physician determined that the physical toll of remaining pregnant would cause the child severe harm.

Not so fast, Doctor, if you want to protect yourself. A physician named Caitlin Bernard treated a young child in that condition—age 9 when she was impregnated, age 10 when Bernard saw her—with medication abortion in Indiana, a rape-and-incest-exception abortion-ban state. Indiana authorities responded to this rescue by launching investigations of an abortion that would never have been needed but for the rape of a little girl that put semen into her. Bernard complied with state law that required her to report the abortion; the state attorney general falsely said she hadn't. Indiana's medical licensing board fined Bernard

$3,000 for discussing the case in public—even though Bernard hadn't named or identified the child, who lived outside Indiana—and reprimanded her.[26] Doctors who practice in states that ban abortion can infer that they are better off letting this impact of semen remain undisturbed where it landed via rape.

The last and rarest major exception to abortion bans permits providers to terminate a pregnancy where the fetus is doomed. One relatively common such peril, ectopic pregnancy, arises when a fertilized egg implants outside the uterus. Ectopic pregnancy cannot result in the birth of a healthy infant. It ends either by spontaneous miscarriage or deliberate termination. Left untreated, ectopic pregnancy can kill the woman who is pregnant by rupturing. A few abortion bans include an exception for ectopic pregnancy; the majority of them don't mention it. Physicians who treat patients with this condition have to exercise medical judgment quickly, their licenses and jobs and liberty on the line, even though the obviously correct response to an ectopic pregnancy is to terminate it pronto. This pregnancy will not go away spontaneously without endangering the life of the person touched by semen.

Let's look at a few grotesque pathologies inconsistent with life that prenatal care detects. Gathering them isn't gratuitous, I think: the exercise shows the plight of doctors who practice obstetrics under abortion bans that provide no fatal fetal anomaly exception. Old school Roe-era opponents of the right to terminate needed ignorance of fetus-dooming horrors that can lurk inside the person they called "the mother" to equate abortion with murder and at the same time call themselves pro-life. Today hospitals that deliver babies have access to diagnostic technology that reveals fatal anomalies with reliable accuracy. In these gruesome settings, a fetus can live only for a short time and in miserable conditions. The person who is pregnant will suffer before it dies. And abortion bans prohibit doctors from taking action to care for their patient.

Take alobar holoprosencephaly. A fortunately rare anomaly (1 in 250 fetuses and 1 in 16,000 live births), it's marked by the failure of the brain to follow the normal developmental path of dividing into two hemispheres. Babies with it can be born alive but cannot survive without extraordinary interventions, such as a ventilator or other life-support machinery, and they never reach developmental milestones. Alobar holoprosencephaly is not an acceptable reason for termination in most states with abortion bans.

Or fetal anencephaly. This anomaly stops the brain from forming and also can thwart development of the skull. "There is no known cure or standard treatment for anencephaly," says the Centers for Disease Control. "Almost all babies born with anencephaly will die shortly after birth." One patient who testified about the impact of the Texas ban reported that her baby with anencephaly "was gasping for air" before dying and that she saw the infant's skin turn purple.[27]

A direr anomaly, acrania, involves a fetus with no skull and no ability to develop one. Nancy Davis testified that doctors advised her to terminate her pregnancy because her fetus would die shortly after birth. Davis agreed and sought an abortion, but she lived in Louisiana. Her fetus, lacking a brain, produced enough detectable cardiac activity to make termination unlawful.[28]

Fetal anomalies shared by unborn twins in northeast Texas looked so horrific on an ultrasound that a sonogram technician fled the examination room. "Organs were hanging out of their bodies, or hadn't developed yet at all. One of the babies had a clubbed foot; the other, a big bubble of fluid at the top of his neck."[29] One kidney for the two of them. No hope whatsoever. "It was, in many ways, a simple diagnosis: As soon as these babies were born, they would die." Unable to afford or manage a 12-hour road trip to New Mexico—two other states, Arkansas and Oklahoma, were closer to home but as places to get an abortion not different from Texas—the semen-impacted patient and her partner waited months for a futile delivery. Surgery to extract the doomed twins took two hours "as doctors sawed through scar tissue from three previous C-sections."

These Texas and Louisiana accounts show what ensues predictably in states with no fatal fetal anomaly exception to their abortion bans, but the role of physicians as deciders is starker in states that recognize it. Antiabortion activists erode the potential of this exception in these jurisdictions by denying the "fatal" part. After all, everything is fatal; nobody leaves this world alive. They prefer to say "life-limiting" instead of fatal and have written standards of care that encourage physicians to treat these fetuses with kindness and respect, keeping them technically alive at all costs—with most of these costs borne by the inseminated person. The purpose of euphemisms like life-limiting "is to make women believe that there's a chance their fetus might survive," wrote Jessica Valenti on Substack, "even if that's never going to happen."[30] Danger and misery for the inseminated human incubator who houses always follows. Like the one for rape and incest, the fatal fetal anomaly exception leaves the impact of semen unremedied where it landed because physicians can't use it to support rescue.

* * *

Forcing people to remain pregnant usually forces them to give birth, but not always. A large minority of pregnancies end in miscarriage. One might think this possibility lies outside the reach of human controllers. Restrictions can withhold abortion and birth control, but they can't withhold anything when a pregnant person miscarries, can they? They can. They do. Controllers seize spontaneous miscarriage as another opportunity to leverage the landing of semen on mucosa.

When a miscarriage expels a fetus or embryo out of the body in a clean and thorough fell swoop, would-be interferers in other people's lives have little to work with. Pregnancy existed and then it ended. But the fell swoop is exceptional. Miscarriages more often occur in stages, with retained products of conception remaining. This material endangers the person in whom it lingers.

A straightforward way to remove this postmiscarriage detritus is a D&C, the abbreviation for dilation and curettage. Expand the cervix to aid entry—that's dilation—and then apply the next intervention, curettage, to clear what's in the uterus. These contents are a source of medical risk to a pregnant person and nothing else: they have no future. Experts favor D&C as a miscarriage treatment when the patient can benefit from a prompt resolution: if she is bleeding heavily, for example, or is in an otherwise fragile condition.

A slower method to resolve miscarriage uses medication. First the patient takes mifepristone to soften the cervix and ease the passage of remains. Then comes misoprostol to generate uterine contractions.

A third method: wait for the body to take care of expulsion on its own. Anatomy often cooperates with this passive approach. In a minority of miscarriages, however, about one in five, the miscarriage will need either Option 1, a D&C, or the mifepristone-misoprostol combination of Option 2, in order to conclude.

Choosing among these miscarriage-resolving techniques is a matter of medical judgment, an exercise in which professional standards take into account what the patient wants for herself. Some people who experience the grief of pregnancy loss would prefer the swift end of surgery, for example, rather than the bleeding-and-waiting pace of medication or the even longer wait that doing nothing demands. Other patients might focus on the nonzero risk of complications following a D&C used for this purpose.[31]

Abortion bans block this therapeutic perspective on miscarriage. Preempting compassion, judgment, and professional best practices, these restrictions look askance on D&C and mifepristone/misoprostol, equating both of them with nonspontaneous abortion, the chosen kind. Abortion bans do not explicitly force physicians to choose the path of passive wait, but they encourage that choice. Prohibiting abortion with the usual limited exceptions tells physicians that if they want to be safe they'll pick the path that comes closest to doing nothing.[32]

In its clinical practice guidelines, the antiabortion American Association of Pro-Life Obstetricians and Gynecologists encourages follower-doctors to remove what it calls "already-deceased fetuses" by cesarean section, a surgery that hurts the patient and imposes risks on her, rather than the faster and safer technique of a D&C.[33] No harm no foul, the antis might suppose. C-sections are so common. Most patients survive them. To that blithe brushoff I'd say that painful incision, painful recovery, and lost time from work or care for one's family always matter to the inseminated person. A decent set of guidelines would care about these consequences of semen on someone else's mucosa enough to refrain from encouraging gratuitous sadism.

* * *

Pharmacists also make decisions about semen impacts outside their own bodies. Instead of protecting patients who are entitled to receive prescription drugs from the interferences of deciders who leverage an impact of semen, about a quarter of U.S. states grant this profession the conscientious-objection option that federal law extends to potential providers of abortion and sterilization. The option is exceptional in the

American workplace. Employees usually don't get to keep their jobs after they've refused their employers' orders and their employer wants to fire them in response. Pharmacists receive exceptional job security normally reserved for a minority of the workforce: government employees, union members, tenured professors.

Here's an illustration of a leveragee at the mercy of a leverager. Amanda Renz went to a Kmart store in Wisconsin to refill her prescription for birth control pills. Standing behind the counter, pharmacist Neil Noesen asked Renz if she intended to use these pills for contraceptive purposes. "Yes," said Renz. "No," said Noesen. He would not refill the prescription. Nor would he tell Renz where or how she could get it filled elsewhere. Noesen was the only pharmacist at Kmart at the time. Renz left the store and headed for Walmart. When the Walmart pharmacist phoned Noesen to transfer the prescription, Noesen refused to cooperate. He later told the state pharmacy board that engaging with his computer screen would have felt to him like participating in contraception.[34]

This drugstore employee decided to override what customers choose and support semen landing as a force he deemed entitled to change their lives, and in his role as a pharmacist he didn't have to say much beyond No to exercise this control. State laws that entitle pharmacists to defy company policy as well as patient health are vague on what exactly the objecting pharmacist must object to. South Dakota pharmacists may refuse to fill a prescription "if there is reason to believe" that the prescribed drug will "cause an abortion" or "destroy an unborn child." A fertilized egg thus is eligible to be considered an unborn child before implantation, no matter that the obstetrics profession defines a later event, implantation, as the start of pregnancy. Options are looser in Arkansas: pharmacists there may say No to "contraceptive procedures, supplies, or information" for whatever reason or lack thereof. The Arkansas statute protecting pharmacists omits any obligation to hold a moral, conscientious, or religious objection. In Mississippi, the veto prerogative that covers pharmacists extends to anything "that violates his or her conscience."[35]

In theory, our pharmacist can also cultivate and indulge antipathy to any of the pharmaceutical products stored behind a counter—drugs that include baldness meds, erectile dysfunction pills, terbinafine for jock itch—but substances that reverse the impact of semen dominate the medications that offend these conscientious objectors. It's not just jobs that defiant pharmacists get to keep; their entitlements extend also to shelter from professional discipline. If a state pharmacy board decides to sanction pharmacists who refused to fill a prescription, for example by suspending their license, state law overrides this professional judgment and prevents the board from enforcing its decision.

Everyday hormonal birth control and emergency birth control lead the roster of drugs that pharmacists have refused to dispense. The possibility that these substances function as abortifacients is tendentious nonsense. Remembering an aphorism favored by the late Mark Kleiman, I'll remark that opponents of abortion have a right to their own opinion but not their own facts. The agency that regulates the distribution of drugs in Europe has determined that levonorgestrel, active ingredient of the birth control drug dubbed Plan B, cannot prevent implantation of a fertilized egg. This drug works by inhibiting ovulation and thickening cervical mucus; it does not destroy an embryo. Accurate labeling by the European Medicines Agency explains what levonorgestrel does (which is make the body inhospitable to conception) and does not do (block implantation).

But because it's impossible for researchers to prove the negative that Plan B has never harmed a fertilized egg, semen leveragers feel entitled to keep the possibility alive in their hearts and minds. Most ignorant false beliefs are none of my business, I suppose. Believe that the moon is made of green cheese or that five is the sum of two and two. I won't try to stop you. Up to the point when you're using your erroneous belief to domineer over someone else and cause harm: that's when you need to find another way to make a living.

* * *

Parents of impregnated minors, along with judges authorized to approve abortions when parents of these minors are unavailable or uncoopera- tive, fill our next tranche of semen deciders empowered to side against the interests of persons whose mucosa this fluid has touched. Like phy- sicians and pharmacists, these people deserve the internet-ism #notall. Some large number of parents and judges, maybe most of them for all I know, mean well. Parents and judges are nevertheless deciders whose choices enlarge the impact of semen on people who are not themselves.

I note what they can impose, rather than any shortfall of deciders' benevolence.

Most states have enacted laws that give parents authority to override what their pregnant children want. Like other instances of semen-leveraging in this chapter, this assignment of power does more harm than good. It makes bad situations worse. I say so with no quarrel about the entitlement of parents to make decisions about the medical care of their minor children, and aware that medication furnished to terminate pregnancy falls under medical care. So too does surgical abortion. As a locus of control over a minor, however, abortion is different in two key respects from other medical treatments that parents can approve or reject.

The first difference: medical intervention will happen to 100% of these patients regardless of what a parent chooses. We're not dealing with parental skepticism about an option like circumcision or therapeutic surgery where the alternative to a procedure is leaving the child alone. Unless she dies first, every pregnant person will face health care and medical providers. Somebody will touch her body intimately for medical reasons soon, no later than in a few months. Parents of pregnant minors are powerless to fend off that touching of their children's genitals. All they can do with their power is limit the future of their daughters.

The other difference that abortion presents, related to the one about medical inevitability that exists no matter what parents decide, is the same semen asymmetry we saw when we looked at doctors who can always say No to termination but end up precluded from saying Yes. States can require parental involvement before a minor can have an abortion but can't stop a minor from becoming pregnant. Now I'll ask you to take the role of a pregnant minor. Termination as a path? Not yours, missy. You're too young. We'll force you to do what adults decree. Obey their veto. But nobody can take official formal action to Nope you out of incubating a baby. Both the decisional capacity of teenagers and the importance of parental involvement get heeded only to favor childbirth.[36]

In other words, state legislatures provision official formal action in aid of only one path, continuing pregnancy. Same person. Same level of physical and psychological maturity. Whether she'll be forced to experience the burden of being pregnant and giving birth against her will is under the control of relatives who can leverage the landing of semen against her interests.

The dominant American position on parental involvement in an abortion decision is mandatory notification, where providers may not proceed until they learn that the minor's parent, parents, or guardian(s) have been told about the abortion to come. About 11 states impose the more burdensome hurdle of parental *consent*. At the other end of this range, a few states require neither parental notification nor parental consent. I live in one of them.

Mindful that informing a parent about plans for an abortion can be dangerous for some pregnant minors, states that require notification or consent typically recognize exceptions or provide the pregnant minor with the option of judicial bypass. Judicial bypass permits the minor to go to court and ask a judge to approve the termination of her pregnancy. Exceptions noted, most pregnant minors in the United States can obtain an abortion only with involvement from their parents. Mandatory parental involvement means the opportunity for parental control.

Again, what's going on is leveraging. Most minors who are not pregnant live under the parental thumb in other ways, but parents who wish to assert dominion over these nonpregnant kids don't have the lever of abortion control that state laws provide. Past landings of semen give parents an extra helping of power over their pregnant children.

Requirements of parental consent implicitly presume that parents are abler than minors to make the abortion-or-not decision. Research has shown that this premise isn't correct. Pregnant teens can decide just as well as their parents.[37] True, American law permits parents to make other medical decisions for their children even if their children would function as well or better as deciders. Abortion is exceptional, however, in that a No to termination decreed by a parent where the healthier and safer answer would have been Yes imposes unique burdens. Not only pregnant teens but children born to reluctant young mothers suffer from this category of parental power to refuse.

From its vantage point of physicians who care for child patients, the American Academy of Pediatrics has studied impacts of this prerogative, concluding in a policy statement that "laws requiring a parent's involvement in a teen's legal abortion are not helpful, and may cause harm." Here is the AAP list of harms. Delayed access to medical care. Illegal and self-induced abortion. Family violence. Homelessness. Suicide. Later abortions, which are associated with increased risks compared to earlier abortions.[38]

Even when parents of teenagers mean well, any communication forced between them and teen abortion patients arrives at a vulnerable juncture. Two conditions, onset of both adolescence and pregnancy of a family member, disrupt settled routines. If you've experienced either condition while living in a family with relatives, directly or through observation of someone else in your household, you may recall the impact. Mandatory parental notification enlarges the force of two stressors. That's in tranquil homes. The stressors in combination have worse effects in troubled families.

From there we have a straight line, an unbroken connection, between impregnation and parental control over teenagers. Semen lands and another set of consequences ensues. Violent parents acquire what looks like a reason, or at least an understandable provocation, to inflict harm on a person who might have done nothing to deserve punishment. Anyone can see this self-entitled anger coming. Justice John Paul Stevens, quoting a trial court, once observed that "a mother's perception in a dysfunctional family that there will be violence if the father learns of the daughter's pregnancy is likely to be an accurate perception."[39] The teen's mother predicted it. The teen predicted it. You, gentle reader, are not shocked to hear it.

Judicial bypass is the cure for pernicious parental control over teenagers who seek an abortion, taking power away from a tyrant at home and moving it to judges. The Supreme Court deemed this fix good enough to rescue mandatory parental notification from unconstitutionality.[40] A minor into whom someone deposited semen can seek help from a decider who might be more benevolent, and probably would bring less emotion to the decision, than her parent. We can infer relative benevolence from the data point that most teens tell their parents when they want an abortion. Those of them who choose judicial bypass know what they are doing, I presume. Controls over the impregnated person continue, however, even when assigned to someone worthy and competent.

Extra trouble for the pregnant minor arises in locations where a large fraction of the judges available to her as bypassers oppose abortion as a matter of conscience. This minor will reach a courthouse where the legally provisioned end run against her parents' hostility is difficult to obtain. After decades of energetic antiabortion activism applied to judicial selection, a growing number of American judges owe their jobs to their announced compliance with ideological criteria that include opposition to abortion.

Fair-minded judges who oppose the right to terminate pregnancy will choose recusal rather than hear minors' pleas under a pretense of neutrality and then command forced birth. But refusing to participate in judicial bypass isn't neutral when it dominates a region or judicial district. Studies of the problem have found swaths of the United States where judges' views make judicial bypass extremely difficult to receive. Back when Roe v. Wade still lived and Tennessee couldn't ban abortion, the majority of eligible judges in Memphis refused to hear bypass petitions.[41] The American sociopolitical condition of urban support and rural hostility with respect to abortion rights means that pregnant minors located away from big cities, like their pregnant adult peers, have a literally long way to go before they can choose termination even when they are lucky enough to live in a state whose interference with the opportunity to undo this impair of semen stops short of a strong ban.

* * *

Predatory inseminators, our next category of people who leverage semen to exert control over others' lives, ejaculate with bad intent. A few of them ejaculate without any obvious agenda and only later leverage this landing of their semen to do harm on purpose. I'll get to one of them in a moment, postponing another subset of predators to the chapter coming up called Lasting Relationships. There we'll meet people, most but not all of them female, upon whom rapists imposed parenthood. Impregnated individuals of that chapter remained pregnant and gave birth. They had their reasons. Other victims of predatory inseminators, the ones who belong in a chapter about abortion rights, prefer to get rid of their pregnancy. Prohibiting or withholding termination strengthens the harm that a predatory inseminator inflicts. Semen makes his rape more powerful and dangerous.

Being able to terminate an unwanted pregnancy is essential to harm reduction: without that opportunity, the transfer of this fluid onto mucosa keeps serious misbehavior of the recent past alive and painful for someone who may have done nothing to deserve durable suffering. Serious misbehavior includes wrongs less severe than rape that can accompany sexual intercourse: deceit, for example, or coercion. Caddishness by an ejaculator isn't as bad, I suppose, but it too gets coddled and abetted when its victim can't eliminate a painful reminder of her experience that she does not want to bear. Governments that restrict abortion support and side with assailants. This withholding worsens a prior wrong that originated in predatory conduct.

Sexual assault during which an adult ejaculates into the vagina of a child and thereby makes her pregnant exemplifies predatory insemination. Child rape—that's the term I'll use here, aware that criminal codes favor more technical terminology—is not the only example of this wrong but it's the easiest to understand as deserving condemnation. The codification of this crime usually categorizes this conduct as worse than the rape of an adult. Some codified crimes are controversial; this one isn't. All decent people disapprove of child rape.

Because in most cases of child rape the assailant knew his victim before he raped her, this predator will know or have reason to know about signs of puberty that communicate to him that the semen he injects risks impregnating her. He might not want to make his victim pregnant. I'm willing to assume that in most cases he doesn't. But when he ejaculates into a child's vagina, he is endangering another person with a deliberate act.

Semen on female mucosa cannot impregnate a girl or woman most of the time—that's how our species is wired—but even though most instances of this conduct won't result in pregnancy, the adult participant knows that the child he rapes cannot protect herself against the risk he has chosen to impose on her. When a predator impregnates a child, his victim needs access to abortion for her health because remaining pregnant and giving birth is dangerous for a child. We met such a child earlier in this chapter, the 10-year-old rape victim that Dr. Caitlin Bernard helped with medication abortion and got punished for rescuing.

The notorious predator Jeffrey Epstein, found dead in a jail cell before he could be tried for crimes that included child sex trafficking, had a big semen-on-mucosa scheme starring himself. A news story published shortly before his 2019 death delved into Epstein's agenda to create a new generation of babies.[42] Epstein talked about his insemination plans with famous scientists of his time including Stephen Jay Gould, Oliver Sachs, Stephen Hawking, and the Nobel Prize winner and quark discoverer Murray Gell-Mann. He told listeners about his notion to establish what he called a baby ranch at a property he owned in New Mexico that would use semen from him to launch superior human specimens. Epstein's goal, according to one informant, was twenty vessels pregnant at all times.

To the extent Epstein offended any of his all-male interlocutors, it was by reminding them of Nazi eugenics. His well-fed and -liquored audience didn't express concern for any mucosa-bearer at the receiving end of Epstein's semen. As a predatory inseminator, however, Epstein had more in mind than master-race ambitions. His taste for underage girls as sex partners almost certainly meant that he'd intended very young women to be the broodmares of his baby ranch. Very young women without counsel or other empowered protectors, because a person with options and the chance to say no would not agree to breed for this man in exchange for his notion of a correct price. But Epstein had leverage.

The respectful attention and conversation from bright-brain luminaries that Epstein received before he could get his baby ranch rolling shows another locus of predatory insemination that, consistent with a pattern we've seen elsewhere in this book, understates the centrality of semen. Epstein's most prominent victim, Virginia Giuffre, who like him would later die by apparent suicide, filed claims alleging not only sexual assault when she was underage but that Epstein offered her money for semen contact that would produce a baby for him to control along with Ghislane Maxwell, his partner in crime. (That accusation never reached the courts, but what this claimant said about mistreatments by powerful men in general warrants belief: Prince Andrew, scion of the British royal family, paid Giuffre an undisclosed amount to settle her claim that, aided by Epstein and Maxwell, he sexually assaulted her when she was 17. Lawyers knowledgeable about this category of litigation speculated that the Giuffre settlement cost Andrew north of £10 million.[43] Individuals who know the truth or falsity of sexual-misconduct accusations because they are the persons accused don't pay out that much for baseless talk.) Predatory insemination led and encouraged by Jeffrey Epstein does not intersect much with abortion—as far as we know, that is: revelations about Epstein's enormous network of sexual misconduct continue to emerge—but it shows the necessity of access to abortion as a mitigator of semen-generated consequences.

Predatory insemination occurs between adults too, not just to child victims. "Your body, my choice," tweeted the neo-Nazi Internet celebrity Nick Fuentes in November 2024 as soon as Donald Trump was projected to win the election.[44] Chapter 1 of this book, on semen as a traveler whose journeys the law tends to leave alone rather than control, mentioned "condom stealthing," a predatory application of semen. Removing a condom or tampering with it overrides the receptive partner's wishes. *Take a dose of my ejaculate where it can upend your life. Whether you like it or not.*

A gender-switched variation on predatory insemination occurs when a female person obtains semen from a male person by stealth and inserts it on purpose into her vagina to make herself pregnant, concealing what she's doing from the boy or man who ejaculated under conditions that would seem to him an insemination dead end. I say "when a female person" rather than "*if* a female person" to remove all equivocation from my disapproval: but whether this conduct actually happens, I'm not sure. Students in my family law class have brought up succubus-like female adventurers who get their hands on semen by seducing a male celebrity or other rich man, carrying away the condom into which he ejaculated with a goal of self-insemination and from there taking advantage of him, but when I've asked them for specifics that I could look up I haven't heard any. Abortion law in the United States doesn't allow the victim of this misconduct to make the pregnancy go away by forcing termination on the impregnated predator, which makes this instance of predation different from my other examples. In all the others, abortion mitigates and lessens the impact of bad conduct. But even here in this scenario that may or may not really exist, abortion is a source of justice in that the reluctant biological father might succeed in persuading the pregnant predator to terminate. Or our malefactor might regret her wrongful act and obtain an abortion to undo it.

Opportunistic predators, a coinage of mine, refers to people who inflict intentional harm by exploiting the intersection of abortion bans and state-generated encouragement of their desire to control or hurt other people. Jon Michaels and David Noll have spotted a wider development in American state law to enlarge the power gap between self-entitled aggressors and individuals who live inside the bounds of a disadvantaged category. The three categories made vulnerable this way, Michaels and Noll explain, are "abortion providers, trans kids, and teachers who adopt inclusive curricula."[45] Governments reward self-nominated bounty hunters in what Michaels and Noll have labeled "vigilante federalism" to recognize the dynamic of state and federal law each supporting the other. Private actors collect money in court for inflicting harms that state governments don't want to do themselves but want done.

When Texas enacted its bounty encouraging interferers to bring people to court for helping someone else get an abortion, it opened an opportunity for control by a category that straddles the border of predatory inseminator and opportunistic predator, an abusive husband or boyfriend who takes advantage of having achieved insemination. His predation: when he learns that the woman into whom he ejaculated chooses to terminate this pregnancy, this man can play a card dealt to him by the Texas legislature and governor. All he needs is information about people close to the woman who knew about the abortion at a planning stage. Friends' responses can be construed as aiding and abetting abortion or intending to do so. Now our vigilante has leverage. He can bring an abortion bounty action in court and collect $10,000 from the helpers.

A *Slate* magazine article headlined "Not Every Man Will Be as Dumb as Marcus Silva" recounted the abortion-bounty hunting of a Texas husband whose wife had called the cops on him twice before leaving him.[46] Witnesses had observed Marcus Silva's rages. While unemployed, Silva went to a work party for his wife Brittni where in front of her coworkers he called her a slut, a whore, and an unfit mother.

Abortion prohibitions gave this predator more power. After he learned from snooping into Brittni's phone that Brittni had learned she was pregnant and intended to get an abortion, Silva trotted to Jonathan Mitchell, the activist who'd created and pushed for the bounty-hunter law, for advice on how to use this weapon. Evidently indifferent to the fate of this particular embryo, Mitchell did nothing to stop the abortion. Instead he helped Silva put together a lawsuit against two friends of Brittni accusing these friends of murdering Silva's child.[47]

* * *

Interferers I'll call highwaymen continue the leveraging of semen by blocking traffic on public roads. They prevent inseminated persons from going to another state for an abortion. We met the constitutional right to travel in chapter 1. Though not explicitly present in the Constitution, this right as laid out by the Supreme Court protects an array of entitlements paid for by other people, including a right to pick up and move to another state and claim taxpayer-funded benefits.

You'd think that if this constitutional right covers travel to another state that's motivated by the desire to benefit from a different legal regime in the form of gaining access to taxpayer-funded government benefits, it must also cover travel to another state at one's own expense, seeking to take no money from anyone. Justice Brett Kavanaugh mused in his Dobbs opinion (while citing no authority) that the right to interstate travel means a right to leave one state for another to obtain an abortion.[48] This reassurance notwithstanding, statutes and local ordinances codified after *Dobbs* have made it illegal to use roads and highways to transport anyone to get an abortion. Highwaymen who know about such travel can collect a judgment of money damages from abortion drivers.

Idaho, the first state to copy Texas's innovation that lets people collect cash in court by suing a fellow citizen for helping with an abortion plan, added another source of control by criminalizing assistance to a minor by helping her travel out of state for an abortion without her parents' knowledge. This criminal prosecution can occur even when rape by a parent of his child started the pregnancy.[49] Another leader-follower on the abortion travel front is Alabama, whose attorney general announced that his state would prosecute what he called "conspiracies to commit abortions elsewhere," meaning support for pregnant persons' travel to another state where abortion is legal. In that announcement, the attorney general also shared his view that Alabama can prosecute pregnant Alabama residents themselves, not just their helpers, for traveling out of state to get an abortion.[50]

A handful of small cities and county governments in Texas have passed ordinances that make it illegal to use roads within the county or city limits to transport anyone to get an abortion. Highwaymen have their eye on Interstate 20 and Route 84, roads that point west toward termination liberty.[51] (We'll see later, in chapter 8, that officials in New Mexico responded to the Dobbs news by inviting Texans to cross the state frontier if they need an abortion.) Other roads in the United States serve the same function. Every state that as of now bans or restricts abortion contains connectors like these on which pregnant people can drive or receive a ride to get away from prohibition land.

Termination of pregnancy is, again as of now, the only motive for helping someone to leave a state that has generated this kind of prohibition. Local governments don't bother or threaten people who transport Texans across the state line to gamble or buy recreational marijuana at a dispensary. Only semen-impacts get leveraged.

* * *

When Brittany Watts, a woman living in Warren, Ohio, suffered a miscarriage in 2023, her experience enabled an array of deciders to control her health and freedom.[52] Pregnancy restrictions over the centuries have historically leveraged the landing of semen to control millions of lives, but usually with a lower number of deciders per pregnancy. Brittany Watts encountered an extralarge number of controllers at the helm. Readers familiar with the state of human rights in the United States will be unshocked by the identity of Watts as a Black woman.

Here's her story, reported in newspaper and television-news reports that drew international attention.

Watts started leaking amniotic fluid when she was in the fifth month of her pregnancy. She sought medical attention from her doctor, who told her that her water had broken. Over the next few days, Watts started to bleed heavily. She returned to the same doctor. At this second visit, the doctor told Watts that the fetus would not survive and sent Watts to the emergency room at Mercy Hospital in Warren. Watts traveled by ambulance, at the doctor's insistence, even though the emergency door of the hospital was just across the parking lot.

After eight hours in the emergency room, receiving no answers and no treatment, Watts left Mercy Hospital—against medical advice, said the hospital record—and went home for more bleeding without care. Another return to the ER followed. Watts pleaded for an induction or an abortion and again received no answers. This time, unknown to her, medical staff were waiting for a ruling from the hospital ethics committee about how to treat her doomed pregnancy: they'd confirmed the fetus would not survive but detected a heartbeat. After a longer stay in the ER, one that lasted 11 hours, Watts left at 7:20 that evening.

The inevitable miscarriage finally happened around dawn the next day. Over the toilet, Watts felt what she called a splash, an emission of blood and tissue that overflowed. Watts scooped up the debris overflow into a bucket and flushed her toilet. She carried the bucket outside and upended it.

Next, though feeling ill, Watts went to a hair salon appointment. The hairdresser asked if she was all right. Watts tried to say she was but apparently she didn't sound convincing, and the hairstylist took her back to Mercy Hospital. There Watts was treated with a D&C, which removed placental remains that the miscarriage hadn't purged, and an intravenous line for her dehydration.

Let's count the semen deciders with control over this individual. Start with the obstetrician, who acted promptly and benevolently at an office visit to help Watts with necessary medical care. Deference to medical authority is mandatory for the inseminated. Next, the less benevolent ER staffers who told Watts to wait.

Another decider was the hospital ethics committee. I've noted that when she left the ER, Watts hadn't known that medical personnel had been waiting for this decider's ruling in response to her plea for an induction or an abortion. Watts also didn't know that near the end of her second day in the ER, the committee had chosen to recommend termination based on nonviability of the fetus (a fact that none of the deciders ever disputed) and a note from a doctor who'd examined her that Watts was at risk of bleeding to death.

More deciders: a nurse rubbed Watts's back during her postmiscarriage treatment for dehydration—and also called the police to report what Watts told staffers she had done with the expelled fetus. A CBS News story said that the police report "was made at the direction of the hospital's risk management team." Passive voice, active deciders. Someone at Mercy Hospital told police about "the need to locate the fetus."[53]

I'll interrupt this tally of semen deciders with power over the inseminated Brittany Watts to mention that caregivers who feel entitled to worsen the plight of their patients are familiar to the nonprofit If/When/How, which studied criminal prosecutions for self-managed abortion in the

United States from 2000 to 2020, near the end of the Roe v. Wade era.[54] Researchers learned that health care providers report what they think of as abortion to police after treating a patient. If/When/How found 61 instances of this cop-calling. After excluding minors, the set contained 51 cases. When state law enforcement investigated persons suspected of ending their own pregnancies or helping someone else do so, a plurality of these investigations (39%) featured reports to the police by health care providers. The next biggest group of interlopers that If/When/How counted—family members, intimate partners, acquaintances—filled a lower percentage of 26%.

Medically trained informers acted out of no legal obligation to drop the dime on their patients. Neither federal law nor the law of any state in the time studied required anyone to report what If/When/How called "a suspected or actual occurrence of a self-managed abortion." These deciders stepped up when they didn't have to. They didn't prevent an abortion but they leveraged past landings of semen to harm patients.

We have more deciders to tally. Police decided to enter Watts's home and search for miscarriage debris. They first checked the yard where Watts had emptied the bucket and then found what appeared to be a fetal corpse when an officer put his hand into the plumbing and touched the trap. Watts hadn't seen it there. To send fetal remains to the coroner for investigation, police officers removed the entire toilet fixture. Several days later, officers came to her home with handcuffs and arrested Watts.

At last we've counted almost, but not quite, everybody whose power over Brittany Watts originated in a trip taken by semen. Trumball County's district attorney, who gave advice to the police about how to proceed with the investigation, chose to prosecute Watts. For which crime, you might wonder. An Ohio misdemeanor. First sentence: "No person, except as authorized by law, shall treat a human corpse in a way that the person knows would outrage reasonable *family* sensibilities." Second sentence: "No person, except as authorized by law, shall treat a human corpse in a way that the person knows would outrage reasonable *community* sensibilities." I added those italics to flag the difference between these two Ohio crimes, neither of which speaks clearly about what it prohibits.

Both crimes lack a definition of "human corpse." Speaking as someone trained to read statutes, I don't know what makes the detritus that flowed into this fixture a human corpse or inclusive of one. Watts didn't know that a fetus, which postmortem inspection showed was dead before it exited her body, had landed in her toilet. I also can't know whether Watts knew she was outraging community sensibilities or family sensibilities by experiencing her miscarriage this way, though I doubt she did. Discussions within communities and families would have yielded the hard-to-answer *What else could she have done?*

We see that Ohio's crime sets up public opinion, genuine or imagined, as another decider. Community sensibilities and family sensibilities were tasked to determine whether Brittany Watts committed a crime. An assistant prosecutor, yet another decider, said in court that what bothered his office was "the fact that the baby was put into a toilet, large enough to clog up the toilet, left in that toilet and [Watts] went on her day."[55] What other options lay ahead for a pregnant woman when a dead fetus exited her body after days of vaginal bleeding and membranes that broke, whose many recent hours in the hospital had given her no relief, this prosecutor did not say. Watts "went on her day," as you and I are doing right now.

I've mentioned unmentionability as a problem for the management of semen: here we have another example of the phenomenon. Someone ejaculated into Brittany Watts. Both he and Watts emitted biomatter from the bottom of their torsos with, as far as we know, no intent to harm or offend anyone. Her emission, but not his, got labeled "a human corpse" by prosecutors who accused Watts of a felony. Responsibility piled onto Watts. Semen traveled without responsibility for the ejaculator.

* * *

This chapter has assigned to semen a central role in consequences that the law imposes on impregnated persons. Is this assignment of responsibility fair? Semen, after all, never acts alone. It's in the mix that starts pregnancy but so too are many other antecedent ingredients. The list of contributors seems almost infinite. Ejaculator and ejaculatee had to meet each other and so did their parents. Ovulation, hormones, the uterine lining, and other anatomical participants are indispensable to the start of a pregnancy. So too are environments and social conditions.

What's fair about this attribution of responsibility, I think, is that semen causes unique material effects that call for examination of it as an instrument of upheaval. Whenever pregnancy exists, semen has landed on cervical mucosa. This landing might have been desired by the person with anatomical receptors, as our Texas professor friends quoted at the beginning of this chapter told the Amarillo federal court, but a person's desire to engage in sexual intercourse didn't make her pregnant the way that ejaculation did. The propulsion of semen from the interior of one person into another isn't sufficient to form a pregnancy but it is necessary.

Transition into the state of pregnancy forces a person to face controls and interferences found nowhere else in the law. The shift from nonpregnant to pregnant pulls an individual out of a relatively safe space, a shelter from formal official interference. We in the United States who aren't pregnant or vulnerable to becoming pregnant enjoy a cluster of entitlements. The government can't punish us without due process. We hold constitutional liberties, including a right to travel to another state. Undoing familiar entitlements to be left alone, the deep and wide constraints that external deciders impose fall on an individual after she transitions into pregnant from nonpregnant.

This switch into being pregnant can occur against the impregnated person's will and after she did nothing to deserve an injurious impact. Abortion provides a relatively easy, safe, and cheap exit from a condition that is sometimes unwanted and always dangerous. Allowing patients and providers to come together for a termination that they both wish to occur rescues human beings from suffering.

Seen in this perspective, legal restrictions that ban or limit abortion leverage the fortuitous contact of semen with a cervix to compel a pregnant person to experience other significant impacts. This compulsion does not have to happen, any more than a person with scurvy must remain affected by that condition by continuing to avoid fruits and vegetables. Pregnancy can be cured easily and safely when law stays out of the way.

If it sounds eccentric to compare semen to scurvy, stay with me a moment. Abortion bans do more than force people to remain pregnant and give birth. Scurvy doesn't force rape victims who become pregnant and have a baby formed through this rape to maintain a co-parental relationship with someone who attacked them severely: in chapter 5, we'll meet a few people who experienced that more-severe-than-scurvy impact. Scurvy doesn't cost the patient wage income after its symptoms are treated. It doesn't imprint the body permanently with the microchimeric cells we met in chapter 2. Fatal in past centuries, scurvy doesn't kill anyone today.

Abortion-prohibition kills people. Because pregnancy is so dangerous, withholding abortion from someone who wants to terminate her pregnancy is worse than withholding vitamin C from someone suffering from scurvy. When a medical repair is safe, effective, and feasible, withholding it from patients wrongs them.

To put people at the mercy of a bad condition delivered to them through their reproductive anatomy does not constitute "letting nature take its course," to quote what Sherry Colb and Michael Dorf had to say about abortion rights in one of Colb's last essays,[56] but an actively imposed mistreatment. Consequences of this mistreatment grow worse when law-based interferences with termination proliferate. Abortion restrictions inflict hurt by strengthening and reinforcing a hazardous contact.

4

"Like Bugs"

In "My Penis," a story John Hughes published before moving to the teen movies he became better known for, a 16-year-old female narrator named Karen wakes up to find herself possessing a penis that emits semen. The emission makes her new body part extra alarming. She'd had to be careful around semen that boyfriends produced, she says, because "sperms are living, you know—they're like bugs, and they get all over." Watching her body ejaculate put the Hughes character in mind of what we've been discussing in the last couple of chapters: before she acquired her own penis, situated at the receiving rather than the emitting end of semen, she had worried about becoming pregnant.[1] Semen contains other sources of disruption beyond sperm cells.

Of its two powers, Make People and Make People Sick, semen as a starter of new human life has dominated this book. Existence versus nonexistence is more significant than the transition into and away from a state of sickness or health. But now it's time to reckon with semen as a source of disease. Saluting John Hughes, whose voice I miss, I'll refer to the pathogens in semen as Bugs.

Viruses live in semen. At least a couple of dozen. Mumps, lassa fever, Epstein Barr, human herpes varieties 6, 7, and 8, herpes simplex varieties 1 and 2, hepatitis B and C, varicella zoster, simian virus 40, and human T-cell lymphoma virus 1 are on the semen-virus roster. The most quoted metastudy tallying up viruses in semen was published in 2017, a couple of years too early for the newer viral arrival of Covid-19, which also lives in this Bugs-friendly home. Semen houses bacteria too—it delivers the sexually transmitted bacterial Big Three of chlamydia, syphilis, and gonorrhea to partners—but while the viruses that live in semen need a fluid for their travel, transport for bacteria can take liquid routes. This difference means viruses are central to a book about semen, bacteria peripheral.

Pathogens fill semen—and not only in research labs and metastudies that count viruses but in real male bodies. A Swedish study of about one hundred men described as "healthy" and "fertile" counted 1,033 strains of microorganisms in the lower third of the male urinary tract.[2] In *The Semen Book*, author Vivien Marx recalled being at a medical conference where a poster announced findings about dangerous inclusions present in semen. Marx was reading the long list when a researcher standing nearby said he marveled at the variety and quantity of the perils. "It is a wonder," Marx reported this man remarked to her, "that women let us in at all."[3]

* * *

As far as observers can tell from attention to its effects, semen departs the human body with an apparent agenda to affect the life of someone other than its maker. Having a purpose that focuses outward is almost unique among human bodily fluids. Breast milk shares this characteristic at a general plane, but where semen becomes *fully* unique—more than almost unique—is in its power to achieve its ends at the expense of the person it touches.

The male reproductive tract functions to produce spermatozoa, protect them from harm, and support their apparent drive to make a difference in the external world by causing pregnancy. Semen as a constituent of this tract helps sperm cells journey toward an oocyte. It caters to sperm by fighting immune-system responses designed to rise up against them. Unless they as travelers can compete by surviving well enough to pursue their reproductive purpose, sperm will achieve nothing. Consistent with the forward-moving agenda it fosters—a goal unshared by other substances that depart the lower torso and can enter the body of another person, including menstrual blood, vaginal fluids, even smegma—semen is chock-full of inclusions and propensities that fight back against resistance.

The fluid that supports the interests of sperm also supports the pathogens that semen houses. Agents of infection, the Bugs of this chapter, share the same imperative to overcome defenses found in the human bodies into which they travel. Bugs have enough in common with sperm to benefit from the extraordinarily nurturing environment that semen furnishes.

In an orderly sequence, one contributor following another, anatomical structures add unique reinforcements to semen. Every player on Team Semen—the testes, epididymis, seminal vesicles, prostate, Cowper's gland, and glands of Littre—adds into the mix what it secretes toward the larger goal of protecting sperm cells from danger and helping them travel to an egg. Two glands, Cowper's and the glands of Littre, bring the first mucinous secretions to the mission.

Their contribution is pre-ejaculate, a substance sometimes thought of as a fellow traveler or anticipator of semen. Pre-ejaculate contains glycoproteins that lubricate the urethra to ease the outward flow of emission.[4] In addition to providing lubrication, this fluid neutralizes traces of residual acidic urine at the tip of the penis with the vagina in mind, as it were. Neutralizing acidity is a key function of semen. Pre-ejaculate makes the end of the urethra a location with a basic, meaning alkaline, pH level. Until this adjustment arrives, the vaginal vault is chemically hostile to sperm. Pre-ejaculate fluid provides a neutralizing buffer.

Total fluid volume of pre-ejaculate is scant, just 1% to 5% of the quantity emitted. Sperm cells, though numerous—140 million are par for a single unit of ejaculate[5]—contribute about the same small percentage of total fluid volume. The source of this best-known inclusion is the testis. Liquids from the prostate gland and seminal vesicles take up much more space; contributions from the prostate gland occupy about a third of the total fluid volume of semen. Like pre-ejaculate as a fluid, the prostate contributes alkalinity, adding bicarbonate buffers. It doesn't stop with adding alkalinity: fibrinogenase from the prostate gland helps semen clot; fibrinolytic enzyme liquefies it.

The last and biggest anatomical contributor to semen volume, bringing more than half the total, are seminal vesicles. Secretions that come from this source include semenogelin, a protein that supports coagulation, and prostaglandins, which induce smooth muscle contractions in the female genital tract. Prostaglandins in the mix thus help sperm travel; sperm aren't very motile themselves as swimmers. Seminal vesicles also contribute phospholipids, which help stabilize the contents of semen against temperature and environmental shock.[6]

Other fluids from seminal vesicles—amino acids, citric acid, phosphorus, potassium—serve a variety of reproductive functions, but the most significant inclusion they contribute is fructose. Sperm need fructose for energy sufficient to keep them swimming. The typical concentration of fructose in semen is very high, more than three times that of another sugar in semen, glucose, and more than three hundred times greater than the concentration of fructose in blood.[7]

Completing the fateful combination, bulbourethral glands add a few drops of mucus to ejaculate. This thick lubricating protein holds these contributions together in one place and also aids their function. Seminal mucus is the right consistency to support the swimming of sperm near the cervix, neither too thick nor too thin. Its viscous jelly-like consistency keeps sperm from leaking out of semen.

By promoting the welfare of sperm, these inclusions in semen make sexual reproduction possible. At the same time, they nourish Bugs. I'll now zero in on reproduction-supportive characteristics of semen that enable it to make people sick, starting with what HIV research reports.

HIV deserves attention today, even decades after significant gains in prevention and treatment during the current century fought it well. The virus still brings illness and death. Outside the United States, HIV kills more women of reproductive age than any other disease. About 1.3 million new infections occurred worldwide in the year 2022, long after the arrival of antiretroviral therapies and a drop in viral loads.[8] When HIV lands, it hurts people during their most productive years. Its timing thus harms not just individual health but economies, societies, and families.

Among the multiple routes that HIV takes to travel from person to person, semen onto mucosa magnifies the virus's power more than any others. More than 60% of HIV transmission occurs via semen; it is "the primary vehicle for HIV-1 transmission."[9] Being in semen makes HIV extra virulent and destructive: "the naked virus," naked here meaning in isolation rather than in semen, is weaker at delivering HIV to target immune-system cells.[10]

What strengthens semen as a way to make people sick with HIV are the same conditions that support its making people. Semen doesn't just hold Bugs; it maximizes what inclusions can accomplish when they land on mucosa. Several characteristics of semen support this function. I've briefly mentioned two, fructose and alkaline PH, and in a moment will move to a third.

* * *

Start with fructose. A virology study of immune responses to HIV in semen confirmed that while improving the mobility of semen's little swimmers by furnishing them with energy in the form of sugar, fructose also helps HIV cells evade antipathogenic agents in the female reproductive tract.[11] Fructose weakens the power of one particularly valiant defender, an antibody named 2G12, to bind HIV cells. The study worked with semen from donors at the University of Iowa selected for being uniformly HIV negative but containing variation in their fructose levels. Its researchers found that semen high in fructose permitted HIV cells to gain infection by hampering defenses of a female-body inhibitor named Griffithsin, or GRFT for short. When the researchers supplemented lower-fructose semen with exogenous fructose, the power of that unit of semen to deliver HIV infection went up.

This power that fructose adds to semen supports other viruses, not just HIV. Earlier research showed the effectiveness of GRFT in preventing infection by herpes simplex virus type 2 and human papillomavirus (HPV) using live animal experiments on macaques and mice. Hobbling GRFT means that fructose feeds disease as well as spermatozoa that rely on it for their sugar-fueled travel via semen.

The second semen trait that supports both sperm and HIV in their separate agendas is alkaline pH. We've noted that, as a setting into which sperm cells travel, the vagina is too acidic to offer these visitors a safe home. Acid pH there kills invaders. Semen provides a counteroffensive to benefit the sperm it brings by nudging the pH of the vagina toward a friendly seven, near the middle of the pH range, up from its starting pH of about four.

Researchers at Johns Hopkins and Northwestern universities confirmed that semen's alkalinity improves the hospitality available to HIV when they stirred a synthesized version of HIV derivative into cervicovaginal mucus supplied by healthy donors. The study design divided this cervicovaginal mucus into two groups, control and experimental, by leaving one share of the donated mucus alone at its original pH of four and changing the other into the pH six that semen delivers during coitus. The researchers found that HIV spread and bonded to cells effectively in the alkaline pH that semen brings to the vagina, and poorly in the unaltered original acid environment.[12]

The last trait or inclusion, like fructose and alkaline pH, also supports both sperm and sexually transmitted Bugs. The presence of amyloid fibrils causes—not "is associated with" or some other equivocation but *causes* meaning generates—a host of human sicknesses, most but not all neurocognitive and all of them serious, including Alzheimer's, Parkinson's disease, Huntington's disease, prion disease, and type 2 diabetes.[13] The roster of diseases supported by amyloid fibrils also includes herpes simplex, Ebola, and gonorrhea.

The connection between amyloid fibrils and ill health is so strong that the presence of these fibrils in all human bodily fluids demonstrates the presence of disease. With one exception. One bodily fluid is unlike all the others. Home of the only healthy amyloid fibrils in the body, semen puts these proteins to reproductive use. How amyloid fibrils in semen support babymaking relates to their support of disease delivery.

Virologists at the University of California at San Francisco who studied amyloid fibrils that fuse HIV to host cells wondered whether this role might have a counterpart in sperm-to-egg fusion:[14] these fibrils are on the scene for both types of durable contact. Their published study included lively video that audiences can observe on a computer screen. Amyloid fibrils and spermatozoa wriggle together, clinging and connecting.

Amyloid fibrils immobilize sperm. That function may seem hostile to fertilization, but it enhances sexual reproduction by a kind of addition by subtraction. The UCSF study found that sperm cells targeted by amyloid fibrils were what the researchers classified as poor quality. After amyloid fibrils target and connect with these suboptimal spermatozoa and immobilize them, immune cells that clear away the resulting debris make room for more promising sperm to compete.

When they land on HIV virus particles, amyloid fibrils in semen shuttle these pathogens to target healthy cells in the mode of little ferries. One transnational study of amyloid fibrils investigating this function named them "semen-derived enhancer of virus infection," SEVI for short.[15] The researchers who identified this major HIV-enhancing effect in semen had been looking for the opposite condition, factors in semen that made HIV harder to transmit. When they injected into rats' tails either the naked virus, meaning HIV with nothing added, or HIV pretreated with SEVI, they found HIV boosted with semen-influenced enhancer was five times more effective in transmitting the virus.

"We were not expecting to find an enhancer, and we were even more surprised about the strength," a study coauthor told Scientific American magazine. "Most enhancers have maybe a two- or three-fold effect, but here the effect was amazing—more than 50-fold and, under certain conditions, more than 100,000-fold."[16] That strengthener of HIV came from the *S* in the study's acronym SEVI. Semen.

Further evidence that semen augments and strengthens HIV is its power to keep and hold this virus in a findable state when tests of other fluids in the body of the same person report no HIV present. HIV can be found in semen of males who have an undetectable viral load in blood, according to the results of a 304-man study.[17] Twenty of the 304 patients (6.6%) had detectable HIV-1 RNA in semen, ranging from 135 to 2,365 copies/ml, corresponding to 23 samples, although they had concomitantly undetectable HIV-1 RNA in blood while they were under antiretroviral therapy. Ten studies have explicitly measured the differences between blood plasma and genital fluid viral loads and found that when blood plasma viral load was undetectable, the viral load in the genital tract—that means in semen—was still detectable in 5% to 25% of people in the studies.[18]

Now, let's move to another virus that joins HIV in finding more nurture and hospitality in semen than even the very nourishing realm of blood.

* * *

Named for the Ebola River, a 250-kilometer tributary located almost exactly in the geographic middle of Africa, the pathogen that causes Ebola virus disease has done most of its harm to human beings at the center of the African continent. So far, the number of people killed by Ebola has been low. In the span between its discovery in 1976 through a big outbreak in the Dominican Republic in 2020, (only) an estimated 15,266 people died, and the limited resurgences since 2020 haven't taken many more.

Ebola has killed relatively few people because it's too deadly for its own good. All viruses need a host to live in: this one kills too fast and kills too many while not being easy enough to transmit, concluded one study of its weaknesses. But although the descriptor "kills too fast, kills too many" lessens the power of a virus to keep going, it's a reason to care about a pathogen. Infected persons die of Ebola virus disease at a relatively high rate: about 50% overall and higher for particularly deadly strains. Vaccine progress continues, but so far most strains of the virus have eluded vaccination.[19]

Its location thousands of miles from this epicenter notwithstanding, the U.S. government has agreed that Ebola virus disease is worth caring about. Congress chose in 2014 to appropriate $5.4 billion for emergency funding. President Barack Obama's request to Congress announced a wide Ebola agenda: to "fortify domestic public health systems, contain and mitigate the epidemic in West Africa, speed the procurement and testing of vaccines and therapeutics, and . . . enhancing capacity for vulnerable countries to prevent disease outbreaks, detect them early, and swiftly respond before they become epidemics that threaten our national security."[20]

Research on Ebola has found supports for this virus that resemble what semen provides to HIV. Amyloid fibrils, the protein fragments in semen that protect and enhance the transmission and infectiousness of HIV, also enhance the transmission and infection of Ebola virus. This inclusion also enhances the ability of Ebola virus to attach to membrane surrounding host cells and its ability to be internalized by those cells.[21]

Semen holds on to Ebola after other bodily fluids have let it go. As far back as 1977, soon after the emergence of Ebola virus disease, researchers could detect this virus in the semen of a patient. In blood too. Not urine, feces, or throat-swab saliva. Just blood and semen.

To document how strongly or weakly each bodily fluid holds on to this virus, the CDC keeps an Ebola chart of fluids produced by the human body. This array reports on published studies for the presence of Ebola in different biomaterials and how long after the onset of symptoms Ebola can be detected. The fluids from which infectious Ebola virus has been recovered are aqueous humor of the eye, semen, breast milk, urine, and saliva. For a dozen other fluids studied, a list that includes emissions from the gut like vomit and feces and what a swab can retrieve from the anus and vagina, Ebola virus RNA provides indirect evidence of the virus's presence. Semen tops the Ebola charts.

Measured by both infectious virus and virus RNA, semen is the bodily fluid in which this virus lives the longest. Breast milk is a distant second: live virus can be isolated from breast milk as long as 15 days after the onset of illness, and the virus RNA method has detected Ebola in breast milk 16 months after discharge from a treatment center. Other fluids vanish from detectability much sooner. Except one. Using the infectious-virus measurement, semen lasts for 82 days after illness onset, not the 15-day durability of breast milk. After discharge from treatment, viral RNA is detectable 40 months later in semen instead of 16.[22] After every other bodily fluid pinky-swears that this virus has gone away, semen tells a more durable truth.

And lest anyone think that detectable Ebola in semen is just a marker of past disease that no longer can infect anyone, researchers learned in 2015 that semen can transmit this virus. Not often—but at least one instance of Ebola virus disease, carefully traced and studied in 2015, could have been transmitted only via semen on mucosa.[23]

Free of symptoms and with no detectable Ebola virus in his blood, a man in Liberia completed his treatment in October 2014 and went on with his life activities. These activities included ejaculating fatefully into a vagina. Investigators tested his blood and semen. His blood test came back negative for Ebola; his semen test came back positive. Genetic sequencing found that viral RNA in his semen matched the viral RNA in his partner's blood. Demonstrating that this result was not an outlier, another study in western Africa found that men can harbor the virus in their semen for at least two and a half years, with the potential to transmit the virus sexually during that time.[24] Semen gives Ebola a much more durable home than blood, its next-strongest shelter.

Ebola viruses can spread when infected semen touches nongenital mucosal surfaces, like broken skin or mucous membranes in the eyes, nose, or mouth. These viruses may be able to survive in bodily fluids like semen *ex vivo* for up to several days at room temperature. In tests of Ebola-spiked human semen in bulk, kept in a dry state under tropical conditions, experiments recovered viable virus in bulk semen at six to eight days and in dried semen at one to four days. Put into semen stored in condoms, the Ebola virus survived to day six.[25]

The durability of Ebola in semen makes this disease an action item even for countries that, like the United States, are located at a great geographic distance from Ebola epidemics. For decades, negative results on a blood test have been understood as signifying the absence of a pathogen. Semen durability undermines this confidence by allowing transmittable Ebola to live and thrive below the blood-screen radar. People who feel healthy, pass the familiar kind of clinical screenings, and are otherwise eligible to enter a country or a bounded multinational region like the Schengen Area in Europe can cross borders bearing Ebola when governments think they are keeping out this virus.

* * *

Gonorrhea, chlamydia, and syphilis comprise the bacterial Big Three of sexually transmitted infections. The CDC counted more than 2.5 million diagnoses of these diseases in 2022, with syphilis alarmingly resurgent.[26] Semen holds all of them. It gives extra strength to gonorrhea.

Of the Big Three, syphilis has the thinnest connection to semen. Lesions rather than an emitted bodily fluid are what transmit the *Treponema pallidum* bacterium most of the time. As we so often see, however, semen deserves more blame or credit for causing change than it receives.

In the pre-penicillin early twentieth century Harry Pariser of the U.S. Public Health Service ran an experiment that injected laboratory animals with semen produced by infected men. These efforts failed to transmit syphilis, and Pariser duly concluded that semen played no role in syphilis infection. A more recent study took a different view of this bacterium in this fluid. Pariser's 1942 exoneration of semen as a deliverer of syphilis "should be taken with caution," the authors said, adverting to their "study results, and those of many other studies conducted earlier" that implicate semen as a transmitter of bacterial disease.[27]

The bacterium that causes syphilis can be present in semen at a high enough concentration to transmit the disease in the absence of direct contact with a syphilitic sore. Its small size and the uncertainty of its findings led a spokesperson for this study to call for more research and conclude that transmission through semen was probably still rare. But possible. One semen sample included in this study found 800 T cells per milliliter, much more than enough to spread the infection.[28]

The CDC reported in 2024 that syphilis numbers had reached their highest height since the 1950s. Soaring infection levels and prevalence mean that even though the Bug that brings syphilis to the human body travels for the most part by sores and only sometimes by semen, the journeys of *T. pallidum* via semen are significant. Chlamydia and gonorrhea fill out the Big Three with semen playing a bigger role in delivery.

Source of the most common bacterial STI, *Chlamydia trachomatis* has the capacity to infect a penis, vagina, cervix, anus, urethra, eye, and throat. Chlamydia can lurk in semen without presenting any symptoms to the person who manufactures this fluid. One study detected chlamydia in the semen obtained from a large minority (just under 40%) of asymptomatic men who had ejaculated in a laboratory for a purpose other than STI testing: along with their female partners, these men had sought treatment for infertility.[29] They had no reason to know their semen contained this hazard.

Gonorrhea is something of a semi-neglected middle child in the family of bacteria associated with sexual transmission. It ranks second of the three diseases in new diagnoses a year and American public health authorities seem to pay it the least attention. Located in semen, however, *Neisseria gonorrhoeae* becomes significant. Most deliveries of gonorrhea involve the transfer of semen, for starters. In addition, seminal fluid as an environment provides extra supports for this bacterium—increased motility, encouragement of the formation of biofilm that makes the pathogen attach to other cells, and enhancement of microcolonies that increase the spread of *Neisseria gonorrhoeae* inside the body.

Researchers studying the bacterium responsible for gonorrhea found that exposure to seminal plasma allows it to move and colonize more easily. An experiment to test its motility showed that 24 times as many bacteria were able to pass through a synthetic barrier after being exposed to seminal plasma. The writers remarked that *Neisseria gonorrhoeae* of the past infected other parts of the human body but "has evolved to thrive in a limited niche," that niche being the genital tract.[30] Semen competed well in an evolutionary struggle to furnish gonorrhea with nurturing conditions.

The authors of this semen-gonorrhea study also noted that exposure to seminal plasma enhances the formation of bacterial microcolonies on human epithelial cells, which can promote infection.[31] These last two findings—*Chlamydia trachomatis*, source of chlamydia, discernible in the semen of asymptomatic men; *Neisseria gonorrhoeae* made livelier when it's in semen—suggest that while our fluid offers unique nourishment to viruses, it also provides a supportive, nurturing home for bacteria.

Bacteria in semen testifies to the possibility of semen as a source of safety for a man himself, not just for the Bugs that happen to find a place to thrive in his body. Consider that men rarely have health problems from chlamydia aside from experiencing fever.[32] Studies suggest semen can inhibit the ability of chlamydia to infect host cells in the genital tract, making men who carry the pathogen less susceptible to infection.[33] Similarly, a study found the prevalence of *Trichomonas vaginalis* significantly higher in women (1.8%) than in men (0.5%).[34] Studies have attributed this disparity in part to the oxidative nature of some male genital fluids that can inhibit certain pathogenic factors, and the zinc concentration in prostatic fluid that can act as a cytotoxic factor.[35]

While bacteria in semen function to make male-bodied persons better off, this inclusion has a particular different impact on female-bodied persons. A headline in the New York Times announced in 2025 that "A Third of Women Get This Infection" and continued with "The Fix: Treat Their Male Partners."[36] The infection that this story noted a third of women get, bacterial vaginosis, has long baffled medical science. It's "poorly understood," wrote the Times reporter, echoing a 2011 medical journal article that had said the "etiology [of this disease] remains unknown."[37] Bacterial vaginosis increases the risk that an infected woman will develop a more serious sexually transmitted disease like chlamydia or HIV. It also can cause symptoms that include vaginal discharge, burning, and itching.

Once again, "sexually transmitted" applied to describe a disease turns out to mean semenally transmitted. The standard treatment for bacterial vaginosis, antibiotics taken by the infected woman for a week, focuses on her body. Antibiotics she ingests clear the bacterial vaginosis but tend not to keep it away; patients often experience repeated reinfection.

Seeking to improve this outcome, researchers in Australia turned their attention to other anatomy. They provided antibiotics not only to female BV patients but to the patients' (male) partners too, giving these men both tablets to be taken orally and topical cream. This partner-focused maneuver worked so much better than antibiotics for the woman alone that researchers stopped the trial early. Although their study as published in the New England Journal of Medicine spoke about the innovation in it as "male-partner treatment,"[38] the shift in therapy that succeeded so well could also be called semen treatment. Topical cream made the penis less dangerous; antibiotic tablets made semen less dangerous. The study helped to confirm an earlier finding that bacterial vaginosis is semenally transmitted. Research published in 2011 had reported "evidence of a relationship between semen exposure and incident BV."[39]

On to another locus of semen Bugs. *Trichomonas vaginalis* is not a bacterium. Nor is it a virus. It nonetheless causes quite a lot of infection. I'll turn to it in a moment. Some context first.

* * *

Social conditions obscure and minify the force of semen as a disease deliverer, as we've seen earlier in this book. Acceptably polite conversations about "safe sex" or "safer sex" rarely define the phrase but carry a tacit reference to physical space between mucosa and semen as a source of safety. Only the absence of semen, or an effective barrier when semen is present, can make sex safe or safer. Mainstream discourse does not say so when it adverts to the riskiness of this substance. Norms, customs, and laws conceal the propensity of semen to wreak havoc when it travels.

We evade, and not only with "sexually" instead of something like "semenally" to modify the word transmitted. Ejaculation onto someone else's mucosa gets classified as Having Sex even though all other acts done for sensual gratification (putting aside practices that set out to draw blood or cut into human flesh on purpose, which I have reason to think amount to a small fraction of the total) are very different in that they tend to leave a partner's biology undisrupted. False parity equates the receptor and ejaculator-inserter of semen, as if each makes an equally consequential impact on the other. Evasion obscures preventable danger.

Semen is a more hazardous carrier of disease than other bodily fluids exchanged during sexual contact. The most notorious pathogen that semen can contain, HIV, is extra destructive when it travels into another person via insemination rather than another route like blood transfusion. The trail of semen destruction lands unequally on human bodies. Even if we exclude pregnancy, whose life-upending consequences we had a chance to consider in the last two chapters, semen causes more harm to women than men. It also causes more harm to Black women and poor women than their white and wealthier counterparts.

This background of social pathology, I think, contributes to the omission of semen from understandings and explanations of how diseases travel. I've made up "semenally transmitted" to bring semen closer to the center of public health discourse that prefers to call infections "sexually transmitted" instead. Offering another new term for this book, I now introduce the acronym dMSMW.[40]

This arrangement of letters builds on older alphabet-soup references to the intersection of identity with sexual behavior. Public health literature on infection transmitted by sexual contact uses MSM to stand for men who have sex with men. MSMW stands for men who have sex with both men and women. With the coinage of dMSMW I return to themes broached in earlier chapters: evasion, concealment, and silence about matters of fact.

The *d* in dMSMW stands for "discreet," a gay-male community euphemism for secretive, closeted, or dishonest. I like dMSMW better than alternatives found in the sources: pnMSMW, said to stand for "potential nondisclosed MSWM," ndMSMW as short for "nondisclosed MSWM," and dlMSMW for "down low MSWM." In all of these abbreviations, homophobia meets unmentionability.

The difference between dMSMW and plain simple MSMW is candor, starting with honesty with oneself. If a man is engaging in acts that transfer semen to another person's mucosa, he ought to do so responsibly. What this obligation entails will vary from individual to individual but at a minimum it demands acknowledgment in his own mind. Because in practice the *d* of dMSMW is likely to signal dishonest or denying rather than benignly discreet, harms follow.

Just as racism and misogyny overlap, a point about which I'll say more in a moment, homophobia and racism come together in dMSMW. In the larger MSM cohort—that's men who have sex with men—Black men differ from white men in a couple of respects relevant to semen travel. A 2006 sampling of Black MSM in Philadelphia age 18–71 found that 44% identified as bisexual and 17% identified as heterosexual. These self-labels are more dishonest-denying-"discreet" than what MSM as a whole call themselves.[41] Black (along with Latino/Hispanic) men are less likely than white men to disclose their sexual behaviors to researchers who ask.[42]

To be sure, justifiable African American skepticism about medical research and advice is amply documented. The reluctance of survey respondents to talk in a forthright way about their sexual behavior probably has roots in racist mistreatments. One study of this gap characterizes it sympathetically, stating in a neutral tone that identity is different from conduct.[43] Its understandable origins notwithstanding, the dMSMW phenomenon remains a source of risk and harm.

People are hurt by behaviors that dishonesty makes harder to guard against. HIV prevention efforts directed at men still focus on men who identify as gay or sexually attracted to men. Intervenors could try harder to reach men who have sex with both men and women but will cop only to their opposite-sex sexual activity, I grant, but there's no obvious public health substitute for an identity label like "gay" that tells the truth about behavior. And so the MSMW cohort misses out on information. MSM who identify as heterosexual are also more likely than gay MSM to have sex while under the influence of drugs or alcohol. Dishonesty to partners follows from dissembling to oneself.

The gendered effects that follow disadvantage women. Researchers have found that men who have sex with both men and women are more likely to hide their male partners from their female ones than to hide female partners from their male ones. In other words, most MSMW happen also to be dMSMW. These men are more likely to take more risks, and disclose less about themselves, when they have sex with— that is to say, ejaculate into—female partners. As a group, men who identify as gay behave more prudently with respect to the risk of sexually transmitted infection than men who engage in MSMW behavior while rejecting "gay" as self-classification. They use condoms more consistently, test their HIV status more reliably, and engage in less sex trading.[44] And to the extent that MSMW are willing to use condoms, they take this precaution more often with their male partners than their female ones. One study in China found that MSMW skipped condoms with their female partners, many of whom were wives, to avoid revealing their sexual orientation.[45] Perhaps unsurprisingly, another study found that men who have sex with both men and women engage in anal sex with their female partners more often than do their sex-with-women-only male counterparts.[46]

When HIV travels between male and female bodies, the unmentionability signified by the *d* in dMSMW—discreet but also dishonest or dissembling—builds on the unmentionability of semen. We're all told that heterosexual "sex" can result in HIV infection. Speaking this way conceals a few truths. Men infect women with HIV more than women infect men: measured as a consequence of each individual "heterosexual act," which I presume means an act that transfers semen from a male body into a female one, the risk of switching from HIV negative to HIV positive is approximately twice as great for the female partner-recipient as her male counterpart.[47] The dMSMW phenomenon, where men who ejaculate into men or receive ejaculate on their mucosa go on to ejaculate into women without disclosing these same-sex physical contexts, obscures another harm of semen on mucosa.

Women suffer more than men from the impact of semen not only because it's they rather than men who can become pregnant but because they are more endangered by genital fluids delivered to them in heterosexual intercourse. Measurable quantity accounts for some of the difference. After vaginal intercourse, semen remains about seven times more copious than vaginal fluid in the female reproductive tract. That's on top of the disease-delivering strength we've been talking about.

Replacing the description of some diseases and infections now called "sexually transmitted" with "semenally transmitted" would speak a truth about which half of humanity is suffering more and which half inflicts more suffering. That particular truth isn't too mentionable. We hear and repeat the phony parity of "sexually," as if people of all sexes or genders who "have sex" participate equally on the transmission playing field.

Racism and misogyny together meet unmentionability in one more disease. Quick, name a Bug, an infection said to be sexually transmitted. Just one, any one you like. I'll pause to give you a second.

You've chosen a disease other than the most common STI in the world, I speculate, the only Bug estimated to afflict more people than gonorrhea and chlamydia combined and that generates well north of two million new infections a year in the United States. Trichomoniasis gives this book a good illustration of unmentionability. I rarely hear the word spoken or see it on a screen. The Nationally Notifiable Diseases Surveillance System monitors several semenally transmitted diseases. All fifty states, five U.S. territories, the District of Columbia, and New York City report incidence data about the bacterial Big Three of syphilis, gonorrhea, chlamydia to the federal government. Hepatitis B, a viral pathogen, too. Not trichomoniasis. The brunt of this disease falls on female bodies while, according to one survey, only 22% of American women are "somewhat familiar" or "very familiar" with the condition.[48] Neither a bacterium nor a virus but a protozoan parasite, *Trichomonas vaginalis* does more physical mischief than the public knows. Its underperceived impacts extend to the body politic as well as the human body.

Like the other Bugs of this chapter, trichomonas lives in semen, and transmission occurs via what still gets called unprotected sex. So far this pathogen resembles others we've talked about here. But unlike the semen-borne journey of Ebola virus disease and HIV, the trich trip is symmetrical. Entry points for trichomonas are the vagina and the urethra. HIV can also travel into another person through the urethra, but that path forward seems to require microtears or other preexisting trauma to the body of the ejaculator. With trich, female mucosa doesn't just receive; it gives.

Ingress and egress. From this symmetry, one might think trichomoniasis presents a good occasion to put semen aside and instead think about other bodily fluids that also seem to have a claim to attention about danger. I'll leave that work to other books. Let's consider how caring about semen can enlarge understanding of this disease.

Start with the name *Trichomonas vaginalis*, a choice that situates this parasite inside female anatomy even though it also lives elsewhere. Its discoverer, Alfred Donné (whose contributions to science exceed his fame: Donné also discovered the blood pathogens that mark leukemia), created the name "trichomonas" without adding "vaginalis." The single-word coinage Donné chose combined "tricho-" for hair or bristle in ancient Greek (θρίξ) with "-monas" meaning single unit. Nothing female in that original name. It was another scientist who added "vaginalis" to "trichomonas," presumably to note the habitat that Donné had investigated.[49] *Trichomonas vaginalis* the parasite causes trichomonas vaginitis the disease. The female-sounding descriptor for this Bug is anomalous, as pathologies with similar names like "vaginitis" and "vaginismus" afflict only people who have vaginas. "Trichomonas vaginitis" in its Latin label notwithstanding, trichomoniasis afflicts male-bodied persons as both sufferers and spreaders. Not in an egalitarian way, however.

Studies of trichomoniasis as experienced by human populations continually report divergences: more women test positive for this disease than men, and Black women test positive for trichomoniasis more than white women. Stark divides: "4.2% among black males," according to one study, and "8.9% among black females" compared with "0.03% and 0.8%, respectively, among males and females of other races/ethnicities."[50] Women who have the disease are also likelier than men to suffer physical symptoms—and here we're talking symptoms that a person of any gender can have, such as a sensation of burning urination.

The pattern aligns with distributions of privilege and suffering. What's going on? If the explanation for the race gap is genetic predisposition, then the genes in question are of interest and deserve more research than they receive. Same for other explanations. If, for example, white men are more likely than Black men to use condoms, as one paper suggests by way of explaining the trich race gap, then that disparity also deserves attention. Sickle cell disease presents an analogy on point. Researchers have protested the underfunding of research on sickle cell compared to diseases that afflict mostly white patients, such as hemophilia and cystic fibrosis, which enjoy support registries and more pharmaceutical investment.[51] Sickle cell appears too black to make a claim on the public fisc. Although it hurts Black people more than white people, however, trich isn't a minority condition. It's #1 worldwide.

Trichomonas offers yet another perspective on the protagonist of this book that shows semen's variety and range. Most of what I've reported in these pages describes a venturesome disruptor. Trichomonas joins other semen adventures that warrant more dialogue and scrutiny than they now get.

Receipt of semen into the vagina delivers the majority of trichomoniasis cases to persons of all races and ethnic groups: although trichomonas is a pathogen that thrives in semen, its impact lands especially hard on people whose bodies don't produce this substance. That's women in general and Black women in particular. Addressing the connection between semen and trichomonas thus steers attention to a disempowered group that ought to occur worldwide: the United States is not the only country where Black women experience an extraordinarily high rate of this disease. The trichomoniasis rank of #1 in sexually transmitted infections supports a distributive justice claim that Black women as patients and an at-risk population ought to receive more money and time from scarce public health budgets.

Trichomoniasis also provides proof of gender gaps in the give-and-take impacts of human reproductive anatomy. Recall two entry points of this pathogen, the urethra and the vagina, and the two modes of semenally transmitted infection, ingress and egress. The female genital tract offers a larger surface for traveling pathogens than its male counterpart. Urethras present a much narrower avenue for entry than vaginas. Trich can enter a female body more easily than it can enter a male one.

Acquisition of the disease from genital contact is part of the trich gender gap, as *Trichomonas vaginalis* does more than just spread itself when it arrives. This pathogen has a distinct process of infection that enables it to trigger cellular damage in host tissue while breaking down host defenses. Adhesion molecules on the surface of this parasite make contact with epithelial tissue of a human host—she's probably a woman, an adult—and achieve the condition of cytoadherence, or sticking to a surface. After cytoadherence, *Trichomonas vaginalis* transforms to an amoeboid form that intertwines with surface cells of the likely-to-be-female host. Damage ensues when the adhered parasite secretes new molecules that separate host cells from tissue, degrade the beneficial chemical phosphatidylcholine, and destroy red blood cells. Proteins located at the surface of the parasite add to the danger: they help to defeat host immune defenses by degrading antibodies and extracellular proteins.

Female bodies are more vulnerable to the degradation-aggression of the trich Bug than male ones.[52] I've mentioned the acidic pH of the vagina as a source of protection from infection for persons with female bodies. *T. vaginalis* elevates that pH value, increasing it to five or more. Higher pH threatens *Lactobacillus acidophilus*, the healthy microbiota that protects the vaginal epithelium. Meanwhile, in male bodies, biological defenses resist pathogenic factors of *Trichomonas vaginalis*. Zinc in prostatic fluid, for example, functions as a cytotoxic factor.

Trichomonas also illustrates the power of semen to give extra strength that we know helps HIV. Contrary to earlier reports that had been more reassuring, trich parasites have been found to be capable of surviving or growing for up to 24 hours in incubated semen—suggesting that *T. vaginalis* may also be able to survive in fresh or frozen semen used for artificial insemination.[53] Live parasites have been found in semen after hours of exposure to air sufficient to kill other pathogens.[54] More study of this neglected protozoan would generate more knowledge of general interest about semen as a disease deliverer.

* * *

The emergence of Covid in 2019 gave pathogens, or the Bugs of this chapter, a new urgency. Semen probably won't deliver the next Covid, if only because fewer people are in reach: airborne pathogens travel more easily than an infection that conscripts fluids and mucosa. But we can expect semen to bring a next *some*thing.

Part of what coronavirus upended was an old continuity that seemed to point reassuringly in one direction: public health would get better as science marched on. It does indeed get better. At the same time, the targets of our therapeutic interventions—by that I include both individual pathogens and infection as a category of peril—also gain strength.

Viruses emerge, evolve, adapt, and reemerge. One study of "deadly viral infections" anticipates large numbers "waiting to infect and adapt," boosted by climate change and poor sanitation.[55] In a book called Viruses, Plagues, and History, neurologist-virologist Michael B. A. Oldstone illustrates the phenomenon of reemergence with bird flu, the variation on human influenza virus that killed more than 40 million people in 1918–19 and has become, wrote Oldstone in 2020, "a new threat to humans."[56] Sure enough, four years later bird flu spread to cattle and from there continued to travel within the vertebrate phylum, infecting cats and poultry along with human beings.[57] Some travelers that emerge and evolve and adapt and reemerge live in semen.

Zoonoses or zoonotic diseases, meaning pathogens that start their path in life by infecting one species and then evolve to infect another, include two prominent viruses that threaten Homo sapiens: HIV and MPX. Origin in chimpanzees qualifies HIV as zoonotic; MPX once had a nonhuman animal in its old name of monkeypox. Both zoonoses live in semen, with HIV faring particularly well—which is to say, from a human point of view, virulently and destructively—in that fluid environment.

Just as viruses have evolved to revive from dormancy and jump to new species, they also evolve to resist efforts to contain them. Coronavirus offers a good example for the moment because we are living under the impact of this virus-prowess right now. That particular virus evolves and evolves once more. Covid vaccination did very well at first, scoring 83% against infection, 92% against hospitalization, and 91% against mortality. A high score on the World Health Organization scale for effectiveness. Over time, all three numbers dropped. Same effect for a booster.

Evolution is the reason. Covid changed to survive. Covid variants that have evolved into potency powerful enough to get past the barriers of vaccines echo a similar effect in vaccination against other diseases like mumps, pertussis, meningococcal disease, and yellow fever. That vaccines become feebler over time can be obscured by their success. They can start out zapping and crushing their target enough to drive a disease into obscurity. When their strength starts to dwindle, there's generally no way to know that this decay has occurred until the disease returns and vaccine-borne immunity has decreased. "Everything of course depends on immunologic memory," said an informant for a science story who had started his vaccine research in 1957, "and we have not systematically measured it."[58]

Bacteria evolve and adapt too, though with patterns and impacts that differ from those of viruses. From the human-health perspective that our species understandably chooses, the two pathogens are alike in that they are both microbes that spread infection by dispersal. They are also different. Bacteria can reproduce on their own; viruses need a host to reproduce. All bacteria are bigger than the biggest virus. Bacteria are nicer to us, if I may anthropomorphize about them, than viruses. Most bacteria perform benign functions in the human body. Only a tiny minority bring disease.[59]

Greater complexity makes bacteria more vulnerable than viruses to human-engineered destruction. Antimicrobial medicines can kill a bacterium by a variety of means. The penicillin family of antibiotics attacks the bacterium's cell wall. Tetracyclines thwart protein synthesis. A younger yet long-established cohort of antibiotics, the fluoroquinolone group, kills bacteria by interfering with their DNA.

You know where I am going when I predict bacteria trouble to come. Evolution makes disease-bearing pathogens stronger and abler to resist intervention. It renders bacterial infections "difficult or impossible to treat," says the World Health Organization, and from there this resistance enlarges "the risk of disease spread, severe illness, disability and death."[60] In one relatively recent year, 2019, antimicrobial resistance was estimated to have caused 1.27 million deaths directly and contributed to 4.95 million deaths worldwide.

Looking to the near-term future, experts predict more winning by antimicrobial resistance and more losing to bacteria by human interventions and human bodies. The old 2019 number of 1.27 million human lives lost to this failure of antibiotics will rise, according to one estimate made by researchers in Brazil, to nearly ten million people per year in 2050.[61]

Some of this strength will result from the power of bacteria to emulate one of the strengths of viruses. The big vulnerability of bacteria has been their big size and physical independence. Antibiotics can hurt bacteria where they live because they contain more mass to attack and offer more external surface exposure. But a growing number of bacteria have figured out how to move into a space distinct from themselves and thrive there the way viruses do. Known as intracellular bacteria, these microbes "have evolved the ultimate resistance against phagocytes, complement, and antibodies: they move right into the host cell and continue their reproduction outside of the host's grasp."[62]

The truism that viruses and bacteria gain strength by evolving makes reference to nature rather than deliberate human intervention, but pathogens can also emerge and adapt as manmade biological weapons. The inaugural director of the Technology and International Affairs program of the Carnegie Foundation has provided a measured assessment of this danger. Some biological weapons seem too costly to be worth the bother, on one hand: for example, assassination that exploits the genetic code of one targeted individual. On the other hand, Katherine Charlet writes, "nations could develop novel or modified pathogens that would spread more quickly, infect more people, cause more severe sickness, or resist treatment more fully."[63]

The possibility that deliberate action could set out to make humanity sick might sound like genre fiction. But deliberate action does just that, as we saw in the last chapter of this book. Abortion bans leverage the landing of semen on mucosa to sicken and sometimes kill human beings. I think it's relatively unlikely that bad actors will exploit Bugs the way they've exploited semen to hurt people, if only because bioengineering villainy is harder to pull off than interference with the right not to be pregnant. Evolution plus the ease of travel in an interconnected world, however, means that the odds that semen will harm human beings in new ways are high enough even if we ascribe good intentions to everyone.

Worse, more sources of illness in semen appear headed our way. We can expect evolution to steer pathogens that now live in semen into both oblivion and a greater degree of danger. We know that at least three conditions present in semen to enhance sexual reproduction—fructose, alkalinity, and amyloid fibrils—nurture and strengthen viruses. We know that semen supports bacteria; we know evolution threatens the power of antibiotics to kill this source of disease. And we know that semen boosts the impact of *Trichomonas vaginalis*, a pathogen that's neither a virus nor a bacterium, suggesting that semen offers plenary hospitality for multiple sources of future danger. The future paths of evolution to come might turn out less eventful than past experience predicts, of course. But even the current roster of disease-makers that thrive in semen needs management.

5

Lasting Relationships

Back in the thirteenth century, Aquinas told us that our original sin comes from semen. He didn't say sperm; he'd never heard of sperm. He blamed semen.

Because "the child preexists in its father as its active principle," Summa Theologica continues, and semen comes from fathers. We persons alive today are steeped in original sin based on our connection not to Eve, our maternal ancestor, but to Adam, the first human inseminator. Aquinas explains that while Eve and all mothers contribute mere "matter" to new children, Adam and all fathers bring "the active principle of generation." Original sin in our species would have ebbed away if only Eve had sinned, adds Aquinas by way of clarification, because original sin as a durable condition arrives inside the next generation only through semen.[1]

Impacts of a secular nature also originate in the travel of this fluid from one body to another. We've seen some of them. Journeys of semen from one body to the mucosa of another body carry diseases, as we saw a chapter ago. Directly before that, chapter 3 covered manmade consequences that exploit a past landing of semen in a vagina to empower outsiders like pharmacists and inseminators and local governments to domineer over inseminated persons. In the chapter before that one, we considered the receipt of semen as a starter that changes lives. Impactful adventures of semen continue in lasting relationships. Touch this fluid or be touched by it on a vulnerable surface, and you can find yourself durably connected to somebody else.

* * *

Surveillance follows semen. People who think they might be or become pregnant, and also those who wonder whether they have or might get a semenally transmitted infection, routinely generate a record of their thoughts, questions, and movements from one place to another that relates to the landing of semen in or near them. Much of that record comes from electronic searches about pregnancy or disease that these people put into words.

Gadgets perpetually next to us maintain attention to where we've been. At the time that I write, this network relies on the instruments we carry, which means that separating oneself from one's device can thwart the gaze. But even an hour or two out of smartphone range is rare for most people these days. The ability of human beings to take a brief break from a physical object is a current condition that I expect the surveillance sector to overcome.

Of the two consequences semen on mucosa can cause—that would be Making People and Making People Sick—pregnancy receives more attention from surveillance than infectious disease because there's more to know in the sense of more to sell. In their survey of profitable technologies that locate and preserve information related to semen on female mucosa, Aziz Huq and Rebecca Wexler start with the tracking of menstrual cycles via smartphone.[2] Almost a third of all women in the United States use or have used period tracker apps on phones. Because all consumers of these apps menstruate, or at least say they do, these people in the aggregate are capable of becoming pregnant.

Semen on their mucosa causes monitoring of more than periods. The Dobbs decision stirred chatter about the high volume of intimate information that these apps collect and exhortations to reject them. Generation X women sounded especially loud in the turn-it-off chorus. Period tracking didn't listen: the technology became more popular after Dobbs, reaching new users at a faster clip.[3] One website counted 2.9 million downloads worldwide in September 2023 of the most successful competitor, Flo, along with more than two million of Flo's two nearest rivals.[4]

The current full name of the #1 app is "Flo Period and Pregnancy Tracker." Even when their brands omit reference to pregnancy, all period tracker apps function to collect semen data when users are impregnated and continue to enter information about themselves. "Fertility apps," writes the privacy scholar Danielle Keats Citron, "ask subscribers to describe their cramps, consistency of their vaginal discharge, temperature, use of contraception, period dates, and miscarriages."[5]

Lasting relationships ensue from this phenomenon because the information that the machines ask users to reveal is both cheap and profitable to store. Period tracker apps make their money through the sale of bundled-together facts; users pay for the services an app renders through the data they provide about themselves. When the product is free to you, as the aphorism goes, you are the product. Stored information can be expected to endure as long as cheap storage endures.

Urging consumers to reject or unplug this electronic grab has been unavailing so far, as I mentioned, perhaps because the machine is good at what it does. Apps are reported to predict pregnancy on average nine days before home tests. The workplace wellness sector has hopped on the gynecology-app bandwagon, offering software to employers who can share information with insurers. Selling fertility treatment as an employment benefit is profitable for businesses that manage self-tracked data. Employees who download fertility-support software presumably volunteered for the surveillance they join, but the tentacle-like reach into medical data collects more information that patients or consumers agreed to reveal.[6]

Health privacy law could inhibit the sale of this data and in this way make the electronic relationship between users and vendors less durable, but current American privacy regulation doesn't cover period tracking apps. Some providers happen to follow policies respectful of consumer privacy, such as storing data locally in the user's phone rather than remotely. Privacy-protective policies are subject to modification that users won't know about, however, and these policies are undermined by conditions in the phone that the apps don't control. For example, many users back up the data they generate in the cloud or neglect to turn off location tracking that can make period-tracker information more informative to third parties.[7] Clicks that consumers need to supply if they want to download any interactive software further waive or modify rights. Danielle Keats Citron observes that for three years, the fertility-tracking app Glow enabled anyone to access to a subscriber's account simply by asking for it. Glow went on to tighten its security, but fertility- and period-tracking apps have remained notoriously indifferent to user privacy.

Intimate data gets aggregated into units that are sold in a market. Data brokers follow thousands of points of information on nearly everyone living in the United States: their travel, their Internet searches, their health conditions and the drugs they take, and how likely they are to experience sets of medical procedures. These collectors trawl through "mobile apps, search engines, advertisers, marketers, and other data brokers; information scraped from websites and social networks; and public records," writes Citron.[8]

Back in the early aughts I asked a savvy friend who worked in information technology why he didn't worry about electronic data about himself that seemed to pile up quietly and exponentially. "Banality and volume," he said. Information about people is uninteresting, yes, and there's so damn much of it. I'd be surprised if you wanted to know the period date that someone typed into her phone. Even if you care about it, this information will hardly ever matter. But sometimes it will be worth buying. Numerically tiny yet qualitatively significant exceptions lessen the protection of the banality-and-volume combination that lets my friend sleep well.

Demand in general keeps data collection robust and potentially dangerous; demand for semen-related data in particular comes from both private customers and law enforcement. Search warrants have generated lists of online searches for abortion providers, geolocation data showing visits to a pharmacy or an abortion clinic after the discovery of a pregnancy, details of a missed period recorded on a period tracking app, and messages about efforts to terminate a pregnancy. Governments have gained access to health records created for other purposes like routine checkups to track women's periods by demanding them via subpoena and also by paying for them.[9]

The practice called "contact tracing" applies to the other consequence of semen on mucosa, Make People Sick. Historians report that contact tracing started in the United States by burdening women identified as prostitutes. Ostensibly to prevent the spread of syphilis, authorities jailed these women and kept track of their sex partners. Patients thought of as respectable—well-heeled, often married, usually male—got identified by anonymizing codes rather than their names. A middle tier on the prestige ladder, standing above sex workers and below the respectable, experienced what most resembles contact tracing as we know it today. Health departments traced this group of syphilis patients without arresting them but did publish their names.[10]

Contact tracing lit up a big bright electronic map in early 2020 when two countries in Asia showed how governments can keep track of who has touched whom. South Korea knitted together seven separate sources of information—location data emitted by mobile devices, "personal identification information," medical records, immigration records, card transaction data, transit pass records, and closed-caption TV footage—into its 2020 response to coronavirus, an effort named the Epidemic Investigation Support System.[11] This exercise in mass surveillance made use of a convenient fact on the South Korean ground: 96.4% of consumer transactions had gone cashless by 2016, enabling multiple sources of data—from credit cards, debit cards, and smart wallets programmed to record travel on public transit—to build crisscrossing trails that found virtually everyone. Machines held close to everyone's body generated and received text messages addressed to individuals as soon as someone tested positive for Covid. The other Asian country that drew attention as a surveiller, China, enlisted smartphones in an unpopular disease-control strategy called Zero Covid. This adventure in contact tracing lasted almost three years. Until December 2022, everyone in China needed an app as a kind of passport for intercity travel and entry into public spaces.[12]

Government surveillance across the early Covid era in both South Korea and China saw to it that all a person had to do to engrave relationship durability into state recordkeeping was exist. Governments in the United States proceed differently. They rarely practice contact tracing for any purpose. In this country, commercial markets fill the role of building and storing durable connections.

Sellers and buyers of data in these markets link people together. Most buyers of this information are sellers themselves, looking for good-fit prospective customers. Nothing personal, so to speak, just a business move that relies on the aggregation of human beings into clusters where their individual identity doesn't matter. But the purchase of data created in response to ejaculation can generate or prolong a relationship that an inseminated individual doesn't want.

Predators who may or may not have impregnated anyone can enlist data collection in the service of domestic abuse. In chapters 1 and 3 we met predatory inseminators, a motley assemblage who inflict a variety of harms that have pregnancy-making in common. The group consists mostly but not entirely of men. Some men rape a child and impregnate her. Some batter their pregnant adult partners. Some medical providers substitute their semen for what their patients chose for assisted-reproduction insemination.

If a predator of the domestic-abuser ilk can seize his partner's unlocked phone for a few minutes, he can install a stalkerware app. That installation gives privacy invaders access to users' texts, emails, voicemails, searches, browsing history, and physical movements. More than two hundred services, Danielle Keats Citron reports, charge subscribers a monthly fee in exchange for providing covert access to people's phones. Domestic violence hotlines in the United States help more than 70,000 people every day: according to the National Network to End Domestic Violence, as many as 70% of callers raise concerns about stalkerware. One study found that a majority, 54%, of domestic abusers tracked victims' cell phones. A security firm detected more than 518,223 stalkerware infections during the first eight months of 2019, a 373% increase from that period in 2018.[13] Semen does not cause this behavior, but it's present: men who choose stalkerware typically have ejaculated into the people whose phones they invade.

National and transnational laws in Europe, along with the choices of a couple of U.S. states, show that law and regulation can act to restrict the sale and acquisition of an enormous mass of information that records the journeys of semen. Legal controls could reduce the bulk of lasting relationships imposed on the unwilling. Consistent with Anywhere It Wants to Go, the phrase applied to semen in chapter 1, however, American law leaves this trafficking almost entirely uncurbed and uncontrolled. Indulgence of both semen and data gathering contrasts sharply with the consequences that people touched by semen as a traveler into their bodies experience. Impregnated people are not left alone.

The pattern of indifference and indulgence for some and surveillance and interference for others returns when we look at location-tracking technology. Most ejaculated-upon persons who set out to end their pregnancies enlist transport. The percentage of patients who traveled out of state for their abortions doubled between 2020 and 2023, from one in ten to almost one in five.[14] Pills and videoconferencing suffice to let a few people stay home for the termination of their pregnancies, but most abortion patients have to leave the house. Most patients who seek medical attention after they terminate their pregnancies with misopristol and mifepristone receive this medication at a location away from their homes.

Travel to obtain help ending a pregnancy can build unwanted lasting relationships with hostile strangers. Relationships imposed on the unwilling in the Roe era seem quaint in contrast to current formations. Members of old antiabortion groups like Operation Rescue used to spend full days near clinics taking pictures of license plates to learn who had arrived in these vehicles. They had to tote cameras and develop photographs rather than just hold up a phone. When late twentieth-century federal legislation discouraged this crude use of surveillance, the surveillants moved on to generate new classes of durable records by leveraging technology. Today automobile license plate readers take photographs of automobiles that traverse roads and streets. These photographs focus on license plate numbers but also capture the camera location, time and date of the photograph, and sometimes images of drivers and passengers.

Just as American data privacy law sides with interferers rather than the people they watch, allotting freedom and prerogative to controllers that resembles the free pass that semen receives, American law enforcement sides with Team Surveillance rather than the freedom of ejaculated-upon persons to travel unsurveilled. Here the relationship started by semen connects possessors of mucosa to police and prosecutors. Since 2022, when American governments gained the power to ban abortion, enforcers of a slew of new crimes have benefitted from the menu of prerogatives for law enforcement. Once states learned that they could criminalize helping someone terminate her pregnancy or crossing state lines for this purpose, several of them did so. Law enforcement personnel enforcing an abortion ban have access to durable evidence that someone traveled for this medical care.

Location-tracking software makes prosecution easier. Post-Dobbs semen-tracking technology includes the geofence warrant, which compels disclosures of information about everyone who passed through a particular location at a particular time or searched the web for a particular keyword. Businesses that respond to a geofence warrant conduct sweeping searches of their location databases and provide a list of cell phones and affiliated users found at or near a specific area in a time frame.[15]

Businesses that sell the blocks of data that surveillance generates operate under conditions of opacity. Some of them sell this information only to government customers and, according to one author, "often go to extreme lengths" to conceal the nature and pricing of their product from the public.[16] The combination of private and public power—"private" in the sense of for sale plus not accountable to the government plus not covered by constitutional limits on state action like the Fourth Amendment; "public" in that it's funded by taxpayers and shares authority with law enforcement and sworn officers—adds up to more force than any ejaculated-upon individual can muster to protect herself. She has to hope that surveillance will proceed with some regard for her rights and interests. Meanwhile, data derived from period apps that law enforcement seeks "may be commercially available, and government entities have already shown an interest in acquiring it." During the first Trump administration, "the Office of Refugee Resettlement collected data on asylum-seeking minors' menstrual cycles and pregnancies in order to track their potential for seeking abortions."[17]

The same synergy between private and public power builds lasting relationships out of genetic data-gathering that threaten individual freedom. Customers enlarge the reach and permanence of semen-derived information when they sign up for DNA testing. A cluster of companies whose brands currently include 23andMe, Ancestry, MyHeritage, Genomelink, FamilyTreeDNA, and GEDmatch accrete what they receive and connect this genetic data with the customer-volunteer's family members. If you're leery of these businesses, as I am, they're not leery of you. Staying out of their sights is out of your control; as a consumer you can't opt out.[18] A thread of semen ties us to the DNA base that these collectors know about and expand.

Demonstrating that law enforcement participation in this data-gathering extends beyond abortion surveillance, police investigators have tapped this trove of information to help solve cold cases. DNA records held by GEDmatch proved crucial to an investigation in California where law enforcement had genetic evidence from crime sites implicating the same individual in dozens of rapes and at least a dozen homicides but had no idea who this person was. GEDmatch data, however, could connect this unidentified perp to hundreds of his cousins. After months of research, investigators had filled in 25 distinct family trees with about a thousand named family members. The thorough, patient slog that followed—first look for men, then look for men in the right age range, then figure out whether these men lived near any of the crime scenes—yielded two suspects, one of whom was eliminated by a DNA test and the other who put out household trash containing genetic identification that implicated him.[19] This triumph inspired law enforcement personnel around the country to both use and enlarge a mountain of factual information that owed its existence to semen.

Let's return to abortion bans as they intersect with data collection as a source of lasting relationships that follow the movement of semen onto mucosa. States whose prohibitions recognize exceptions to the ban or permit abortion at an early stage of gestation use abortions as occasions to collect and store information about ejaculated-upon persons. Utah, for example, has created what it calls an "abortion module" that patients must click through in the form of mandatory online training familiar to students and white-collar workers. After she engages with quiz questions to the satisfaction of this software, the patient can receive a certificate of completion. Next she has to wait 72 hours.[20] The durable module lives on.

Texas goes further. Whereas data-generation in Utah applies to actual abortion, the Texas rule orders physicians to gather information about what it calls "abortion complications" (but might well be no such thing) and send these assertions to the state department of health and human services. Multiple physicians as well as the hospital in which they work are tasked with dubious and redundant reporting. Because Texas can punish informants for failure to report but not for misattributing medical consequences to abortion, these individuals are steered to generate noisy post-insemination data about patients whose mucosa has been touched by semen.[21]

* * *

Biological parenthood is next in our review of lasting relationships that semen creates when it travels. Whereas stored data maintains relationships that need machinery to persist, the parenthood consequence of ejaculation endures person-to-person. Long after seminal fluid has dissolved into oblivion post-landing, the tie of semen on mucosa keeps people together, connecting individuals whose bodies once touched this fluid at the same time. The connection has the capacity to stay in place whether the persons who possess these bodies like it or not. Impacts of shared semen press into human lives and make a claim on the future.

Ejaculate into a vagina and in more than half the U.S. states you're eligible to join a government-controlled network called the putative father registry. The Supreme Court first expressed its approval of a putative father registry in 1983 when it ruled against parental rights for a genetic father who'd had the option to sign up in a registry maintained by the state of New York but had not done so.[22] Registries invite men to assert their interest in a baby they may have fathered.

Most men who add their names to these state databases know about the birth of a child, but that knowledge isn't necessary. A putative father registry doesn't try to establish parental rights or entitle anyone to anything. Instead it's a place to declare that semen landed on mucosa and that the ejaculator seeks a lasting relationship.

Data collection generates other lasting relationships from semen on mucosa before any baby is born. The consequences of semen that generates babies can be sorted into three categories. First, obligations to bio-children impose a connection on parents to their children that these parents might or might not want. Second, children are tied to their bio-parents, again on a like-it-or-not basis. Third, the two persons whose semen and mucosa came together to make these children are connected to each other. Adoption, a complement to biological parenthood, creates new ties that do not of themselves terminate semen connections. I'll review these interrelations in turn.

The first relationship: Parents are connected to their children. Make a baby with your body via semen on mucosa, and the law will impose obligations on you. You might try to renounce this baby soon after its birth, as Justice Amy Coney Barrett said to a lawyer during the *Dobbs* argument at the Supreme Court. Barrett expressed this idea as a question—"Why don't the safe haven laws take care of that problem?"[23]—framing "that problem" as an unwanted lasting relationship between a parent and a child. Safe haven laws are on the books in every state. What they contain varies but all of them tell parents who wish to abandon an infant without risking criminal prosecution that they may drop their baby at a site accessible to the public, such as a fire station.

Let's put aside for now the literature documenting multiple problems that safe haven legislation fails to "take care of,"[24] and assume that tossing a baby into a government-furnished receptacle leaves new parents and their children healthy, wealthy, and wise. Relinquishment doesn't end the lasting relationship that semen creates. For starters, most states give the relinquishing parents a window of time to change their minds and reclaim the baby, a choice that seems humane given the desperation and distress that relinquishers may feel but also one that keeps the connection alive. In my home state of New York, this period runs for 30 days. It's shorter in most other places. Making the abandonment permanent right away, as Alaska does, is rare.

Safety for the infant requires some kind of in-person handover, preferably while video cameras in the reception area or building lobby roll. The balance between protecting the baby and supporting a fast exit with no lasting relationship for the parent seems hard to strike. Soon after the Supreme Court decided Dobbs, a graduate student reported on the extraordinary lack of information about American safe haven laws in operation. Governments in the United States at all levels know nothing about motives that impel new parents to relinquish newborn infants—a deficiency that I admit probably comes with the no-questions-asked territory—but also basic data that could be gathered without intrusion: how many babies get relinquished this way, their state of health, where they end up.[25] Lack of information about safe haven laws in practice obscures how they actually function. Maybe they end parental ties to children and maybe they don't. Nobody keeps track.

On to child support obligations, which endure at least 18 years after the landing of semen on mucosa and can go on longer. We visited this topic as a consequence of Seed the Starter in chapter 2, paying attention there to its impact on inseminated-upon people and inseminators as individuals. Here in this summary of lasting relationships between people that follow from the transfer of semen, I note the function of child support in data collection and state surveillance. One assessment of "the longstanding and widespread phenomenon of exorbitant child support debt owed by noncustodial fathers to custodial mothers in low-income and predominately Black families" describes child support debt as not only a severe economic burden but also a "financial bubble." What Tonya Brito means by "bubble" is that for very poor noncustodial parents "this debt is artificially inflated, largely uncollectible, and potentially destructive."[26] It's durable, too.

Babymaking stays costly for years after the birth of a child even if someone else pays for the shoes and afterschool uniforms and pediatrician attention we referenced in chapter 2. The focus of this chapter, people's dealings with other people, adds relational legal liability to the consequences of semen landing on mucosa. Criminal sanctions can punish parents for neglect or abuse of people who exist as a result of this movement from one body into another. Tort law puts them on a cash hook for this mistreatment.[27] Parents confident they won't be accused of parental misbehavior might well be right, but the risk of liability when deciders condemn conduct remains a durable consequence that continues until their children reach legal adulthood.

Another twist on durable liability extends beyond the harm parents do to their children to the harm that their children do to others. Like liability for neglect and abuse, liability for children's misdeeds befalls parents only rarely; immunity is the norm. Immunity won't always protect the parent of an errant child, however. One survey of the liability landscape finds the justifications for parental immunity "rotating," hard to reconcile with one another, and rooted in fear.[28]

Liability attributable to the child-parent connection extends in yet another direction: your children can sue you for harms they attribute to your neglect of their welfare. Courts impose this duty on parent-defendants. Again, not often, but they do.

One durable connection that originates in semen travel and ties children and parents together all the time, rather than on the rare occasions when courts impose criminal or tort liability on parents, is the creation of a birth certificate. People can't opt out of being named on a child's birth certificate the way they can keep their names off marriage licenses by choosing not to marry or property records by declining to buy property. Unlike marriage and property ownership by acquisition, biological parenthood can befall persons independent of whether they want that status. All the creation of the new status needs is a landing of semen on mucosa. From here, the state makes a permanent record that it could not have generated absent that landing.

The high level of privacy that state law bestows on protecting birth certificates, where individuals must be family members to access these records, does not undo or negate this semen-created bond. Having one's name listed on the same birth certificate puts people together even if this document is extremely difficult for an outsider to look up. Each birth certificate unites at least two individuals—usually three, but a minimum of two—as governmentally recorded members of a family.

Durability of a birth certificate takes us to adoption, a relatively rare route to parenthood. Around the world, the large majority of child-parent relationships originate in a transfer of semen that unites two participants, an ejaculator and an ejaculatee, in a shared physical relation. We saw in chapter 2 that only a small minority of children under 18 in the United States became members of their families via adoption. Adoption is even less common in other wealthy countries. It's important to the sociolegal study of our fluid, however.

Adoption might appear to challenge both the preoccupation with semen that pervades this book and the theme of semen-derived lasting relationships that fills this chapter. If a person can become a parent without ejaculating into anyone else or being ejaculated into, then semen as a constituent of parent-making seems peripheral rather than central. As for lasting relationships attributable to semen, adoption presents an apparent exception. Our ejaculator and ejaculatee made a baby together but another person, someone who might not have ever been touched by semen, becomes that baby's parent through adoption. Well, let's take a closer look.

Adoption of a child can occur only after official, formal relinquishment or forfeiture. The new relationship that it launches requires the termination of another one. (Adults can be adopted by other adults without any relinquishment, but here we are talking only about the adoption of children.) Anyone who becomes a parent via the travel of semen from one body to another keeps that parental relationship by default, which is to say the relationship lasts until there's a reason for it to end.

Calling one adult a "biological" father or mother of another person, as adoption discourse tends to do, makes direct reference to insemination. Every biological father inseminated someone else; every biological mother received semen on her cervical mucosa. Although the adoptive-parent relation is understood to rest on volunteering than biology, that connection too is biological in that anyone who adopts a child becomes the parent of someone who exists only because biomatter traveled from the interior of one person to another.

Instead of making the original semen-rooted relationship less durable, adoption strengthens this force. Let's return to the birth certificate. Adoption layers complications onto this record. Superseding the original birth certificate that named one or two biological parents, an amended birth certificate adds the adoptive parents' names and erases the original ones. Both documents linger in state storage largely inaccessible to seekers—and they are even more inaccessible to adopted children, who unlike the nonadopted majority cannot obtain their original birth certificates under the law of most U.S. states—but always enduring.

Emotional and psychological consequences for biological mothers continue this theme of durability that follows the relinquishment of a baby for adoption. Observers wishing to think that adoption is a gentler or more merciful route to nonparenthood than abortion must reckon with the durability of the original relationship as a source of pain. "Women are less interested in placing their child for adoption today than ever before," observed the adoption-law scholar Malinda Seymore, writing in 2023. The small number of relinquishers overstates the desire to give up a baby for adoption, because most people who relinquish originally planned to choose either keeping their baby or abortion— and their original plan failed. Seymore cites a study that found "when women were denied access to abortion for an unplanned pregnancy, ninety-one percent parented rather than relinquished for adoption."[29] Low rates of relinquishing babies into adoption suggests that this path is distasteful for most people who face it as an option.

To an interlocutor inclined to say that relinquishment of one's new baby isn't for everyone but could work well as a choice among others on the possibilities menu, pleasing the minority of biological mothers who volunteer to take this path, I have contrary data to relay. Relinquishment doesn't succeed in the sense of allowing a connection to be cut without pain. Durable consequences that often follow relinquishment include depression, shame, negative self-image and self-reports of feeling unlovable, and difficulties in attachment to both romantic partners and children born after relinquishment.[30] Birth mothers benefit from continued post-adoption contact and experience less grief when they know that their children are happy in their adoptive homes, Malinda Seymore continues, but score worse in grief resolution when they lose contact with these children. In many states, the promise of continuing contact that adoptive parents make to birth mothers is not enforceable.[31]

On to the second category of lasting relationship occasioned by semen on mucosa, the connection to their parents imposed on children. One hundred percent of parent-child relationships originate in transfers of semen to which the child did not consent. The bromide that children "didn't ask to be born" is yet another reference to semen that omits the word semen. We didn't ask for the episode of ejaculation that formed us; we're stuck with its consequence. Estrangements that divide parents from children appear common (almost a third of my friends, for whatever my limited personal experience might be worth, have chosen no contact or very limited contact with their mothers), but dislike or repudiation doesn't cut off the formal and legal recognition of child-parent relationships.

People have children for reasons that mostly "serve their own interests," writes David Benatar, a philosopher known for his work on antinatalism, the stance that making a baby is wrong. "Parents satisfy biological desires to procreate. They find fulfillment in nurturing and raising children," and maybe a kind of old-age insurance policy. "Progeny," Benatar continues, "provide parents with some form of immortality, through the genetic material, values, and ideas that parents pass on to their children and which survive in their children and grandchildren after the parents themselves are dead."[32]

These motives are understandable, from the parents' perspective anyway, but don't cure the problem of an unconsented-to imposition. Consent by the child is missing from all begettings of children. Antinatalist gloom might or might not be correct, but Benatar must be right when he says that human existence befalls us without our permission. It's another durable connection derived from semen on mucosa that can be unwelcome and it lasts as long as the begotten person lives.

Fatherhood started by the donation of semen outside a preexisting sexual relationship illustrates the force of this fluid as a launcher. Journalists who interview prolific donors attest to the lasting nature of semen-spurred relationships. Durability takes different forms. The donor who told the BBC he'd generated about eight hundred children by selling semen for £50 per dose using Facebook mentioned his ego and a sense of competition.[33] Whatever one may think of this motive or its claim to accuracy as an estimate of children begotten—eight hundred is a big number—it generated the durable consequence of more people.

Other men who sell or give away their semen in large volume report connections that they feel to the children and the children's mothers their effluvium touched. Semen donor Ari Nagel, credited with the number 138 as counted in April 2023, told a reporter that the quantity of his bio-children coupled with their location all over the world prevented him from being "a full-time dad. But my presence is more than what the anonymous sperm donor can do."[34] Another high-volume donor, pseudonymed Louis, attributed his unconventional parental status to coming from a broken home and a self-diagnosis of autism. This insem-inator went on to meet 40 of his bio-children and claimed to be close with some of them.[35] In February 2024, one man, Kyle Gordy, recited his count—61 children, 11 of whom he'd met; 9 more on the way—and what he thought he'd accomplished beyond ejaculating: "I enjoy helping people and seeing the kids grow up and seeing them happy."[36] Semen enabled these men to start permanent connections whose quality I would not presume to judge although I will presume that they include pain among the children so generated, not just pleasure.

Now let's check out bio-parents stuck with each other. I'll start with unwilling fathers. Searching case law, one author found two men and one boy forced into fatherhood and the attendant obligation to pay child support despite not having consented to the act that led to insemination.[37] A woman in Alabama assaulted a friend while he was unconscious and became pregnant.[38] A 15-year-old boy engaged in sex-ual intercourse with a 34-year-old woman who later gave birth to their child.[39] A woman performed oral sex on a man while he had a condom on. She saved the condom and its contents and later gave birth to the man's child.[40]

Unwanted fatherhood has also befallen ejaculators who engaged willingly in sexual intercourse with partners but lacked willingness to become parents. Assurances by women that fatherhood would not ensue do not protect men reliably from the ascription of this status. In a Michigan case, the female partner in male-female intercourse said she was using birth control *and* was infertile, one lie about risks not being enough;[41] a woman in Indiana obtained semen from a male friend after signing a contract releasing him from the financial responsibility of fatherhood and then filed an action against him seeking child support.[42]

Research published in the Journal of the American Medical Association about another unwanted consequence following insemination worked with the number 519,981 as a denominator. That's the estimate of how many vaginal rapes occurred in states with abortion bans from July 1, 2022, when the Dobbs era began, until January 1, 2024. Next the researchers multiplied 519,981 by the (low but nonzero) probability that these rapes resulted in pregnancy. The exercise counted 64,565 pregnancies formed by rape during that 18-month period in abortion-ban states. Almost all of these pregnancies, 91%, occurred in states whose bans provide no exception for rape. The study concluded that almost three million women in the United States have experienced a rape-generated pregnancy.[43]

This much enormity making my mind boggle a bit; I'll claim that small numbers in the form of individual experiences are necessary for an accurate reckoning of this consequence. Verified accounts confirm the formation of lasting relations between rapists who ejaculated and the possessors of mucosa. Let's look at a few of them.

When Kellie Eizenga, a resident of North Carolina, was fifteen, a 25-year-old man named Timothy Bobbitt ejaculated into her vagina. Because Eizenga was too young to consent to sexual intercourse, the age of sexual consent in North Carolina being 16, Bobbitt's act constituted statutory rape. Bobbitt pleaded guilty to *attempted* statutory rape (italics mine) and received a sentence of 94 to 122 months, or approximately eight to ten years, in prison. What Bobbitt did was more than an attempt, as Eizenga became pregnant during the time Bobbitt was having sex with her and genetic testing established that the baby to whom Eizenga gave birth was Bobbitt's biological daughter.

Three published decisions by the North Carolina appellate courts show that Kellie Eizenga wanted nothing to do with the man who'd impregnated her.[44] She resisted Bobbitt's multiple attempts to gain joint custody or visitation of the person his semen had formed. State law gave both her and Bobbitt hope in the struggle. In North Carolina, persons convicted of first- or second-degree rape that generates the conception of a child may not bring a claim for custody or visitation of that child.

Good news for Eizenga. The good news for Bobbitt was that he had been convicted of (only) attempted statutory rape. His criminal record might have made him look less than fit to family court judges mindful that statutory rape by him was fully achieved, or more than attempted—but Timothy Bobbitt had a legal entitlement to seek custody and visitation of the child formed by the landing of his semen onto Kellie Eizenga's mucosa when Eizenga was underage.

A younger victim of statutory rape, impregnated at age 12 by an 18-year-old acquaintance, also rejected termination and gave birth. Tiffany Gordon told family members she believed that "my son was innocent." The offender served less than a year in prison for this crime and soon after his early release drew a 5- to 15-year sentence for raping another girl. A Michigan court gave this inseminator joint custody of the baby he'd made by rape, ordered that his name be put on the baby's birth certificate, and revealed Gordon's address to him when directing her to live within 100 miles of him as a legally recognized father.[45]

Acceptance of pregnancy and motherhood seems different from acceptance of a shared-parenting relationship with a malefactor, but most American states show indifference to the difference by requiring a criminal conviction of rape before a rapist-inseminator can be denied custody of the child he generated by his wrongful act. "We do not require convictions for termination of parental rights for such reasons as child abuse, neglect and habitual drug offenses," noted one lawyer-activist who fended off the custody initiative of an inseminator never convicted of the rape she said he'd committed.[46]

So while a criminal conviction by the inseminator can cut off unwanted paternal relations, the plea deal struck in Bobbitt v. Eizenga reveals how vulnerable women remain to the enduring relations created by rape. A 2022 NBC News story reported an especially durable such connection. Crysta Abelseth was 16 in 2005—younger than 17, the age of consent in Louisiana where she lived—when John Barnes, then 30, ejaculated into her. Abelseth told a reporter that she'd reported this assault in 2015 after a trauma counselor told her she wasn't too late, yet the police did nothing to investigate her complaint. In a public statement, the police department confirmed that it had indeed never assigned the complaint for investigation: "our department absolutely dropped the ball," it announced, "and we simply must own our mistake."[47] Whatever it might mean to own this mistake, that acknowledgment didn't sever the connection between Abseleth and Barnes.

Durability of co-parenthood derived from rape continues in most of the country. In a 2015 statute called the Justice for Victims of Trafficking Act, Congress moved toward weakening that durability by encouraging states to adopt as a legal standard clear and convincing evidence of rape rather than a criminal conviction as grounds to cut off inseminators' claims of durable parenthood. More recently, amendments modified the unofficial-but-influential Uniform Parentage Act promulgated by the National Conference of Commissioners on Uniform State Laws to provide that in a legal proceeding where "a woman alleges that a man committed a sexual assault that resulted in the woman giving birth to a child, the woman may seek to preclude the man from establishing that he is a parent of the child."[48] Neither effort, however, has enough force to shift the default of a continuing relation between ejaculator and child.

* * *

Sharing custody of a child means sharing power. Over the child, for starters. Parents have brought to court a growing array of quarrels. Multiple bones of contention about children in common show the depth of the semen connection. Because my home in central Brooklyn offers a ringside view of one in particular, I'm drawn to it as an illustration.

Strife can arise between ex-spouses who disagree about enrolling their children in one type of religious private school, a yeshiva. (The word "yeshiva" comes from a Hebrew root meaning "to sit," a verb that may imply passivity in the face of authority. You heard from me on the subject of Orthodox Judaism and semen back in chapter 1. All my schooling from kindergarten until college took place in a yeshiva.) In typical versions of this dispute, one parent has retreated from the Orthodox Jewish community in which the couple had lived while the other has remained. The anti-yeshiva side of this recurring quarrel gained supportive attention when The New York Times started in its headlines to refer to some of these schools as "failing."[49]

One lawyer with experience representing parents who object to keeping their children in yeshivot has written that allocations of custody do not necessarily determine which parent gets to make this decision. Reviewing losses in court experienced by the more secular combatant, Julie F. Kay writes that parents who favor religious observance frequently win no matter the custodial arrangement. If the pro-yeshiva parent has sole custody, he can get his way because judges think he is empowered to call the childrearing shots. In the more common setting of joint custody, judges reason that pulling children from yeshiva would disrupt their education. And when the secular-minded parent has sole custody, "the court acquiesces to the noncustodial religious parent's assertion that the child's extended religious family or community will reject any child who attends a public or Modern Orthodox school that does not require strict adherence to religious orthodoxy."[50]

For the sake of neutrality, let's assume the moral and educational equivalence of a religious and a nonreligious school for the child fought about in this dispute. Let's also attribute good faith and good intentions to both adults. Parent A changed their mind about religion. Parent B regards this change of mind as the betrayal of a commitment. The dispute will cut deep, cost money, and assign power to external deciders. Neither parent can proceed alone according to the dictates of their conscience; a past landing of semen on mucosa locked them together.

Only one of us can win. My remark that sharing a child means sharing power extends to more than power over the child. This relationship gives authority not only to outsiders like family court judges but also to parents over parents. Years of teaching family law have taught me that intraparental quarrels challenge the coherence of joint custody, a concept the course must cover. Joint custody means shared prerogative for adults whose dyadic relationship ended while their children were still young. When these parents can't agree, they can end up in court. The high price of litigation means that any fight they couldn't settle away from judges must be, to them if not others, existential or central to an indivisible religious identity. To circumcise an infant or not. Vaccination or not. Psychotropic drugs for a child's depression: what's more prudent, abjuring them because they might be harmful or embracing them because they might save a life?

To call this strife disagreement understates how intensely it can penetrate: the word disagreement has a connotation of manageability that is absent here. Individuals connected to each other by a past transfer of semen, forged by this heat into the status of co-parents, have each gone

on to become the other parent's bitter enemy. This turn of events is probably rare, but I have observed it and read about it in reliable narratives.
Any painful and durable riven-yet-connected relationship that could not
exist without ejaculation belongs in this chapter of a book about semen
reckoning.

If I have a right to contact you, then you must live with the unpleas-
antness of this contact when I initiate it. If you have the right to visit my
child—a person who might be (but isn't always) your child too—then I
must arrange my life in accord with this right of yours. If you and I share
custody of a child while living separate lives, then major childrearing
decisions both empower and weaken us whether we each like this forced
sharing or not. Parental rights, all of them mirror images of burdens,
can cause both ejaculatees and ejaculators to suffer when the transfer of
semen starts a pregnancy that results in the birth of a child.

* * *

Ejaculation, in sum, forms relationships that endure. Adults connected
to each other through the children they share rather than affection for
each other are a fixture of the Western literary canon. Think of Medea
and Jason, characters alive in Greek mythology for more than three
thousand years. Sexual jealousy at the center of *Medea* is presumably
even older.

Durability itself endures and expands. We still read venerable tales of
permanent unwanted connection between semen-on-mucosa sharers,
or we can if we want to, and through our societal participation in ejaculation we add to the quantity of what continues. That which endures
generates more connection. Modern adoption preserves and extends the
original impacts that created biological parenthood. Records of genetic
testing keep track of past journeys by semen. Technology like geofencing
or stalkerware sides with continuing durability and against any participant who wants to move on or away. Along with social customs and the
force of law, machines reinforce semen permanence. They stand against
oblivion, erasure, and forgetting.

6

Pleasures and Satisfactions of Semen on Mucosa

Making the best of semen calls for attention to the happiness it generates, not just the risks and harms that have populated the last couple of chapters. Pleasure is what human beings pursue. Jeremy Bentham gets the most credit from English-speaking readers for taking pleasure seriously but before Bentham came up with his felicific calculus, the Enlightenment thinker Cesare Beccaria wrote that the correct way to judge law or policy is to look for *la messima felicità divisa nel maggior numero*, the greatest happiness for the greatest number. More pleasure, less pain. We've spent pages on pain. Time to consider the journey of semen onto mucosa as desired and desirable.

Let me try to be clear about what I mean to include when I bring up semen pleasure. On one hand, I take people at their word when they say what they want and don't want, and so I'll deem a semen-related experience pleasurable when human beings say they like it, appear to pursue it, or sacrifice to get it. Is desire authentic? Might people prefer a condition that hurts them to an alternative state with that condition absent? If something that feels good has a pernicious external effect, for example wrecking the planet with climate change, can it still count as pleasure? When we think we want something, do we really want it? Yes, yes, yes, yes. At least in this chapter. The philosophy of pleasure agrees.

On the other hand, I'll complicate this acceptance with a value judgment: I care about safety, broadly understood. Safety isn't the only constituent of pleasure. Too much of it could even cause pleasure to diminish, I understand. Outsiders can acknowledge excitement and even a degree of danger in a semen felicific calculus. That said, we've seen in the preceding chapters that one broad category of semen danger lands unequally and asymmetrically on human beings.

Semen danger accompanies the greatest contribution to pleasure that this substance makes, the launch of pregnancy that results in the birth of a child. We know about a taste for babymaking from revealed preferences: most people become biological parents before they die. Answers to surveys that ask respondents whether they want children and if so how many confirm the fact of this pleasure, and the baby-making that most people pursue in turn confirms the accuracy of their answers.[1] With regard to insemination, individuals walk the walk and talk the talk.

If actions reveal preferences, as I am presuming they do, then semen as baby-starter appears extra desired and desirable in that the half of humanity that suffers the physical pain of childbirth and a risk of death from semen as babymaker engages in a higher rate of babymaking than people who participate as inseminators. The Centers for Disease Control regularly surveys a nationally representative sample of persons aged 40–49, an age range that captures almost everyone who will achieve biological parenthood, to learn about American fertility trends. In its most recent report—which is consistent with earlier studies as well as a pattern around the world—the CDC found that 84.3% of women had given birth and only 76.5% of men had fathered a child.[2] Explanations for this gap vary but all are consistent with semen on mucosa as renderer of pleasure.

This bottom line about pleasure noted, semen as babymaker brings dangers to women that extend beyond the physical detriments of pregnancy. Longitudinal studies of parents report that the transition into fatherhood provides more happiness and satisfaction than transition into motherhood.[3] A set of surveys that reached more than 18,000 participants found that fathers scored higher on happiness than both mothers and men without children.[4] Current trendspotting stories like "Why More Women Are Choosing Not to Have Kids" attribute the decline in the American birthrate, about 2% each year on average since 2007 with a steeper drop in 2021 blamed on the Covid pandemic, to reassessment of the pleasure-pain balance among potential child-bearers.[5] Reassessment follows readily enough from the Supreme Court's 2022 decision that added manmade danger to the risk and pain present in every pregnancy. One-third of women aged 18–39 told polltakers a year after Dobbs that they or someone they knew personally had decided not to become pregnant "due to concerns about managing pregnancy-related emergencies."[6]

To the extent I'll value danger in this chapter's treatment of semen as a source of pleasure and satisfaction, then, I'll want to protect vulnerable people from the whims of deciders who don't have skin in the game.

We met controllers in chapter 3. These people leverage the impacts of semen on mucosa to make hurtful decisions without suffering consequences in their own bodies, and their power shows no sign of going away. Individuals for whom the transition to parenthood includes physical pain and risk of dying have a greater stake than bystanders in semen applied to this purpose. They deserve preferential attention in the felicific calculus.

A final inclusion in my working definition equates pleasure with the abatement of pain. This understanding also aligns with the philosophy of pleasure as expressed by the Stoic philosopher Epicurus, who wrote that pleasure is a condition where "the body is free from pain and the mind from anxiety."[7] Negation or amelioration of a bad condition counts as pleasure.

* * *

Orgasm, proclaimed "the peak of pleasure" by the Dictionary of Psychology,[8] is as good a place as any start to thinking about semen as a source of happiness. The emission of semen is closely associated with orgasm. For an ejaculator, this sensation can feel like the hit of a short-sharp-spiked recreational drug. Studying male volunteers wired to instruments that depicted their brain when they ejaculated has confirmed that the brain region that lights up most during ejaculation is the mesodiencephalic transition zone, a region of the cerebral cortex that also registers the delights of cocaine and heroin.[9]

This finding of intense pleasure used manual stimulation from the subjects' female partners to induce ejaculation into a container rather than onto mucosa. Male-bodied persons can enjoy ejaculating onto nonmucosal surfaces and typically experience orgasm when they do. Pleasure from solitary masturbation to orgasm probably deserves to be counted among the pleasures of semen, but in this chapter I'll focus on ejaculation that makes intimate contact with another person. It's the perspective I'm qualified to take. Lawyers, of which I am one, focus on relationships: societies, governments, dealings between people. Experiences that have no impact on another person are only rarely any of the law's business. I am at a further distance from the sensation of solitary ejaculation of semen from never having experienced it: I can understand how it feels only from what I hear or read. I also do not know whether or how much the pleasure of ejaculating alone is offset or complicated by something negative that equates to pain in the felicific calculus.[10] And I can't grasp in a personal way the separation, or metaphoric daylight, between the distinguishable experiences of emitting semen from one's body and reaching orgasm.

The epistemological circumstance of my having lived in only one type of gendered body (a condition that would also limit a writer who emits semen, albeit in different ways) and the occupational identity that steers me to focus on dealings among human beings come together to center reception of semen in this chapter's analysis of pleasure. To matter here, semen must venture into someone's body. Requiring receptive mucosa as a criterion for inclusion widens as well as narrows what counts in the pleasure tally because it cares about what ejaculators' partners feel.

Ejaculation delivers pleasure to these partners. One study of sexually active heterosexual women found that for some of them, receipt of a high volume of ejaculate made their orgasms extra intense.[11] Any volume of ejaculate at all looks like evidence of the ejaculator's pleasure, which an affectionate companion could find pleasing to observe.

Observed ejaculation as informative of how a male-bodied person feels when he ejaculates brings us to the combination of distance and closeness present in pornography's "money shot" or "come shot." As with "barebacking," a term I'll use when I move to another semen-related pleasure, I'm choosing idiom rather than a clinical phrase deliberately: semen throughout this book is social as well as medical.

Viewers seek this inclusion when they consume pornography. "If you don't have the come shots, you don't have a porno picture," said Stephen Ziplow, writing in 1977 from the vantage point of a movie maker. "Plan on at least ten separate come shots."[12] Decades later, ejaculation recorded on film still marks the climax of a scene and closes a narrative.[13] Titling its documentary about a video-sharing website "Money Shot: The Pornhub Story," a choice Netflix made in 2023, is yet another reference to semen that omits the word. The popularity of money-shot content in porn suggests that this commodity delivers visual pleasure to customers. Whether imagery of semen exiting a penis records authentic satisfaction as experienced by performers who get photographed I wouldn't presume to say. Let's assume it doesn't. It still does cue audiences to think about their own pleasure.

Semen delivers pleasure more interestingly through what the science journalist Jesse Bering has called "the antidepressant effects of seminal plasma."[14] This variant on semen pleasure isn't an elixir that causes a thrill on contact. Instead semen brings comfort and satisfaction. It eases and lessens distress when it lands on mucosa; it makes people feel better. Researchers found this category of pleasure when they surveyed 293 female undergraduates to investigate an association between what these subjects reported about their exposure to semen and their level of depressive symptoms.

Students who said they engaged in heterosexual intercourse and answered "never" to a condoms question scored as freer from depression than peers who "usually" or "always" used condoms and those who did not engage in heterosexual intercourse at all. Members of the never-condoms cohort, women touched intimately by semen on the regular, also reported fewer suicide attempts. Another study found that semen-exposed women scored higher on tests that measure cognition and concentration.[15] Summarizing this research on his Scientific American blog, Bering mused that semen might be "a sort of natural Prozac—whether obtained vaginally, anally or orally."[16]

These findings may help explain the persistence of barebacking, or no-condom anal sex shared by two men. For observers concerned about the spread of HIV, barebacking may appear pathological—even today, when the risks of semen on anal and vaginal mucosa can be greatly reduced with drug prophylaxis, and more so when this practice occurred in the fatal-illness years of approximately 1982 to 1996. Researchers working in the pre-PrEP era (PrEP, an abbreviation for pre-exposure prophylaxis medication, is discussed at greater length in chapter 7) asked men who engaged in barebacking why they chose to do it. When they ought to know better, the question implied. Respondents said that the transfer of semen delivered a sense of deep connection. That too may sound pathological. Desiring something that can kill you or your partner seems dangerous in a pointless way. But if semen is a happiness vector, as Bering observes, then the desire to take and give it where it will penetrate most deeply isn't perverse.[17]

Women who wish to become biological mothers have reason to want semen too, not just the genetic material in it, because semen on their mucosa delivers pleasure by improving the prospects of the pregnancy they want. One multicenter study that directed randomized participants to either engage in or abstain from vaginal intercourse while receiving transferred embryos concluded that exposure to semen increased the odds of successful early embryo implantation and development.[18] A meta-analysis of eight controlled studies including 2,128 women found that in vitro fertilization fared so much better with seminal plasma on the vagina and cervix at the time of "ovum pickup or embryo transfer" that the study authors spoke about an impact on the clinical standard of care, writing that this interventionist application of semen should "be considered as a straightforward, non-invasive, and rather cheap treatment to improve implantation in IVF."[19] Researchers at the University of Iowa found that vaginal exposure to semen (only vaginal; the study also looked at oral exposure and found no effect) reduced the risk of preeclampsia, a common and potentially painful pregnancy complication that reduces pleasure.[20]

Veering a short distance from mucosa in the semen felicific calculus, I'll note that semen also has generated pleasures by stimulating the human imagination. A jeweler and sculptor told a journalist that she'd expanded her business to include semen after a couple of years making ornaments out of customer-supplied fur, breast milk, locks of hair, and cremated remains of people or pets. The TikTok video that showed this artisan mixing semen into clay went viral. Both this sculptor and another artist said that the semen idea had come from their customers, suggesting demand for an unusual usage.[21] "Natural Harvest: A Collection of Semen Recipes," a cookbook, received good reviews on Amazon when it was published in 2008. During the First World War the British Secret Intelligence Service, MI6, found semen effective as invisible ink.[22] I'm unsure where to classify the mucosa-inclusive application of semen pursued by one @AaronEvansXXX, a persona identified on social media as an Indianapolis police officer eager to receive dozens of strangers' "loads" without pause in his rectum. That pleasure seems to combine physical sensation with performance art.

* * *

Then there's the pleasure for which semen is indispensable rather than merely entertaining or enjoyable. Once again we find semen undermentioned in contrast to the sperm in it. In the assisted reproduction commercial market, where customers pursue insemination to start a pregnancy, we don't hear men referred to as semen donors, a term I used in chapter 5 of this book, even though semen rather than sperm is what clinic employees first store and manage, what the donor knows is present in his donation, what customers can identify when they open a package they've paid for, and what gets inserted into a vagina with an instrument like a syringe. Nor does anyone offer to donate semen to anyone else, except maybe facetiously. (Monty Python, remembered in chapter 1 for saying "every sperm is sacred," almost made that joke. You can find online the sketch featuring Terry Jones at a blood bank imploring management to accept his donation of urine. The doctor in charge of donation brushes him off. "Spit?" whimpers the Jones character. "Earwax?") Vendors dealing in semen don't call themselves semen banks in parallel to the blood banks that also sell a bodily fluid.

This familiar silence notwithstanding, semen too, not just sperm, is always necessary for babymaking—even the variety of babymaking that sets out to address azoospermia, the condition where a father-to-be produces healthy sperm but can't generate a pregnancy by ejaculating because his gametes are blocked from reaching his semen. The fix for obstructive azoospermia is testicular sperm aspiration, where sperm cells drawn from the patient's testicles with a needle meet ova in the lab. This workaround sounds like impregnation without semen but it's not, because it never happens without a semen sample to test. Insemination via testicular sperm aspiration could in principle occur without any prior travel of semen into a vagina but in practice the intervention follows a diagnosis of infertility. Testicular sperm aspiration as a treatment for infertility is always preceded by instances of vaginal intercourse that included futile ejaculation. Human beings owe their existence to biological fathers who ejaculated onto mucosa. This connection means that the desire of human beings to make children is a desire to enlist semen.

The focus of this book on law and policy enlarges the evidence that insemination delivers satisfaction. Consider the state-level regulatory trend that requires health insurers to pay for interventions to treat infertility. The trend hasn't reached a majority of states, but big jurisdictions including California, Illinois, New Jersey, New York, and Texas are on the list. It didn't arise from nowhere. Someone lobbied lawmakers to reach this result. That someone wouldn't be the usual suspect of

American health care, insurance providers: businesses that will get stuck with the bill rarely ask governments to burden them with mandates. This variation on semen transfer must make governments as well as individuals happier.

Government policies that encourage people (read women) to make babies, ascendant around the world as I write, prove another level of pleasure attributable to semen on mucosa. National governments that reward babymaking with cash increase the satisfactions of this journey. Those maneuvers from the state doubtless add to distress too, but a government-funded transfer that covers what prospective parents already want but cannot easily pay for adds to the pleasure side of our ledger. Babymaking furnishes another helping of pleasure by easing worries about population decline. Presumably American state governments are pleased in a flesh-and-bloodless but real way when, for example, a credit rating agency rewards them for their state's high score on birth rates.[23]

* * *

First-person narratives by women that relay how much the author craves insemination support a conclusion about semen as a source of pleasure in the Epicurean sense of diminished pain. We can classify assisted reproduction via semen donation as pleasurable with reference to what I've described as revealed preference: most people make babies with their bodies before they die. Popularity implies pleasure.

Semen banks—a term that should exist, like "semenally transmitted" to modify infection or disease—sell this fluid to a diverse customer base. Social change has enlarged the sale of semen beyond the old clientele of infertile heterosexual couples, a cohort that spokespersons for the banks said comprised only 20% of the market in 2021. Most semen-bank buyers, about 60%, are gay women. The remaining 20% have been labeled single moms by choice.[24]

Recipients and seekers confirm that semen delivers pleasure in the sense I use in this chapter, something that people prefer to the alternative of not having it and are willing to pay money to experience. Through this utilitarian lens, an essay with the phrase "I'm grieving" in its title offers testimony to semen as a source of pleasure: grief will morph into pleasure when it abates. The author of that essay and her wife set out to reduce their grieving with semen from a stranger.[25]

Another female customer married to a woman paid indirect tribute to semen pleasure in an Esquire article where she described her search for a sperm donor as reminiscent of "a high-stakes mashup of the worst parts of online shopping—the doubt, the unpredictability—and online dating, with its anxieties and disappointments and unintentional hilarity."[26] She laughed at her effort to read self-characterizations by donors and try to pick one. "When it comes to the opposite sex, I don't have a type or even criteria for red flags," she wrote. "I'm a lesbian. The entire male species is a red flag to me. And yet, here my partner and I were, in close conversation with a part of the population that neither of us had intimately interacted with in years; and here we were, forming pointed opinions about men on the fly." The writer ended her story by saying she and her wife, keeping their focus on the pleasure of babymaking while shifting their means to this end, chose to look for semen away from a sperm bank.

Single women, straight and otherwise, join the seekers of semen acquired to land generatively on their mucosa. First-person accounts of this quest testify to the depth of that desire. One of these narratives, titled "Fertility Treatment Cost Too Much So I Had Sex with a Friend," did the math on what the clinic she chose had laid out for her. Assuming four ovulation cycles as a necessary minimum, the price would be $6,000 to $7,000 if she enlisted an anonymous donor and $8,000 from an acquaintance.[27] If the cliché about First World problems comes to mind, fair enough, but single women old enough to consider this possibility and young enough to become pregnant without heavy technology are a relatively low-paid lot. Again, revealed preference about pleasure. Investment in the pursuit of semen by people who forfeit other good things to get it demonstrates the pleasure of insemination.

Like other distributions of pleasure and pain in the United States, the struggle to acquire semen has a racial constituent. "Black men account for fewer than 2 percent of sperm donors at cryobanks," a headline from the Washington Post announced. "Their vials are gone in minutes."[28] According to a count taken in October 2022, in the four cryobanks that each held semen from more than a hundred donors, only 12 donors out of 748 were Black. One informant told the writer that while on the phone with a sorority sister she'd put vials from a Black donor into her online shopping cart. Reaching the checkout screen, she learned that this semen was sold out. Her friend at the other end of the call had clicked faster.[29] Compromises mentioned by participants in this market testify to a pain-pleasure tradeoff. Black customers have reported deciding, with some reluctance, to accept semen from mixed-race donors. One cryobank chose to drop its ban of donors who'd had sickle cell disease.[30]

In addition to the compromises they choose as individuals, Black participants have brought mutual aid to this pursuit of pleasure. Black women in the market for semen have found peers in "professional settings, support and prayer circles, and online forums on platforms such as Facebook, where women trade notes about finding the right doctor, the hormonal side effects of fertility treatments, and rituals like eating French fries and other high-fat foods after embryo implantation."[31] Among the uses of Facebook by this community is a group called Fertility for Colored Girls that has thousands of members and chapters in 16 states. These supports exist to enlarge pleasure. [32]

* * *

Semen producers who turn over this fluid to benefit semen seekers demonstrate yet another pleasure of semen in contact with mucosa. Here pleasure is more straightforward than what semen seekers receive. For women who want to become pregnant and search for the sperm they need, semen acquired by donation fills a unique void. The pleasure that semen gives them is fulfillment of an urgent ambition and the easing of distress. For semen producers who donate this fluid as a pregnancy generator to recipients outside a sexual relationship, the felicific calculus operates more gently. Semen donation does not (I presume) originate in feeling deprived of something important. Unlike egg donation, it causes no physical pain to the producer at the time of extraction.

We heard from some of these donors in the last chapter, which focused on the lasting relationships that semen starts by landing on mucosa. I quoted these men to present their ejaculation in a perspective I think doesn't get enough regard—their identity as human beings who have plans and goals. Donating semen to a bank is regarded as a quick shallow episode, barely even a transaction and certainly not an undertaking. I'd agree with any eye-roller who wants to note that the contribution ejaculators make to babymaking is relatively cheap and convenient. Looking at semen through the lens of pleasure and pain that occupies this chapter permits consideration of what semen donors want and receive when they donate without exaggerating their importance to sexual reproduction.

Let's check back with our small sample of chapter 5. Donors told journalists about an array of pleasures they received by giving away or selling their semen. Taking action as problem-solvers gave them satisfaction. One of them reported pleasure from being sought out by some of his bio-children. Another donor said that he was happy to see happiness in the children he'd met.

To these men's happiness, we can add happiness of women who receive donated semen. Researchers studied this happiness in 2014 when they distributed a questionnaire to semen-seekers who had signed up with Pride Angel, a British website set up to foster communication between seekers and donors, asking them about their experiences. Informants reported another array of satisfactions.

Some women who obtained semen by online donation praised the Internet for giving them access to more prospective donors than they could otherwise meet. They also liked the chance to investigate and to decide whether they preferred closeness or distance. A smaller fraction expressed discontents, of which the most common was what informants characterized as dishonesty among donors; that testimony references the pain half of our felicific calculus..

The researchers gave themselves credit, rightly so I think, for looking at something new. "Whilst studies have examined the experiences of women who use clinic donors, to date there has been limited research investigating women's motivations and experiences of searching for a sperm donor online."[33] Their study investigated pleasure.

* * *

Semen's felicific calculus invites attention not only to what semen provides but what it *can* provide. This point of view invites observers to think about semen policy. Policy change will occupy the next part of this book, but pleasure in this chapter offers a chance to introduce policy here. Happiness and satisfaction of human beings as a goal supports and justifies actions to enhance the good things that this substance can deliver.

Semen policy, as I envision it, commits itself to the greatest good for the greatest number. If this approach to semen sounds like a no-brainer in the mode of *Oh, did we miss an alternative, like the worstest bad for the smallest or leastest number?*, think again. Choosing semen policy isn't obvious or inevitable. Because any substance that generates significant and preventable consequences qualifies for regulatory attention, the path of policy identifies an action item for the government. Having power that regulation can control or mitigate means that Anywhere It Wants to Go, the attitude toward semen documented in chapter 1, needs reconsideration. Semen policy also rejects the tradition of unmentionability that started this book.

Finding the greatest good for the greatest number requires consideration of pleasure and pain. Semen is a unique source of both impacts. The review in this book has emphasized the pain half of the calculus because pain is where law, where I come from, can do the most good: the great power of regulation is enhancement of safety and safety means shelter from risk and harm. Equally important to keep in mind is happiness, the point of the felicific exercise.

How to investigate, measure, and assess the pleasures of semen is the next question. I announced my methods preliminarily when this discussion began. Actions, in my view, reveal preferences: when people do something, I'll presume that the effects of their chosen actions please them. I also listen to what people say they want. Following the Stoic tradition, I equate the abatement of pain with pleasure.

Having explored pleasures of semen that extend beyond babymaking, I think semen policy ought to aim its efforts at that particular consequence. Again, one reason for a choice I make in this book is concern about relative competence. I don't know how semen policy can deliver this fluid to recipients as an orgasm intensifier. The artisans we've met who use semen in recipes or to make jewelry can find raw material on their own with little loss to overall human happiness. Because the generation of new people is so important at so many levels, semen policy has ample work to do on that alone. I'd focus on insemination as a maker of babies.

To my mind, the impacts of insemination differ in valence or quality. I wouldn't apply scarce policymaking energy to enlarge perverse or antisocial pleasures. On the question of which pleasures are perverse or antisocial, I favor liberal tolerance but only up to a point. Earlier in this book, we learned that the predator Jeffrey Epstein had a plan to please himself by establishing what he called a baby ranch populated with young uterus-bearers into whom he would inject his semen, twenty pregnancies at a time. To hell with that pleasure. On the related constituent of pain, I've noted that female bodies suffer more from insemination than do male ones, and from there I think it's correct to give extra deference to the preferences of female-bodied persons. Girls and women live directly rather than indirectly with the consequences of pregnancy controls.

The regulation of semen as a pregnancy starter has an almost infinite menu of possibilities. For example, by way of a thought experiment chapter 1 of this book suggested that the law could impose fitness demands on semen comparable to the more familiar and uncontroversial interferences that set out to protect fetuses and embryos. For now, let's focus on a more feasible goal that insemination policy already works to pursue: enhanced collection and delivery of semen donated to start a pregnancy outside of a preexisting sexual relationship. Pleasure and pain are at stake.

* * *

Two paths to insemination by semen donation are available in the United States. The first path involves institutions that call themselves sperm banks or cryobanks. I speak here about "paths" rather than options or alternatives because our protagonists might be able to reach only one. But both exist. Both paths can be improved in the sense of made more likely to increase happiness.

Cryobanks and their customers have chosen a route regulated by the Food and Drug Administration, which means they have accepted the imposition of safety controls. At present, establishments that deal in "human cells, tissues, and cellular and tissue-based products," a group that includes semen, must study the substances they process for listed diseases. They must screen (in contrast to test) each semen donor for two additional diseases and review his medical history.[34] The FDA also performs onsite inspections of cryobanks. On top of these demands are voluntary standards of organizations that some cryobanks belong to and higher standards in a few states. As a source of semen for a seeker and a place to donate for a producer, interacting with a bank is formal—contractual, covered by licensure and regulation, and presented to customers as something of a medical-health service rather than just a sale.

The alternative path to donating and receiving that delivers semen is simpler on the surface. No formal compliance. No guarantees, promises, or disclaimers unless both the donor and the recipient agree to them. No freezing of semen. Lawyers who advise the donor or the recipient about the deal would have reason to tell their clients about the risk that a court would decline to enforce these agreements. Uncertainty is another way to say opportunity: informal sperm donation permits a range of options to flourish. Find a friend, enlist an acquaintance, log onto social media, or float a pertinent search-word or two into the Internet.

Both formal and informal donation of semen generate pleasure for donors. Researchers who asked semen donors why they chose to donate divided respondents to their survey into formal and informal camps. For men who donated semen in the formal mode, filling out questionnaires and ejaculating in a laboratory, these pleasures "included being legally and physically protected, evading paternal feelings or social consequences, and having a simple, standardized procedure in terms of effort and finances." Donors who provided semen on an informal basis supplied a different and complementary set of pleasures: they liked "engagement, the possibility to choose a recipient, lack of rules and regulations, having contact with the donor child, and having an (intimate) bond with the recipient."[35]

For both the formal and informal tier of donors surveyed about their motives in another study, a majority assigned "very important" to the response of "I want to help others." Respondents in both groups also said they agreed with other pleasure-related goals: "to enable others to enjoy parenting as I have myself" and "to do something valuable and worthwhile," along with the wry remark that "my sperm would go to waste otherwise."[36]

Now, let's widen the felicific calculus to include downsides of both formal and informal semen donation. A paper called "The Case for an Unregulated Private Sperm Donation Market" rightly challenges the truism I mentioned that equates regulation with safety. In it Jacqueline Acker observes that although cryobanks must cooperate with safety-minded regulators, donating semen to and receiving semen from these institutions adds risks for both recipients and donors that are much less present in private donation. A cryobank could mix up vials of semen or store them negligently, jeopardizing inseminated customers. It might experience a data breach or receive a government subpoena that would threaten the privacy of donors.[37]

The risk of acquiring a sexually transmitted infection from informally donated semen continues the theme of pleasure balanced against pain. Most states require cryobanks to freeze the semen they collect rather than deliver it unfrozen to purchasers for the good reason that frozen storage provides time to test donated semen for STIs. As Acker notes, however, fresh unfrozen sperm is more efficacious as a pregnancy starter. Negotiated agreements in contrast to government regulation to enhance participants' interests present the same possibility of working out both better and worse. Every approach to happiness as policy comes with costs.

Both the formal and informal paths to insemination by donation call for improvements that regulatory choices can install. Customers of cryobanks and the children formed by semen sold there could be allotted a right to access more complete records. State-level reforms offer a catalogue of possible expansions that policymakers ought to consider. They might think about a national donor registry; better disclosure to customers about the risks of semen donation; biographical materials about donors furnishable later to customers and their children including, for example, medical, educational, and criminal felony conviction history with names redacted; and limits on anonymity.[38]

Improvements to regulation can take the form of removing restrictions, not just adding or tweaking new ones. An example of major regulatory addition-by-subtraction occurred in 2024 when the FDA announced its plan to drop its 1980s-vintage ban on semen donation by men who have sex with men.[39] Technological progress I'll explore in chapter 7 supports this regulatory turn.

To the formal versus informal perspective on semen donation, Jacqueline Acker adds the pertinent observation that cryobank regulations written as consumer protection are hollower than they look. For example, a requirement that these institutions screen semen to detect disease doesn't enforce itself even where it is on the books, and it isn't always found there: the map of state-level cryobank regulation includes jurisdictions that demand little screening by the sector.[40] Or consider the risk of fraud and deceit, which looks like something suited to the regulation toolbox. Dishonest ejaculators can describe falsely what they offer in both formal and informal semen markets but the formal sector offers significantly more opportunity for financial gain from lying.[41] The informal path of semen donation, living as it does at a distance from regulation, needs less regulatory repair.

I am inclined provisionally to improve the informal semen-donation market with policy in two broad stances. First, the law ought to clarify and enforce tort and contract remedies for injured participants. Less directly related to state action, the Internet can do more to distribute information useful to market participants. Model agreements between inseminators and inseminated persons, guidelines for semen safety prepared by expert nonprofit organizations, social media sites that connect people who want to donate with people who want semen, and narratives that recount past experiences with both the formal and informal paths to insemination have a ready home in our screens.

* * *

Improving the markets for insemination enlarges human happiness not only by delivering semen in arrangements that people want but also by enlarging possibility. Human beings gain pleasure and lessen pain when they gain power over the movement of this fluid from one person into another. In this perspective, the picaresque journeys of chapter 1, wherein semen can roam anywhere it wants to go, become quaint and obsolete. We are, or ought to be, in charge of this substance. Let us make the best of semen.

PART II

What Is to Be Done?

7

Water Management Informs Semen Management

Management of semen might seem impossible. Cope with semen, sure. We routinely face its bad and good consequences. Semen can be welcome enough for us to strategize how to obtain it, as the last chapter reported, and dreaded too. But manage? The prospect sounds like an oxymoron in the literal Greek sense, *oksus* and *moros* at the same time: when it roams anywhere it wants to go, the substance shows how sharp or "oxy"—(from ὀξύς or *oksus*, Greek for sharp)—it can be. Semen inserts itself pointedly into numerous environments. Dull blank resignation in response to this force earns the *moros* (foolish: think "moron") part of the word.

But management of semen is possible. If you've ever been a supervisor in a workplace, or reported to an okay boss, or negotiated with your parents, or taken teenagers on a trip that went well enough, then you know the balance of hold-the-line assertion and realistic acquiescence I'll be describing in this chapter. People yield to semen but also stand up to it for interests they feel are at stake, imposing a degree of control that's less than total but always present. The propensities of semen and what we want from the substance come together in mutual impacts. Nature and artifice meet in every intervention.

Human experience with water as it relates to weather and geography offers ideas and role models to expand semen management. We know from daily life how water-weather-geography delivers both what we have to tolerate and what we can push against. In my native and current home, outer-borough New York, local climates routinely obstruct what people want to do with their day. My neighbors and I put on coats and footwear that mitigate rather than overcome the drawbacks of our environment. Residents of my block deal with our mostly lousy weather by buying and storing clunky umbrellas and snow shovels and bags of rock salt. Brooklyn resembles most of the world in this respect: few of us on the planet are lucky enough to live in Lima, Cape Town, or the southern coast of California. We peer at phone screens to look at forecasts that constrain our journeys. We cancel plans, or take the proverbial rain check, in response to edicts from the weather that won't budge. At the same time we're not passive.

Just as management of water-weather-geography reminds us at a general level that human beings don't simply roll over when faced with natural forces that seem opposed to what we wish, managements of semen that are well underway remind us that we're already asserting control over this substance. Chapter 1, "Anywhere It Wants to Go," gathered examples of rolling over—some of them relics, others that continue. We yield to semen, on one hand. We put it in its place, on the other.

In this chapter I'll roll out instructive experiences of humanity gaining power over water, the fluid most important to its existence. What people have done about, with, to, against, and for water has counterparts that planners can apply to semen. Aligning water intervention and semen intervention follows a problem-solving orientation that can inspire more action.

Admittedly a polluting and despoiling lot, our species increased its health and wealth and happiness when we moved water around. Humanity thought big and reaped rewards. To my mind—and not only to mine—the ancient fable of Icarus and Daedalus does more than warn humanity about the peril of trying to overcome an environment: it invites us to imagine what we can do. "Think of the difference it made!" wrote Anne Sexton in a poem that praised Icarus for putting on wings and heading for the sky.[1] Initiative beats obedience and quietism. Similar to semen in this respect, settings that contain water-related danger offer opportunity.

Look around. As I write and you read, water waits for our summons nearby in pipes. Reservoirs built by human effort gather rainwater ingeniously for drinking and irrigation. Aqueducts carry water from reservoirs. In New York City, water supplies are powered almost entirely by gravity. Pipe networks move steam into buildings. Steam traveling this way heats residences, humidifies hospitals and museums, and can even power air conditioning. In California, an elaborate network of reservoirs, canals, and pumping stations spreads water throughout the large state. The water tower is a type of reservoir mindful of time: water typically enters these towers at night when demand is low and leaves them during the day when demand goes up.

As water and weather wreak their will, or their nature if you like, on us, we wreak right back. "Water gushes out of the faucet," a chemistry text chapter begins. "Honey oozes out of a squeeze bottle," the text continues. "Gasoline flows out of the pump."[2] True. It's equally true that no liquid ever put together a faucet or a squeeze bottle or a pump. We cope with, harness, and exploit the conditions that constrain and propel every fluid we live with.

Management aimed at weather and geography is more overt and transparent than the interventions we apply toward managing semen. But the efforts are similar. Human beings want to thrive and be safe. Both our geographic locales and our bodies have good claims to improvement-minded energies that put a fluid in order.

Structures like levees and dams and wind farms bow to geographic conditions that were present before these modifications arrived, and at the same time do more with weather or a body of water than just defer to it. They engage with environments and substances to deliver changes that people need. Human beings everywhere have agendas about geography. In dealing with these agendas they've wished and prayed and shirked, but they've never limited themselves to wishing or praying or shirking.

Connecting semen management techniques to controls on water, weather, and geography calls for candor about the record. I praise ingenuity and problem-solving aware that human action has ravaged the planet's water and weather. Heedlessness, negligence, and refusing to make short-term sacrifices or political tradeoffs toward repair of past lapses all loom large. In highlighting water management precedents that can inform the challenge of living better with semen, I endorse an outlook rather than blind replication. I expect semen management to make mistakes going forward. Law, policy, and governments ought nevertheless to assert dominion over semen just as they have asserted dominion over water. The gains of this management effort exceed what the alternative, Anywhere It Wants to Go, has provided in response to semen on mucosa.

* * *

For grandeur and ambition in water management, consider the dam. Historian of the environment Trevor Turpin wrote a book titled simply *Dam* and rhapsodized about it using italics: "The terms that come to mind are *power, strength, achievement, domination*—not all of them complimentary!—as well as *civilization*, both in general terms as a level of cultural development and encapsulated specifically by the phrase 'hydraulic civilization.'"[3]

Ambition about how to constrain and engineer a body of water to enhance human prosperity that the dam embodies offers a precedent for semen. Contemporary assessments of the dam report successes. A paper that adverts to balancing and judgment in its title, "The Environmental and Social Acceptability of Dams," credits dams for producing cleaner carbon-free energy. Dams also irrigate cultivated land, supply drinking water to communities that need it, reduce the risk and magnitude of floods, replenish low water-table levels, support waterway navigation and reservoirs for tourism and recreation, make fish farming possible, and protect estuaries.[4]

Water management starts by managing location. Every fluid calls for at least containment; it can't be allowed to flow uncontrolled. Semen and water, both necessary to life, require not just containment but also orderly movement and redirection. Humanity has risen to several location-related challenges.

For thousands of years, containments of water have taken into account the variety of what people want on different occasions. Roofs, for example. Our ancestors who invented the roof knew that everything that this installation keeps out—not just precipitation but sunlight, birds, insects, bird and insect droppings, projectiles that gravity or a stiff breeze sends to hit our bodies—is something we might desire to touch us at another time, under another set of conditions. And so every roof has a particular size and purpose. It extends only from point A to point B; it stops when protection ceases to be desired or easy enough to achieve. Same with awnings and umbrellas. Same with semen barriers like condoms.

Another parallel that semen management shares with water management is perpetual undertaking to do better. Our forebears slept under chunks of sod that they hoped would keep water from falling on their heads. Then they, meaning we, figured out that other materials—clay, thatch, concrete, tin—do a sturdier job in and on a roof. We don't stop. Partitioning water away from our bodies as a kind of self-defense makes a claim on human cleverness that we maintain without pause.

Consider the ever-developing endeavor of flood control. For more than a century, levee-building has dominated flood control strategy in the United States. What levee-building builds is a structure located near water that rises above the local ground elevation. This technology dates back before the Bronze Age.[5] Levees function to keep water from destroying or overpowering what people need to live prosperously in settlements or societies. Houses, streets, crops, and possessions are all vulnerable to water damage.

Embankment, a mass that's taller and bulkier than a nearby body of water, is the defining characteristic of a levee. Like the ancient birds that inspired human-aviation ambition, embankments formed by nature gave our settlement-building ancestors ideas for flood control. These people observed that sediment tends to get pushed to the sides of a river as it flows. Banks fill with dirt and silt to rise slightly above the riverbed.

The builders of ancient levees copied nature as embankment-maker when they piled up mud for flood control. Earthen materials—soil, sand, rock—continue to fill today's levees. Reinforcements in the form of wood, plastic, and metal blocks can be added. For levees that seek stronger flood protection, there's concrete.

Federal regulations that govern flood insurance identify a distinction between a levee and a levee *system* that's pertinent to the semen management parallel. A levee is "a man-made structure, usually an earthen embankment" designed and constructed to reduce risk from flooding, while a levee system understands flood protection as using "a levee, or levees, and associated structures, such as closure and drainage devices."[6] The two have separate tasks. Levees engage with water by standing in its way. Levee systems continue this engagement by recognizing that human needs don't stop after the structure carries out its task of blockage. They manage the movement of water to another location.

This division between two functions—a barrier to water and a design to divert water from where it flows—recognizes two approaches to flood management that also apply to semen, containment and diversion. Barriers that block the flow of semen are even older than the levee. Our species has applied itself diligently to the challenge of blocking semen from traveling from one body to another via sexual intercourse, keeping records of its ideas.

Variations on a theme of condom are old enough to show up in the old source I noted when I mentioned Icarus: Greek mythology includes condom mythology. Minos of Knossos, a king of yore, meant no harm to his mistresses but found himself killing some of them unintentionally by filling their vaginas with what turned out to be snakes, scorpions, and woodlice when he ejaculated. Distressed about his peculiar emission because it blocked him from fatherhood, King Minos was grateful to receive a sex tip: ejaculate into the bladder of a goat, said his informant, after which experience he'd be cleansed and could produce semen suited to babymaking. According to the Greco-Roman writer who reported the story in the first century BC, Antonius Liberalis, the condom-like intervention worked. King Minos followed the suggestion then engaged in sexual intercourse with his brave wife, and over the next years became the father of many children.[7]

Bronze Age archeology, cave art, and writings from around the world present a varied array of sheaths applied to this task during the last eleven thousand years. Today's latex and rubber were preceded by fabric wraps, tortoise shells, oiled silk paper, and animal parts: skins, innards, bladders. Even mammal horns have put semen at the barred end of a barrier. Modern enhancements of the condom follow the levee strategy of considering the relation between materials and design on one hand and the goal of containment on the other.

Just as engineers who built levees figured out that grass seed in the soil helps resist the erosion that comes from contact with water and that judicious additions of metal make soil-and-rock combinations abler to stand up to a flood, the perpetual condom-improvement undertaking seeks better materials and finds them. Ancient Egypt used linen. Ancient Rome retained linen and improved on it by making condom material also out of goat and sheep bladder and intestine.[8] In a similar overlap between established and new fabrics, entrepreneurs in the United States sold condoms made of animal tissue while working with vulcanized rubber, a product of the Industrial Revolution credited to Charles Goodyear. Rubber condoms in turn gave way to latex in the early twentieth century.

The modern condom testifies to the importance of what human beings want by continuing to take form in different materials and shapes, each presenting a mix of traits. Latex condoms are cheap and agreeably thin. Users who are allergic to latex (about 4% of the population) or who value the transfer of body heat between partners can buy condoms made of lamb cecum. This material is known colloquially as lambskin:

it's actually not skin but an intestinal pouch. Lamb cecum blocks sperm and semenally transmitted bacteria but is too porous to provide safety from the smaller-sized HIV.

Offering another array of upsides and downsides for users to consider, polyurethane plastic reached U.S. condom customers in 1994. Polyurethane plastic is thinner than latex, more transparent, more neutral in smell, and compatible with an oil-based lubricant, on one hand. It's more expensive and slightly more likely to break or slip in use, on the other.

At the moment we've got quite an array of condom options. Latex for the majority, old school animal biomatter available for users who like warmth or have a latex allergy, and plastic for the small fraction of the population who are both allergic to latex and committed to blocking HIV. One might have thought the condom menu had enough for everyone; it continues to grow. Consider polyisoprene, approved by the FDA in 2008 as something of a return to latex but prepared in a laboratory to keep out allergens. Users report that a polyisoprene condom feels pleasantly "stretchy" like latex rather than plastic "baggy."[9] It too is more expensive than latex. Choice and more choice.

When looking ahead at the condom-materials landscape of the near future, researchers found high promise in graphene, developed in 2004 by physicists who won a Nobel Prize for their work six years later.[10] One manufacturer has bragged that graphene is 20 times more resistant than steel and five times lighter than aluminum. The first graphene condom sold in the United States rolled out in 2023.

Barriers block semen situated inside the vagina too, not only on and around the penis. The female condom also continues to evolve. Natural rubber latex, polyurethane plastic (whose drawback of feeling baggy goes away when a penis isn't being wrapped), and synthetic latex are all available as materials for this internal obstacle to semen. One manufacturer in China launched a female condom that gets pushed into the vagina in the form of a capsule. Once inserted, the capsule dissolves. The condom then unfolds and releases foam to hold its thin polyurethane film in place.[11]

In this recurring pattern that characterizes the management of both water and semen, a barrier is invented and used. Ideas for improvement emerge. Some of them catch on. Ingenuity continues. In a counterpart to evolution as a phenomenon that alters organisms, new materials and designs of the condom thrive when they offer fitness, which means that the novelty they bring to the market is useful for the task of blocking this fluid effectively and agreeably. Progress proceeds. We don't stop. Anywhere It Wants to Go remains influential, but history of the condom shows "a history of the human spirit,"[12] where human beings domineer over semen with full confidence and a sense of entitlement.

We can do it, says the condom track record. *We're in charge. We'll block semen to get our way and please ourselves.*

* * *

Diversion, the levee-related maneuver applicable to semen that complements containment, has a bounteous and pertinent history in floodwater control. For both water and semen, diversion has tended to seem feeble in contrast to containment. Politicians and residents in an affected geographical region feel vulnerable after a flood that levees failed to control and crave a better barrier to replace the one that let them down. The next wall will hold up, goes the hope. Just make it stronger, thicker, taller, newer. The geologist Nicholas Pinter has called the desire for another vertical barrier a "seemingly instinctive response after flooding."[13] But diversion remains desirable and necessary.

Even a mighty barrier can't withstand flooding as well as a barrier backed by diversion. Failures that made Hurricane Katrina devastating in 2005 spurred a redesign of levees to protect New Orleans that ended up mitigating an impact of water to come, Hurricane Ida in 2021. Some of the post-Katrina improvements focused on making levees function better as barriers—reinforcements or "armoring," higher and wider seawalls, more effective pumps—while others expanded the diversion of water from the city.[14]

Stormwater drains illustrate another type of diversion. Water gathered in stormwater basins and pipes heads to a larger body that could be a natural formation like a river or creek, or a human-built collection of water inside a treatment plant. This variation on diversion is known as redirection. Practiced today, redirection sets out to keep pollutants found in groundwater—chemicals, oils, pathogens, trash—from harming health when this water is ingested, with flood protection another goal.

Mindful that the accumulation of water near a building can threaten its structure, advice to owners of houses recommends diversion as a management technique. One guide encourages attention to clues about unwanted wetness—think mildew, mold, mosquitoes, overflowing gutters, soggy ground, drowned plants, drifting mulch, and flaking walls in the basement—to explain the diversion remedy for water flowing onto a parcel of land. Maybe your neighbor has practiced this remedy on you, the guide continues. Check out the yard slope next door. It might be higher than yours and tilted down toward you on purpose. Water diversion ideas for homeowners include sump pumps, rain barrels, rain gardens, cleaner gutters, French drains (this design starts with a trench two feet below the soil and puts landscape fabric on top), sealing a driveway with landscape foam, and raising the height of one's land.[15]

The semen counterpart to diversion of groundwater deserves somewhat more favorable consideration than it receives. Genesis 38, referenced a couple of times in this book, warned Old Testament readers that coitus interruptus can provoke enough wrath to earn a death penalty from God. Modern sex education continues this opprobrium for a contrary reason: pulling out just before ejaculation was wrong in Genesis because withdrawal supported an agenda deemed bad, while in recent decades we're told it's wrong because it will fail to advance a good goal. I've been reading about birth control for decades and, best as I can recall, I never came across one encouraging or positive word about withdrawal until I went looking for it. Chapter 1 interpreted hostility to withdrawal as a scolding to ejaculators for their hubris and insufficient deference to Anywhere It Wants to Go. Now I move to withdrawal as diversion, provoker of a similar antipathy.

According to research published in the medical journal *Contraception*, when opposite-sex couples of reproductive age engage in sexual intercourse for one year with no birth control, 85% of them will experience pregnancy. Using typical adherence to condoms as their birth control method—"typical" meaning imperfect, real-world, human error included—takes the pregnant fraction down to 17%. Typical adherence to withdrawal for the sake of contraception, same definition of typical, causes pregnancy at almost exactly the same rate, 18%. The most popular barrier method of birth control has a slightly better record than diversion but only slightly.[16]

Calling semen diversion "better than nothing," the *Contraception* article continues, understates its accomplishments. It probably deserves disapproval as a birth control method for sexual intercourse beginners. They need practice in the timing of ejaculation and maybe other lessons borne of life experience before they'll attain command of the technique. Withdrawal deserves less disapproval for other demographics. Researchers report reason to think that in the current century, practitioners of the technique have gotten better at withdrawing. Married couples appear to be good at averting pregnancy this way. Unmarried couples become more skilled over time.

Another reason to judge the performance of diversion practitioners charitably is that coitus interruptus calls for only ordinary skill instead of high prowess. If we credit the studies that have found no sperm in pre-ejaculate fluid (conclusions have been mixed), then transfer of pre-ejaculate into a vagina does no harm when avoiding pregnancy is the goal. Ejaculators' timing needs to be only good enough rather than worthy of a swashbuckler. The old sex-ed talking point that pre-ejaculate swims with potential is only slightly truer than the false warning intoned in my youth that there are no safe dates on a menstrual-cycle calendar. You Can't Be Too Careful. You can be just that, in a harmful way, when you rule out diversion without due regard for the evidence and omit due skepticism toward the alternatives.

* * *

"Make more of it" is another imperative common to our two fluids. It's perfectly consistent for the same substance to be too copious in one setting and too scant in another. Substances exist to serve us in varied capacities. Human experience with water shows that the same fluid routinely calls for interventions that achieve the opposite effect of what other interventions do.

Too Scant asks more of managers than Too Copious. Containment and diversion, while demanding extensive ingenuity, vigilance, and expense, engage at a relatively simple level with the propensity of fluids to roam. As commands to a liquid, both "Don't move [there]" and "Move [from here to there]" regard the substance as stable, more of a fixture than something to analyze. All liquids share a propensity to flow, leak, seep, travel, and moisten that which is dry. Containment and diversion manage these traits held in common. Make More of It, applied to both water and semen, forces closer attention to where the particular substance comes from and what it includes.

Semen quantity or volume is a variable that provides information about semen quality in one aspect, the ability to travel into the female reproductive tract and fertilize an oocyte.[17] Too little semen per unit of ejaculate will fail to achieve fertilization. Urologists pursue Make More of It as a treatment by paying attention to more than the quality of semen aimed at mucosa; they also need sufficient quantity for the analysis they achieve under a microscope.

The spirit of can-do management we've seen throughout this chapter gave rise to the silastic seminal collection device, a condom-like wrap ("silastic" is a trademark portmanteau combining silicone and plastic) that can contain semen emitted in vaginal intercourse rather than through masturbation-generated ejaculation into a cup. The silastic seminal collection device delivers a larger share of semen volume than alternative containers—and, demonstrating the connection between semen quality and quantity, this material also performs extra well as a preserver of sperm motility.[18]

Desire for more water in the form of rain has preoccupied our species at least since the start of agriculture. In the second century Marcus Aurelius included in his Meditations a prayer to Zeus for rain. The religion I grew up in and reminisced about in chapter 1 has a still-recited *tefilat geshem*, prayer for rain, which morphs into a prayer for dew after the spring transitions to summer. This prayer chooses to praise God as deliverer of rain and precipitation rather than ask the deity directly for this favor. Expressions like "O Allah, shower upon us abundant rain, beneficial not harmful, swiftly and not delayed" and "Look on our dry hills and fields, dear God, and bless them with the living blessing of gentle rain," published on a website called Catholic Rural Life, favor more pointed beseeching.[19] One mountain village north of Barcelona revived prayer in this century to Our Lady of the Torrents, known there as a virgin hero with power to intervene.[20]

"Make more of it" as a water intervention took a technological turn in the mid-twentieth century. American scientists who invented cloud seeding started their work by reflecting on the origin of every raindrop and snowflake. Units of precipitation all need a particle that's not water—a tiny bit of dirt or soot—to form. When water vapor encounters one of these starters, it crystallizes into a solid state, a droplet. We still haven't achieved rain or snow when that happens. A droplet becomes bigger by colliding with fellow droplets in the sky. The size of this formation determines its precipitation category or label. At its starting size, between 0.0001 and 0.005 centimeters in diameter, a droplet is too light to fall. It graduates from droplet to raindrop when it reaches 0.5 millimeters in diameter. Then it's big and heavy enough to land as rain or snow. Cloud seeding makes more rain by adding more particles to the atmosphere.

More starters = more rain is the idea. Working in a General Electric laboratory, a team of researchers that included Bernard Vonnegut, brother of the author Kurt, chose silver iodide as the particle substance. This compound was safe in the sense of not known to do harm when ingested—it still has a clean safety record—and effective in that it hastens particle formation. Without intervention, water vapor located near a bit of dust (or bacteria, sometimes) needs an ambient temperature of −40° Celsius to crystallize around this starter. Substitute silver iodide for dust, however, and formation can occur in much warmer settings. The General Electric team formed ice crystals in temperatures as warm as minus five.[21]

This innovation achieves Make More of It through another helping of human effort. When suitable clouds are present, the pilot of a twin-engine airplane can release silver iodide or another compound into them using flares on the plane's wings. That's the most popular method. A plane can seed clouds by flying above and below them. Ground-based generators offer an alternative to aviation in mountainous topography and venues where the judgment of a pilot is less needed. These generators seed clouds from a tower frame structure, typically with flares or rockets.

Aided by improvements in data collection and model design, current evidence supports a Yes answer to the question about whether this intervention works. Studies of snow as the yield in contrast to rain have found cloud seeding especially availing—and snow furnishes more than winter recreation: when it melts, it turns into a source of fresh water. The affirmative answer to Does It Work is modest in size. Cloud seeding won't cure a drought. But it does produce precipitation.[22]

The ledger of costs and benefits that this technology brings includes effects beyond the creation of rain and snow. Airplane flares and ground towers that shoot rockets are sources of environmental pollution. Precipitation-making that occurs in nature—the spontaneous formation of droplets from water vapor put in contact with particles—isn't a virginal idyll, however. Smoke particles generated by wildfires that blazed in the western United States while I wrote this book make clouds denser and less likely to yield rain.[23] Particles created by pollution are smaller and more numerous than the big bits of sea salt, dust, and pollen that launch droplets in nature. Droplets that are too small can suppress rainfall.[24]

Cloud seeding serves environmentally useful functions. Governments have tried, with some success, to use it as a way to put out forest fires. Hail is destructive to property, especially crops; cloud seeding that focuses primarily on increasing rain has the incidental good effect of lessening the size of hailstones.[25] Keeping objects of property, especially food, intact rather than destroyed benefits the environment.

Now we move on from making more. "How about less?" can be directed fairly at both semen and water. The first part of this book showcased semen as a unique source of risks and burdens. Semen is always on the scene when unwanted pregnancy occurs and it's usually present when HIV, the deadliest sexually transmitted infection, travels into another person. Less semen would mean fewer instances of these bad consequences. The other liquid of this chapter can also accumulate in excess.

The problem of too much water worsens as climate change progresses. Increases in temperature on earth have generated devastating floods. Hotter temperatures are connected to flooding because the atmosphere of a warmer planet holds more water vapor. Enlarged volume of water vapor makes the ensuing rainfall heavier. When rain falls more heavily, flooding becomes more severe.

Climate change ought to inform the agenda of this book. As a challenge to fluid management, "make less of it" complements "make more of it" as applied to both water and semen. Commonalities shared by the two fluids could inform progress on both fronts.

* * *

Neutralizing unwanted characteristics, another intervention that manages fluids, offers another round of parallels between water and semen. Unwanted characteristics found in water that have enlisted the energies of improvers fall into two broad categories: (1) salt and (2) inclusions I'll group together under the rubric of pollutants or pollution.

Though often unwanted and sometimes deadly as a constituent of water, salt differs from pollution in that it's an inherent or original condition. It got there first, so to speak. Salt water covers about 70% of the planet; only 2.5% of water on our planet is the fresh kind, safe to drink. Human action takes salt out of water drawn from oceans and seas to make water safer for people to swallow and more supportive of livestock and planted crops. With 69% of this fluid volume used by agriculture (human beings in households consume only 12%), desalination not only neutralizes unwanted characteristics in water but leads to the production of food.[26]

The second broad set of unwanted characteristics in water arrives when something foreign meets a supply of this fluid and gets mixed into it, rendering it less useful or desirable. Innocent with respect to the inclusion of salt in water supplies, human action is often responsible for this other constituent. Enter intervention, the recurring theme of this chapter, which for this inclusion sets out to eliminate the pollutant and its effects from water. As an ongoing initiative with room to expand, semen management can find renewable inspiration from the record of progress on both desalination and the cleanup of water pollution. I'll start with the historically older undertaking of desalination.

Humanity noticed thousands of years ago that salt in water lessens its value for irrigation and human bodily consumption. No matter where they live, people know that seawater is relatively copious, available in much greater quantity than the fresh kind. A couple of thousand years ago Aristotle, familiar to this book as a writer who commented on semen, wrote that salt departs when water is heated: "Salt water, when it turns into vapor, becomes sweet." With equal accuracy Aristotle observed that "the vapor does not form salt water again when it condenses."[27] Writings published around the same time in ancient China report desalination techniques. About a thousand years before Aristotle, desalination via boiling of salt water may have been practiced by Minoan sailors. The Danish physician Thomas Bartholin speculated in 1680 about desalinating water by freezing it; so did Chinese farmers. Precursors like these took a long time to gain documented operational effect but since the middle of the twentieth century, following post-Second World War investments especially in the United States, desalination has been achieved through the "turns into vapor" approach that Aristotle recognized.

Thermal technologies heat sea water and collect the condensed vapor, or distillate, that ensues. Distillate becomes fresh water. Several methods of heating salt water to generate desalination are in use around the world today. Of them, multistage flash distillation produces the most fresh water; another thermal technology, vapor compression distillation, offers a smaller capacity alternative for hotels and industrial applications.

These thermal approaches to desalination that Aristotle would have understood (though he didn't know how to make them happen) take salt out of water effectively but at a relatively high cost: heating water is expensive. Human ingenuity applied to desalination has marched ahead to the "membrane" approach, which needs less energy to clear salt from water. Of the membrane methods to turn salt water into fresh, reverse osmosis is the most frequently used in the United States. Reverse osmosis feeds salt water to meet fresh water in a membrane assembly to the fresh water, forcing the water to flow in a reverse direction that leaves dissolved salts behind. The method yields less fresh water than thermal technology but has a lighter energy footprint and increasingly can be fueled by solar and wind power.

For semen-improvers open to learning from the water record, desalination achievements show the value of multiple intervention options. Let's stick with the binary of thermal versus membrane technology. Alternative ways to remove salt from water permit deciders to take into account an array of variables, including the characteristics of salty feed water to be treated, which energy sources will power the desalination machines, where the product water has to go (industrial applications versus human drinking, for example), and how much product water is needed. Balancing these variables has steered the Middle East, for example, to favor thermal over membrane desalination. In this region, where fossil fuels are relatively cheap and membrane technology has a hard time with high local temperatures and the harsh salinity of available water, the higher cash price of thermal desalination is worth paying. Elsewhere, the cheaper and environmentally sounder membrane technology of reverse osmosis makes more sense even though it takes salt out of water less thoroughly. Similar variety and multiplicity can and should inform the neutralizing of semen's unwanted characteristics.

Like desalination, the task of removing contaminants from water also calls for more than one intervention. A Centers for Disease Control description of how untreated water in the United States is made safe to drink explains filtration and disinfection, which like desalination turns out to encompass multiple levels and processes. In a first step for water treatment, coagulation chemicals—salts, aluminum, iron—bond with dirt to make larger particles. These to-be-filtered particles that coagulation made bigger get enlarged again via mixing and sometimes more chemicals: after this stage the particles are called flocs. Flocs, now heavier than water, sink to the bottom of the treatment tank.

Filtration in the sense of physical separation is next. Different pore sizes and different materials in the filters—sand, gravel, charcoal—catch different contaminants. Carbon filters remove bad odors. Onward to disinfection. More variety there too. Chemicals including chlorine, chloramine, and chlorine dioxide are the main killers at work, but ultraviolet light and ozone also disinfect water. Again, semen-improvers can find multiplicity to learn from rather than a simple application like a sieve.

According to the World Health Organization, water at a level of basic quality taken for granted in my country and others—located where human beings live, available on demand, and not contaminated with fecal matter—is available to most people on Earth, about 5.8 billion of us. The other two billion people on the planet experience deprivation of clean water to different degrees. About 1.2 billion can reach it within a round trip of 30 minutes. Another 282 million have access to clean water if they travel farther. Some rely on unprotected wells and springs. At the least fortunate tier, 122 million people drink what they draw from untreated lakes, ponds, and rivers.

Water in this existence is deadly. It sends into human bodies cholera, diarrhea, dysentery, hepatitis A, typhoid, and polio. Among these conditions, the one that sounds gentlest would be diarrhea. Yet diarrhea kills about 829,000 people a year worldwide—either directly when they've drunk dirty water or indirectly when clean water is too scarce to be expended on handwashing.

Readers who take for granted access to H_2O at the temperature they favor and plenty of choice among soaps and hand-sanitizing liquids might think that initiatives that try to furnish clean water to people who lack access to it are banal. It's not rocket science, goes the phrase. But this pursuit of safety takes on a real challenge. Water management has achieved spectacular gains, and it ought to accomplish more. Semen management too.

* * *

"Sperm washing" as a description of another technology brings our two fluids together in a single term. "Washing" in everyday life, away from the laboratory, uses water to achieve cleanliness. Nonliteral washing extends this improvement initiative to semen. As we've seen elsewhere in this book, the word sperm in "sperm washing" serves as a euphemism: what gets washed in the sense of agitated or manipulated in a centrifuge is semen rather than sperm.

This intervention works to enhance biological parenthood through improvements in artificial insemination. Washing semen removes less-than-motile sperm cells and other undesired inclusions in seminal fluid to increase the odds of successful impregnation. The technique has fared especially well for HIV-discordant couples in which the male partner is HIV positive and the female partner HIV negative.

Manipulation of semen to neutralize the unwanted characteristic of HIV in it was pioneered in 1992 by clinicians in Milan. The birth of an HIV-free baby followed five years later. Today, couples who use semen-washing intervention to suppress the transmittal of HIV can count on a successful result. One meta-analysis looked at assisted reproduction involving semen that had been treated for HIV prevention in 11,585 cycles of assisted reproduction experienced by 3,994 women. How many HIV transmittals followed? Zero.[28]

In contrast to the high-ish price of semen washing, a similar yet different technology is relatively cheap. This intervention frames the unwanted characteristic as inability to fertilize a human ovum. Here I have in mind over-the-counter supplements sold as sources of sperm improvement.

To stick with my water analogy, those pills and powders and gummies are comparable to chemicals that treatment plants put into water first to make filtration more effective by enlarging particles and then by destroying the pathogens that remain. Water treatment chemicals are supplements even though people who add them probably wouldn't favor that label. As an inclusion, it achieves neutralization by addition rather than the subtraction that a filter performs.

Do please note my view that semen-health supplements differ from variations on chlorine added to make water safe for drinking. Retail businesses that sell them certainly manifest less commitment to the rigors of science. Unlike water treatment chemicals, supplements are hustled to the public. Their ads overpromise. All that said, however, they work. (Always? Perfectly? Effective alone, unaided by any other intervention? Come on: be fair. Nobody holds chlorine and chloramine in water treatment plants to that standard. And I am not telling you to consume or ingest them. I wouldn't.)

One medical journal article reviewed randomized studies of antioxidants taken to improve semen health, seeking to measure what the authors called "major semen parameters." Motility, density, morphology, and quantity of sperm showed improvement in most of these studies. The authors concluded that vitamin C, vitamin E, and CoQ10 are especially helpful treatments for infertility.[29] That supplements are easy to obtain—they are a couple of clicks away at your keyboard as well as on the shelves of brick and mortar stores—shows that semen management technology can proceed minus the elitism and exclusion that often accompany high-tech medicine.

* * *

The Clean Water Act offers ideas for clean semen. This law, which started life under the more lumbering name of the Federal Water Pollution Control Act of 1948, focuses on observable, measurable, and controllable sources of water danger and safety. Water starts out clean and is vulnerable to pollution, the Clean Water Act presumes. Its method of decreasing pollution and increasing safety identifies two objects of attention: pollutants, which harm water by entering it, and polluters, the people and businesses and governments located near important bodies of water that will toss pollutants into that water if not steered away from that bad path by regulation. The law calls its targets of direct management "point sources."[30]

Manufacturing, shipping, oil and gas extraction, mining, and feedlots can be significant point sources. So too can governments—local sewage treatment plants, for example. The approach to water pollution written into the Clean Water Act forbids point sources from discharging any pollutant into surface waters without a National Pollutant Discharge Elimination System permit. This law tasks the Environmental Protection

Agency with reducing harmful elements in water through a permission-to-discharge system. State environmental agencies issue these permits.

Pollutants are unwanted characteristics. Congress wrote a broad definition of the term that includes "dredged spoil, solid waste, incinerator residue, sewage, garbage, sewage sludge, munitions, chemical wastes, biological materials, radioactive materials, heat, wrecked or discarded equipment, rock, sand, cellar dirt and industrial, municipal, and agricultural waste discharged into water."[31] All unwanted. The Clean Water Act works to neutralize them.

Turning to semen, improvers of this substance can follow the reasoning of "point sources" as they keep in mind the spoonful of emitted fluid that holds so much power over the people whose bodies it touches and distant phenomena, controllable to a degree by planned human action, that make semen better and worse. Interventions that touch semen directly are the counterpart of the Clean Water Act's point sources. Interventions that change semen by touching something at a distance work with metaphoric wetlands, separate from and ecologically connected to semen at the same time. Similar to how violent shifts in weather have (somewhat) expanded public awareness of anthropogenic climate change as a call to action, our sensory perception of this substance reminds us of what we are trying to improve.

The semen intervention that parallels point sources of the Clean Water Act is laboratory treatment to neutralize the unwanted characteristic of HIV. Semen washing, the technology of isolating healthy sperm cells suitable for assisted reproduction by removing unwanted inclusions, touches the liquid being made safer just as point sources of pollution touch waters of the United States. The substance gets improved directly. Like the National Pollution Discharge Emission System permits that the EPA authorizes state environmental agencies to issue, the intervention spells out and follows a plan to manipulate liquid that contains hazardous material. Water cleaning and semen cleaning share perspectives, priorities, and methods.

* * *

Pre-exposure prophylaxis illustrates the feasibility and big upside potential of semen management. Shortened into PrEP, this term stands for a class of pharmaceuticals used to ward off HIV. At the time I write, PrEP is available as a pill taken on either a daily or event-exposure basis and an injection whose protection lasts for months. Approved for HIV prevention in 2012, it went generic in late 2020.

This relatively new drug won fast enthusiasm from medical providers and regulators as a force in worldwide public health. A World Health Organization report concluded that patient who asks for PrEP ought to receive it and confirmed that medical providers should consider it for populations identified as high priority: men who have sex with men, transgender women, adolescent girls and young women who have engaged in condomless sex with a male partner, and people who inject drugs. The Centers for Disease Control has estimated that taking PrEP would enhance the lives of 1.2 million people in the United States.

Efficacy and safety data depict PrEP as something of a wonder drug. Decades after the launch of antiretroviral therapies that perform well at their task of keeping AIDS at bay, HIV still stays permanently with persons who acquire it and is something to be avoided. AIDS, the disease preceded by HIV infection, is now killing about 13,000 Americans each year—not a huge number but significant, comparable to heroin overdose deaths. Before death, the disease is unpleasant to endure. Antiretroviral progress has increased prevention but once AIDS arrives, conditions that drew horrified public attention in the 1980s—wasting, opportunistic infections, skin lesions, neurological illness—remain. The virus can mutate, jeopardizing the future of HIV patients who are doing well on these therapies today. Elsewhere on the prevention front, the promise of a vaccine against HIV hasn't yet arrived, which makes PrEP uniquely valuable.

Pre-exposure prophylaxis for HIV prevention has been researched extensively with resounding results. People not infected with HIV who take this drug compliantly can enjoy high-risk sexual behavior confident that their T cells, also known as CD4 cells, are impervious to HIV. They will remain HIV negative even after repeated intimate exposures. The CDC is uncertain whether to consider PrEP's success rate 99% or 100%. Worldwide in the decades-plus that PrEP has been in use, the number of seroconversions has been in the single digits. It took a rare strain to get through the barrier. Building on technologies that already exist, scientists aware of PrEP's remarkable track record are, at the time I write, working on newer intake methods, including longer-lasting injections. If you stay on PrEP while HIV negative (a negative serostatus describes the only population that receives the prescription), you won't become HIV positive no matter what physical experiences you have.

Although guidelines written for prescription writers and the public tend to omit this word, semen is what PrEP works with and whose unwanted characteristics it neutralizes. The abbreviation MSM, whose S in the middle stands for sex rather than semen—MSM = Men [having] Sex [with] Men—follows the practice we've found in this book of using "sex" to describe something people engage in when a more precise description would mention the transfer of a particular fluid onto mucosa. Advice from the CDC and other informants continues to treat tops the same as bottoms in this recommendation for PrEP, proceeding as if a man's "having sex" with another man rather than receiving semen in his rectum exposes him to HIV. In function, PrEP is all about the semen.

Like some of the water interventions we've looked at in this chapter, PrEP neutralizes unwanted characteristics of a fluid. So too does doxycycline, a counterpart to PrEP. Doxycycline as pre-exposure prophylaxis addresses semen less pointedly than its HIV-preventative big brother because it thwarts bacteria rather than a virus. Recall that semen can contain and deliver the bacteria that deliver syphilis, chlamydia, and gonorrhea onto anal and vaginal mucosa. Although it doesn't nurture bacteria as strongly as it nurtures viruses like HIV, semen is still a host for bacterial infection. The newer use of an antibiotic that has been serving human health for decades to provide safety from dangers found in this substance offers another inspiring reminder of how interventions put effluvia in their place.

Patients mindful of bacterially transmitted STIs can fill a prescription for "doxy" and keep pills available to take just before or after mucosal exposure. After reviewing four randomized controlled studies that found this prophylaxis efficacious in blocking transmission of syphilis, chlamydia, and gonorrhea (evidence of benefit was especially strong for the first two diseases), the CDC made a recommendation that providers offer doxycycline as a preventative to men and transgender women who have sex with men and who have had one of these bacterial conditions.[32] The medical center that led this research chose a prouder tone for its headline: "Why Doxycycline Is a Great Bet Against STIs."[33]

Continuing to move along the axis of nonpoint sources, the concept I've borrowed from water management, we find another intervention to neutralize the unwanted characteristics of semen in hormonal contraception. We're further from semen now but still touching it, so to speak. Interventions that act on female reproductive anatomy fend off pregnancy after semen has landed on mucosa. Here, the characteristic being neutralized is one that, unlike HIV or pollutants in water, might be very wanted. Contraception foregrounds the wishes of the person who faces the detriments of pregnancy. If she doesn't want to receive the initiative of sperm but does want to be touched by semen or is willing to accept that touching, she can neutralize an unwanted characteristic of the fluid with prophylaxis.

Since 2010, governments in the United States have supported this neutralizing by paying for it. All insurance plans in the Health Insurance Marketplace must provide FDA-approved contraceptives without charging a copayment when the patient obtains them from an in-network provider. The Affordable Care Act is in this respect a counterpart to the Clean Water Act. If you are reading this book while located in the United States, you can take a break from my prose and help yourself to safe water that's safe to drink by turning on a tap. You don't have to exchange or give up anything for the water safety you enjoy, except remotely as a taxpayer. (If these words reach you when you are outside the geography of my country, odds are you enjoy the same entitlement financed in a similar arrangement.) Like water, like semen. American legislation offers you protection on comparable terms against the semen superpower of Make People.

The human entitlement to semen safety extends to prevention from its consequences. That safety must be paid for. If we individuals can't afford it, and sometimes even if we can, governments should pick up the semen-safety tab similar to how they pay for clean water. We're free to welcome semen if we want—cherish it, chase it, nurture it—and free to regard sperm as addressable inclusions.

As a species, we know that semen will land on mucosa; as individuals who live in human bodies we can anticipate occasions to support and encourage that journey along with occasions when we'll care more about lessening its risks in our lives. Like water, semen moves. Like management of water all over the planet, semen management faces reality. The engagement that I urge in this book has been robust for centuries.

Thinking of semen as a fluid that we can manage to maximize our happiness similar to how we manage water moves us toward more of that happiness. The history of water-control initiatives testifies to the practicality and determination of which human beings are capable when they pursue prosperity and better health. Keeping focus on the fluid—where it travels, what it can do to us, what it can do *for* us, how to optimize its quantity and quality—frees policymakers from distractions that thwart our capacity to please ourselves. Semen is our instrument, a thing for humanity to control and enjoy.

8

Regulating Semen: Every Hazardous Substance Is Valuable

I'll be the first to agree that the term hazardous substance could sound insulting. Especially so when the substance comes from, and gets close to, the gendered human body. For law and regulation, however, "hazardous substance" is the opposite of an insult.

That's because governments as regulators can lower the boom and ban every product or object they think deserves opprobrium. Whenever it lacks a good enough upside, harmful material in the United States gets taken out of people's lives by legislation that prohibits its possession or sale. For example, selling garments that contain asbestos is now illegal, full stop. Hazardous substance as a designation is very different. It means that someone with authority to ban the substance concluded that ample benefit is there. Warning in the adjective applauds value.

Here are a few officially recognized hazardous substances you might know and enjoy. Gasoline probably comes within a few feet of your body during your day: more than 90% of U.S. households live with at least one personal motor vehicle and registry records of 2023 reported that only about 1% of these vehicles were the pure electric kind.[1] Maybe you swim touched by chlorine, a hazardous substance used not only in pools but to bleach paper and cloth, to sanitize industrial waste, and in household cleansers. Ordinary consumers buy and store propane and butane. Lubricants, dyes, detergents, pharmaceuticals, and pesticides often include benzene, another hazardous substance. Formaldehyde is a main ingredient of disinfectants, germicides, and embalming fluid that does many other good things, including control of mildew in wheat and rot in oats. All of these hazardous substances offer benefits greater than their hazard.

Substances labeled hazardous by the law are all useful, desirable, desired, and risky. In this sense, these products are just like semen—except that semen is *extraordinarily* useful, desirable, desired, and risky. Now, let's check out what earns this regulatory label.

The Federal Hazardous Substances Act addresses material that "may cause substantial personal injury or substantial illness during or as a proximate result of any customary or reasonably foreseeable handling or use."[2] Semen fits this definition of hazardous substance. Another statutory definition on point understands the related term "toxic" to mean "the capacity to produce personal injury or illness to man through ingestion, inhalation, or absorption through [a] body surface."[3] Another good fit with this book. Even better when we understand "man" to include all persons. Courts and agencies read the word this way.

Regulators apply the Federal Hazardous Substances Act to control much less potent, consequential, and life-changing objects of attention than semen. If liquids like pool cleaners, paint thinners, adhesives, and brake fluids are hazardous substances, then so too is the fluid that can generate pregnancy and infection. Regulators have nonetheless left semen alone. That stance of theirs is correct and deficient at the same time.

It's correct on one hand because the application of federal hazardous substance rules extends only to interstate commerce, which means that the network of regulation applies only to substances that are sold across state lines. Semen is indeed sold and bought from one state to another, but interstate commerce is absent from the day-to-day journeying of human semen from one body to another that occupies this book. Quotidian semen is much more significant in volume and impact than semen for sale.

On the other hand, the regulatory toolkit contains more than prohibition, and regulators outside the federal government can put this toolkit to use. Regulation of semen can take forms other than attempts to ban or impede it. Once we recognize that regulation offers more than interference with what people want to do, we become abler to borrow thoughtfully from hazardous substance precedents on point.

* * *

Multiple agencies share the work of hazardous substance control but one in particular, the federal Consumer Product Safety Commission, has consumer in its name and "consumer" aligns with the agenda of this book. In the United States, this word signifies layperson or ordinary person. Consumers are human beings with options, tastes, and vulnerabilities.

They vary. Some American consumers of products or substances have been dealt a good hand. People might be fortunate in the sense of sophisticated, rich, savvy. If they're not extra lucky in this way, the hand they got dealt is still pretty good because they're lucky enough to live in a country whose consumer law proceeds from a premise that people deserve some protection from risk. This entitlement can be applied to contact with semen.

In a publication posted on its website that describes what the Federal Hazardous Substances Act requires, the Consumer Product Safety Commission takes the vantage point of a layperson who wants safe interaction with a hazardous substance. I'll summarize this publication, *What Requirements Apply to My Product?*,[4] by paraphrasing its content into three bullet-point questions that would occur to the consumer of a risky fluid:

- Containment: When I wish to be near this substance but also prevent it from having an impact on my body, which barriers and distancing strategies are effective?
- Post-impact remediation: Should my body be touched by this substance in a way I don't want, or that I regret accepting, how can I undo or lessen the effect of this contact?
- Information: What do I need to know about this substance to reach good decisions about interacting with it?

Regulation can generate practical answers to these questions, as I'll show in this chapter, and do so with full sex positive panache. Awareness of semen as hazardous is entirely compatible with the pursuit of sexual pleasure gained by intimate contact with a male body. Say it with feeling: Every hazardous substance is valuable. Regulation makes the best of these substances by balancing opportunity and constraint. Benefits that include but are not limited to the physical plane might require an opportunity to ejaculate but they don't necessarily require anyone to receive an injection of preventable danger.

I'll take the three questions in turn, spending the most time on the last one about information. Semen fits extremely well with disclosure and transparency, the central features of information as a regulatory category. Information guides choices.

Commercial kinds of hazardous substances are regulated with mandatory information-delivery—I'll show you examples of these rules—but information reaches endangered persons especially effectively when the substance is semen because people can act on the information they learn. Synthetic chemicals usually arrive at the human body before the person to be touched learns about the risks these materials deliver. Their arrival is often covert. It's deciders who don't experience direct physical contact with the hazard—think plant managers, remote authorities who control drinking water, medical providers, sometimes parents—who choose how this substance will land on someone else's body. Only rarely will the individual exposed to a hazardous machine-made chemical know about risks of physical injury it poses before its danger ripens. Stealthy contact with semen does happen, as we saw in chapter 1, but recipients typically can tell when this fluid is headed their way. People at the receiving end of semen may be able to use what they've learned about it in their own interest.

Information too often absent when that fateful touching of mucosa by semen occurs is knowledge about the nature of the substance that mucosa-possessors need for their safety and protection. Regulation can generate that information and increase the odds that it will reach vulnerable people. But let's take care of body surfaces first—that's containment and post-impact remediation—before we move to the mind.

* * *

Containment of semen as an aim of regulation parallels regulations that mandate the containment of hazardous substances. Regulators routinely require and encourage barriers that protect human bodies.

Covid-19 brought one important type of barrier into everyday conversation. Although this disease has only a thin connection to semen, as we saw in chapter 4, one statement by a regulatory agency made early in the Covid pandemic about personal protective equipment applies aptly to our hazardous substance: "PPE acts as a barrier between infectious materials such as viral and bacterial contaminants and your skin, mouth, nose, or eyes (mucous membranes)," the Food and Drug Administration announced in early 2020. This barrier "has the potential to block transmission of contaminants from blood, body fluids, or respiratory secretions."[5] Exactly what semen calls for and what regulation can help supply.

Regulation pursues containment by mandating obstacles. For example, mucosa and other vulnerable geography of the human head—eyes, face, ears—must be protected from "flying particles, molten metal, liquid chemicals, acids or caustic liquids, chemical gases or vapors, or potentially injurious light radiation," says the Occupational Health and Safety Administration.[6] OSHA's criteria for personal protective equipment cover the hazards of semen by addressing risks from "absorption, inhalation or physical contact."[7]

The containment strategy requires a physical divide between a hazard and the vulnerable human body but doesn't stop there: separation must also function reliably, and so containers get regulated for quality. The Environmental Protection Agency defines a container as "any portable device in which a material is stored, transported, treated, disposed of, or otherwise handled."[8] That's a broad definition: it's written to cover a 55-gallon drum, a big tanker truck, a railroad car, a small bucket, or a test tube.[9] Anything that functions to keep material separate from what the hazardous substance could touch qualifies as a container that has to be strong enough. Regulations demand adequate strength.

Standards that govern quality of barriers and containment spell out safety criteria for a container that can inform strategies to improve semen barriers. Whatever holds hazardous material must be in good condition, holding together with integrity. Once it has aged or deteriorated enough to fail in this task of separation of a hazardous substance from what it touches, it has ceased to be safe. It mustn't leak. Another criterion for safety focuses on how a container and the hazardous substance in it touch each other. Regulation understands that incompatibility between the substance and the barrier can cause an adverse reaction, such as an explosion.[10]

Analogous considerations apply to barriers that separate semen from mucosal surfaces. Containment as a strategy starts with the premise that all persons are entitled to block semen from their mucosa whenever they want. The barrier category describes materials and strategies that separate this hazardous substance from the human body surface it endangers. Barriers must respect the truism that names this chapter: every hazardous substance is valuable. Semen offers uses and pleasures that no alternative can provide. Containments of this hazardous/desirable/desired substance therefore must be amenable to removal and restoration by the vulnerable person.

Only one barrier to semen in use today fends off the dual Make People and Make People Sick possibilities that have filled this book. It's possible to count the protection offered by condoms as triple rather than dual by dividing Make People Sick into two separate categories: the condom is effective in real life against what one review regards as three risks: (1) HIV, (2) other sexually transmitted infections, and (3) unwanted pregnancy.[11] Any plan that attempts to make the best of semen should put this object front and center until better technologies supersede it. Governments—that's us taxpayers—should pay for condoms and work to optimize their distribution.

Give away condoms for free, I propose, and make the giveaway program easy to locate and use. It's a feasible path already underway. Many billions of condoms have been handed out worldwide since 1991. The 2012 peak of 2.5 billion annually hasn't been equaled, but these schemes distribute more than a billion and a half condoms a year.[12]

Studies of condom distribution schemes provide evidence that these giveaways succeed. At one U.S. campus, researchers who interviewed 355 students found that most respondents knew where to find free condom dispensers and had a positive opinion of this distribution.[13] A majority of the sexually active respondents said they intended to take a condom from a campus dispenser in the next six months.

Away from higher education, every state in the United States is now doing what I want it to do by giving away condoms. All states provide condoms at pickup locations and most also use postal mail for free distribution on request. Some states limit their distribution scheme to one offering only; others provide a couple of options like nonlatex polyurethane or more than one size. Consumers who wish to block a future journey of semen can click to learn how many condoms they can order at a time and an estimate of how many days they need to wait.[14]

The previous chapter of this book explored condom innovation as a source of health and safety comparable to water supply innovation, another effort that also enlarges health and safety. Our record of optimism and cleverness in water management, I argued, demonstrates that as a species we can make our lives better by engaging productively with a fluid necessary to life. Regulation oriented toward improving semen containment can strengthen this kind of initiative by encouraging creative thought.

Take for example the 2013 contest that the Gates Foundation sponsored for innovation in condom design. The competition awarded prizes of $100,000 each to eleven winners. Easy to roll one's eyes at what might look like a publicity stunt that's cheap for the wealthy sponsor and to note an apparent absence since that year of earth-shattering transformations on the condom front. But the initiative made progress. Foundation officials put inventors from around the world in touch with one another, and the 812 submissions both demonstrated and enlarged a level of interest in semen containment. "There's not one magic bullet," as a program officer said to a reporter,[15] but attention and a degree of accomplishment improved this barrier.

Governments can spur the same hustle with grants and mandates that steer research toward better condoms and condom-like containments of semen. I imagine regulators would bring to the work of assessing new ideas considerations that overlap with but differ from what judges in the Gates Foundation contest liked: less attention to dazzle and more to compatibility with existing conditions, maybe. The goal of semen containment benefits from both perspectives. Regulations written to effect safety statutes, including but not limited to the Federal Hazardous Substances Act, can expand the investment that private organizations pursue.

Joining condoms in the containment category is the pharmaceutical intervention PrEP, a complementary success story for this semen management strategy. PrEP needs little to no introduction here. We met its achievements in the previous chapter. It's succeeding as a source of containment; for people who take it, PrEP works like a charm.

With this achievement continuing to grow, the next step for distribution of PrEP and condoms that regulation should take is to improve interactions between the two. Providers of one barrier rarely provide the other and harm follows from this separation in distribution. One meta-analysis found men who have sex with men using PrEP were 25 times more likely to acquire gonorrhea, 11 times more likely to acquire chlamydia, and 45 times more likely to acquire syphilis than their counterparts who do not use this drug. Condoms could improve these results.[16] Applying a hazardous substance perspective to semen regulation helps to unite these two interventions and optimize their enhancement of public health.

A category of regulation applied to hazardous substances, "secondary containment," sits at the border between barriers and our next category, post-exposure remediation. Secondary containment fosters safety by ordering attention to spills before they happen.[17] Multiple EPA and OSHA regulations mandate this safeguard. "Here's the scenario," says a blog in its advice to the regulated about how to comply with one demand for secondary containment: "Your primary container fails (e.g., a drum/ barrel, IBC tote, storage tank—you get the picture). The spill is heading directly toward a drain that connects with the public sewer system." Immediate peril. "But you're not too concerned, because your secondary containment stops the spill from spreading."[18]

Again semen presents parallels to familiar, sensible controls on hazardous substances. Secondary containment of semen can guard against the hazards that ensue when primary containment fails. Primary containment is exemplified by the condom; for secondary containment, we can add interventions that remedy the rupture or slip of a primary-containment barrier during vaginal or anal intercourse. Post-splash protection against the hazards of semen includes levonorgestrel, or the morning after pill, and post-exposure prophylaxis, sometimes dubbed PEP, the pharmaceutical sibling of PrEP that's prescribed to be taken immediately after sexual intercourse with a goal of preventing the transmittal of disease. Prompt low-cost treatment for semen-transmitted infection also falls in this category.

People who use condoms as disease prophylaxis can prepare for the risk that primary containment failure will fail by proceeding the way regulation of hazardous substances teaches and keep a prescription for PrEP or doxycycline, the antibiotic. That use of secondary confinement can fend off HIV and bacterial disease respectively. Emergency contraception offers the same preventive function when condom rupture puts a person in danger of becoming pregnant. These sources of safety are available on a nonsecondary basis too, with no broken condom in the picture. But when they take care of people after a barrier fails they offer the same protection that environmental and occupational safety law provide.

Multiple sources of regulation can contribute to enhancing primary and secondary confinements of semen. Being in charge of pharmaceuticals puts the Food and Drug Administration at the center of postexposure interventions, but it's not alone. Education regulation can make primary and secondary confinements of semen more available to students both by promoting awareness of them and writing rules to expand their distribution. Authorities that control jails and prisons can ensure that incarcerated persons have access to these preventatives. Insurance regulation can write coverage mandates. These three are just the first that come to my mind; other regulators hold pertinent authority. Governments could invite a wide breadth of agencies to consider what they might do to advance semen containment, similar to plenary directives aimed at the entire executive branch like *apply cost-benefit analysis* or one I'll consider later, *plain language*.

* * *

To enhance post-splash remediation of the hazards of semen, regulators can learn from a panoply of well-established rules. Federal regulation recognizes that hazardous substances can land on vulnerable human bodies even with maximally feasible obstruction installed in advance to block this impact. For illustration, here are some regulations that deliver protection from three liquids when, following the pattern of semen that we've observed in this book, these substances splash or flow dangerously onto the human body. Semen calls for post-contact attentions comparable to those that established regulation already gives to blood, chemicals used in laboratories, and agricultural pesticides.

To protect people from the hazardous substance of a stranger's blood, the Occupational Health and Safety Administration rule called Bloodborne Pathogens directs employers to be vigilant against the prospect that this bodily fluid will occasionally escape containers and splash onto a worker. All employers whose employees are at risk of exposure to blood are tasked to prepare a written Exposure Control Plan that sets out to reduce this risk. In putting together this plan, employers must follow whatever current protocols the United States Public Health Service recommends for postexposure treatment when barriers fail.[19]

The rule governing bloodborne pathogens presumes that every instance of escaped blood is potentially dangerous. Semen regulation ought to share this understanding despite the low odds of injury from both fluids. Most contacts with someone else's blood convey no infection and will cause no harm to the contacted person. Most transfers of semen onto mucosa neither impregnate anyone nor deliver a disease. These events nevertheless warrant the adjective hazardous. The word does not mean certain to injure when it lands: it means risky at a sufficiently high level. Both semen and blood qualify for this characterization.

OSHA provides another semen-regulation role model by imposing controls on laboratory chemicals that resemble those governing accidental exposure to blood. Its rule, named Occupational Exposure to Hazardous Chemicals in Laboratories, mandates written preparation called the Chemical Hygiene Plan.[20] The agency also requires training of employees who work with hazardous chemicals, including training on how to discern that these substances have seeped or leaked notwithstanding barriers. It obliges employers to teach workers how to protect themselves from this impact.

Continuing this recognition of the worker as an individual who matters, OSHA entitles employees to employer-furnished medical attention at their behest following exposure or possible exposure to a hazardous chemical in a laboratory. Presumably the doctor who examines a worker and concludes that risky contact did occur would take professional steps to undo what the substance did to the mucosa bearer. Barriers are always necessary and never sufficient.

As for pesticides used in agriculture, another hazard that can land on human mucosa even when barriers are in place to block it, the Environmental Protection Agency joins OSHA as a source of post-splash protection. Like semen, pesticides can touch the human body by means that include "application, splash, spill, [and] drift." The EPA gives these four examples of how a hazardous substance affects human lives as a nonexclusive list. Regardless of how these pesticides travel onto mucosa, responsibility for the hazard that regulation imposes obliges employers to protect the person whose body is touched.[21]

Poison control as practiced in hospital emergency rooms offers further instruction on the role of pharmaceutical products as responses to the danger occasioned by exposure to a hazardous substance. The American College of Emergency Physicians, though not a regulator itself, supports regulation by publishing a recommendation of antidotes that hospital emergency rooms ought to have on hand, in what quantity, and with what degree of ready access. Before the ACEP issues these expert guidelines, it holds post-exposure treatments to data-driven criteria for efficacy and safety. Exposures that pharmaceutical interventions undo include lead poisoning, severe hypoglycemia, opioid toxicity, acetaminophen overdose, and black widow spider venom.[22] Readers bothered by references to poison in a discussion of semen may recall the aphorism by the sixteenth-century Swiss philosopher-physician Paracelsus: *Alle Dinge sind Gift, und nichts ist ohne Gift.* All things are poison, and nothing is without poison.[23] Semen included.

Regulations that demand fire extinguishers provide another example of secondary containment in action. Prevention does not suffice: if human strategy could prevent or limit every unwanted fire, then regulators wouldn't need to bother with mandating this post-exposure preventative. Bother they do. The Coast Guard demands fire extinguishers on motorboats and school ships and aircraft. OSHA requires safety instruction in usage from employers that provide fire extinguishers in the workplace. Fire extinguishers are necessary for airworthiness as defined by the Federal Aviation Administration. Federal regulations that cover shipyards, mine safety, trucks and buses, and housing for farmworkers all insist on fire extinguishers as a source of safety after danger arises.

Management of semen calls for the same reasoning. Hazardous substance regulation teaches that barriers that block the flow of a hazardous substance are necessary and desirable; it also knows that barrier protections will occasionally fail. Antidotes or first aid required by hazardous substance regulation demands has three important counterparts when the substance that has a dangerous impact on mucosa is semen. First, post-exposure prophylaxis, sometimes abbreviated PEP, undoes the impact of HIV risk. Second, emergency contraception also wards off a risk, here the risk of pregnancy. The post-exposure preventative used most is what's known informally as the morning after pill or Plan B, typically made of levonorgestrel. Abortion is the third counterpart to the poison antidotes and fire extinguishers that regulation demands.

PEP and emergency contraception parallel the secondary containment of environmental regulation in that they contemplate and manage the future and the past. Abortion is entirely retrospective, all "post." Law and policy now offer support for all three post-splash rescues. Expansion of these protections can accomplish more.

Post-exposure prophylaxis against HIV complements the pre-exposure protection we met in chapter 7. A side-by-side chart published for the lay public by the National Institutes of Health tells readers that pre beats post. Answering the question *How Effective Is It?*, the chart gives high marks to PrEP—a reduced risk of 99% for sex and "at least 74% for drug use"—and a gloomier take on pharmaceutical protection after the fact: "PEP can prevent HIV when taken correctly, but it is not always effective. Start PEP as soon as possible to give it the best chance of working."[24] This summary tells a larger truth about exposure to all hazardous substances, not just HIV: precaution is better than intervention post hoc. But as we've had frequent occasion to observe in this chapter, life-altering fluids arrive onto mucosa even when extraordinarily effective barriers exist. Making the best of any hazardous substance must include remedies deployable after exposure.

As for levonorgestrel, anyone of any age can buy it where it's sold, no prescription needed. A second drug that prevents pregnancy after exposure to semen, ulipristal acetate, is marketed by prescription under the trade name ella. Ella is even more effective than levonorgestrel, especially for users who weigh more than 165 pounds.[25] Both medications fend off pregnancy well. They deserve promotion and publicity that regulation can enlarge.

Of the three post-splash measures that undo harmful impacts of semen after it lands, abortion needs the most expansion. The other two, PEP and emergency contraception, still get withheld now and then, but they are easier to obtain than abortion and are treated far more leniently by the pregnancy deciders we met in chapter 3. Criminal codes, at least for now, leave these interventions alone while they meddle heavily with abortion. The other reason that abortion needs extra attention from law and policy: pregnancy is extra dangerous. Becoming pregnant is more significant than the *chance* of becoming pregnant that emergency contraception wards off. And due to happy progress in antiretroviral therapy, more bodies are now imperiled by pregnancy than by HIV.

At the national level, Congress can make semen safer through the repeal of two statutes on the books as I write that worsen the hazard of this substance: the Hyde Amendment, which forbids spending federal funds on abortion, and the Comstock Act, which forbids using the U.S. mail or another common carrier (a label that includes courier services like UPS or Federal Express) to send any article or object "designed, adapted, or intended for producing abortion, or for any indecent or immoral use."[26] Enacted in 1873, the Comstock Act is thought of (at the time I sign off on this book) as dormant, a zombie law; prosecutors haven't used it in many decades. Until it's repealed, this law remains dangerous because it can be exploited to endanger patients who live in states that ban abortion.[27]

The other statute that stands in the way of post-splash remediation for semen-caused harm, the Hyde Amendment, is alive and kicking as a federal-level interference. Its impact falls extra hard on poor women. Because Medicaid, the nation's health care scheme that insures the poor, is funded mostly by the federal government rather than the states (the split is about 69% to 31%) and governments of poorer states fail to make up the shortfall, the Hyde Amendment in operation withholds abortion coverage from the majority of poor people in the United States. Repealing this law would increase safety from the main risk of our hazardous substance.

While the nation waits for Congress to get rid of two dangerous federal statutes, state governments can improve post-splash remediation of semen's impact on mucosa. We know what they can do from what three of them are doing—and in particular what they stepped up to do in 2022 after Dobbs came down. In that fateful year, California promptly appropriated $110 million for abortion, making some of these funds available to out-of-state residents as abortion support grants. The governor of New Mexico looked eastward to a neighboring antichoice state and announced plans to build a new abortion clinic near the Texas border. In Maryland, the landing of semen became safer via a new law that authorized nonphysician clinicians—nurse practitioners, nurse-midwives, physician assistants—to provide abortions and added an appropriation to pay for abortion training.[28]

I value these post-Dobbs supports for abortion that California, New Mexico and Maryland chose because they are material and physical and that's how my preferences run: but making the best of semen needs theory and principles too, and the hazardous substance perspective also comports with the expression of ideals. The governor of Michigan connected abortion with both anatomy and an abstraction, "the economy," when she announced a tagline: "If you don't think abortion is about the economy, you probably don't have a uterus."[29] State constitutions offer space for abortion ideals to intersect with values that inform transactions like cash budgeting and the construction of an abortion clinic. New amendments to these constitutions around the country have united the right not to be pregnant with other human rights.

State governments also can make semen less hazardous by supporting individuals who provide or seek the post-impact undoing of harm that abortion delivers. Journeys to obtain an abortion from one state that bans the procedure to another that permits it can receive more than just nonprosecution or tolerance from the destination. New York, for example, has modeled what a pro-choice jurisdiction can do to help inseminated persons who live under legislation that forces them to remain pregnant and give birth against their will. Made public when Dobbs was still in its leak stage, this May 2022 response took form in three new laws. The first of them prohibits New York courts and law enforcement from cooperating with efforts to arrest or extradite abortion providers. The second provides a legal cause of action to counter the antiabortion bounty that Texas codified before Dobbs. The third prohibits insurers from taking action against New York health care providers who assist in reproductive health services via telehealth or virtual medicine.[30]

Nongovernmental organizations have for decades supported the delivery of abortion to people cut off from this rescue after semen landed on their mucosa. They focus on needs. Some pregnant women need money; donors like me give money to charities that pay for abortions. Some pregnant women need mifepristone and misoprostol; the Dutch physician Rebecca Gomperts founded a nonprofit that sends abortion pills all over the world from an offshore pharmacy that makes cheap and effective generic drugs. American governments can finance abortion thorough grants to these NGOs, a move that would counterbalance the money they've ladled onto charities that promote authoritarian social goals.[31]

* * *

Information about hazardous substances as a regulatory strategy and pursuit invests in guidance, answering the consumer's hypothetical *What do I need to know about this substance to reach good decisions about interacting with it?* by enlarging informed choice. Human beings might want variously to reject, postpone, accept, recoil from, or embrace the prospect of being touched by semen when it's offered.

Different people favor different impacts and individuals' wishes can change over time. Their choice; their call. The abortion-rights catchphrase If/When/How, the name of a nonprofit that describes its mission as reproductive justice, applies to the possibility of contact with a life-changing substance just as it applies to the possibility of becoming pregnant.

Urging and encouraging interventions that deliver information about semen here, I have in mind two directional routes, one that gets laid out in advance by content suppliers and the other dynamic and interactive. At the first level, an official or scripted plane, state and local governments create curricula for schools. These materials address semen, albeit with indirection and evasion familiar from the early pages of this book. The second level of information delivery that regulation can improve is self-propelled education, the optional way to learn that adults and teenagers out of school turn on and off according to their own interests, needs, and curiosities. Each route for information delivery has strengths and vulnerabilities; both are essential to semen education.

Like other phenomena paired in this book, the two paths of school curricula and self-education influence each other. Adults write curricula based on what they know or believe from a vantage point that has access to more eclectic information than what children can receive. School curricula, in turn, teach information to adults. What children get taught in public schools about semen is the only instructional content about this subject that must clear government hurdles before it's distributed to the public. Preclearance slows the pace of education and brings in political compromise, but it also decreases the risk of misinformation in an electronic ecosystem that liars, trolls, provocateurs, bullshitters, powerful entities with bad intentions, fools, and malware can reach.

The great American judge Learned Hand (1872–1961) wrote in one of his decisions that he opposed lowering the "treatment of sex to the standard of a children's library." Adults who read because they want to deserve better, Hand believed.[32] They do. At the same time, adults also deserve to benefit from the caution and scrutiny put into curricular materials officially approved for children. Information on matters of fact reaches the public best when two sets of advantages come together: the expertise, (relative) rigor, and you-can-look-it-up transparency present in government-supplied texts and the lively, wide-open, and flickering Internet, where participants follow their desires and quit clicking when bored. Regulation supports both ways for people to learn about semen.

* * *

Scripted curricula ought to convey information about semen to young people in school. I've come up with six facts. To show the feasibility of everything that I want, I've assembled examples from current real-life curricula that have been relaying all of these points. Here is my list.

[1] The impacts of semen are pregnancy and sexually transmitted infection.
[2] Be careful about semen on mucosal surfaces, especially those located in the vagina and the anus, because these locations allow semen to make its impacts.
[3] The movement of semen into a vagina or anus is desirable and proper only when both the ejaculator and the recipient want this contact. Both get a veto.
[4] Semen can be blocked with a barrier.
[5] Many impacts of semen on mucosa can be undone.
[6] Semen is a source of pleasure, not just danger.

Commentary on each of the points follows in a what-why-how format.

[1] **What**: The impacts of semen are pregnancy and sexually transmitted infection.

This sentence is the foundation on which all of my regulation-by-education plan rests. It explains that semen is a hazardous substance. Semen makes people and it can make people sick. No other material qualifies for this description. While I'd like my coinage of "semenally transmitted" to catch on, here I use the more familiar "sexually transmitted" because in this sentence I am talking about the centrality of semen to that descriptor. Current educational materials use "sexually transmitted" to cover numerous consequences that they can and should attribute to semen.

Why: Risks deserve attention when they are significant. Their significance can be measured with reference to two separate and independent respects: first, the magnitude of the harm should the risk ripen; second, probability that harm will occur. *How bad* and *How likely*, in other words.

Semen's two impacts qualify as important under both. Earlier chapters of this book reviewed the reasons to consider both pregnancy and sexually transmitted infection to be extremely costly. Even for recipients who crave semen, people we heard from in chapter 6, semen is risky. Its dangers ought to be known.

As for the chances of harm from contact with semen, this consequence is likely enough to warrant regulatory attention. Let's look first at semen as the substance that makes people. Most women experience at least one pregnancy over their lifetime and women outnumber men. Both majorities are narrow but they point to more than a quarter of the human population who will be touched in a pain-causing way by the arrival of semen on mucosa. Insemination that launches a pregnancy is painless for the ejaculator most of the time, but causing someone else to become pregnant can be costly to him too.

The next likelihood to consider under this "why" rubric addresses semen as a substance that can make people sick. How many of us become infected with semenally transmitted disease is harder to know than how many of us give birth. In chapter 4, I reported data showing that semen is extraordinarily hospitable to pathogens. We know that a large fraction of people with STIs received their disease directly from semen that arrived on their mucosa. Even when sexual contact via a different deliverer—saliva, vaginal fluids, a sore—causes an infection, past hospitality from semen in someone else's body probably nurtured the pathogen.

Sexually transmitted infection will land on most people in the United States before they die. The Centers for Disease Control has estimated that 20% of the U.S. population has such an infection on any day of the year. Almost half, or 46%, of new sexually transmitted infections sicken young (for this purpose, I mean aged 15–24) persons.[33] Any disease that affects the young this much is especially significant, as illnesses that befall younger people are more disruptive of education, early earnings, the start of careers, and family formation than conditions that affect older people. Long-term effects that harm younger people blight more years of life.

How: Stay the course. Every approach to sex education that I've seen, even the uninformative Abstinence Only about which I'll say more in a moment, identifies pregnancy and sexually transmitted infection as objects of teaching attention. The main modification I advocate for instruction is to focus on semen in addition to sex. Transfers of semen onto mucosa cause 100% of unplanned pregnancies. These transfers don't cause 100% of sexually transmitted infections, but no other bodily fluid delivers disease onto mucosa as effectively as semen. Educators ought to name the substance when they cover the risk of pregnancy and STIs.

[2] **What**: Be careful about semen on mucosal surfaces, especially those located in the vagina and the anus, because these locations allow semen to make its impacts.

Why: Mucosa is semen's partner in impact-making. For semen to cause change, mucosa is just as indispensable as the star of this book itself. Mucosa of the mouth and throat matter too; information about this source of risk should also be available. But those sites are less urgent. Among the surfaces on which semen lands, the vagina and the rectum outrank oral mucosa.

In this perspective, semen is idle—in a benign sense of the word, similar to indolent as a descriptor of cancers—whenever it lands someplace non-mucosal. This characteristic means that people who receive semen on their mucosa are safer when they know about the possibilities of sending semen to a biological dead end. Their partners in this transfer, people who ejaculate, have experience with non-mucosal landings of their semen. Even the fraction of them who obey some variation on the order not to masturbate that I mentioned back in chapter 1 have likely emitted semen onto non-mucosal surfaces while they slept. Ejaculators learn from experience that putting semen someplace idle is feasible and consistent with a good life. For ejaculators who do not receive semen on their own mucosa, education on this point is necessary but less personally urgent. Semen receptors, a mostly female cohort, need to know about the unique vulnerability of a couple of body sites.

How: Decades after the 1982 launch of federally funded "abstinence only," shorthand for an approach to sex education that urged administrators and curriculum planners to cultivate as much dishonesty, evasion, conservative ideology about male and female gender roles, veiled theology, and denial as they could foist on teens and children in apparent commitment to belief that ignorance about sex keeps young people celibate and safe, evidence that this strategy is perverse finally started to erode the initiative. Findings by public health researchers show that Abstinence Only accomplishes nothing good.[34] Any secular metric you look at—teen pregnancy rates, teen STI rates, teen psychological health—either got worse or did not change in states that have followed this path. Although governments in the United States haven't been guided by the data here, public opinion aligns with science: the alternative curriculum favored by the Centers and Disease Control and the World Health Organization, comprehensive sex education, is more popular than abstinence among parents and teachers. I'm also heartened by a bit of rebranding: proponents of Abstinence Only seem to have dropped the eighties name of their program. They switched to "sexual risk avoidance programs" and now avoid saying "only" when they recommend abstinence.

Children can understand surfaces as receptors. Toys teach them that a protuberance fits into an opening. If you've ever held Lego blocks in your hand, you've experienced the concept. Shoelaces enter eyelets. One set of contrasting surfaces we think of by its brand name, Velcro, puts together smoothness and a hook: the word combines "vel" for velvet, the soft receptive surface, and "cro" for crochet, the hook or penetrator. Skating combines friction and smoothness. Familiar receptor-meets-traveler precedents like these provide a foundation to understand the relation between semen and mucosa. Each needs the other for an impact to result.

Mucosa can be mentioned to school children. The World Health Organization's *School Health Education to Prevent AIDS and STIs: A Resource Package for Curriculum Planners: Teachers' Guide* names mucosa. In its lesson plans, this guide tells teachers how to answer the question of how semen travels from semen into the body. Answer: "through the mucous membranes that line the vagina, penis, anus/ rectum."[35] Elsewhere the guide repeats this reference to mucous membranes as the locus of HIV vulnerability.[36]

[3] **What**: The movement of semen into a vagina or anus is desirable and proper only when both the ejaculator and the recipient want this contact. Both get a veto.

Why: Veto power over the transfer of semen from one body to another is the item of my six that's not like the others. I've written the other five as matters of fact, while "desirable and proper" expresses a value judgment. When a value judgment is widely accepted as correct in a universal sense, however—think of the Golden Rule, for example—it becomes eligible to join a list of teachings.

Legal rules enforce the value judgment I've stated. The law criminalizes sexual assault and, in parallel to codified crimes, also provides that persons who suffer intentionally inflicted harmful or offensive contact can recover money damages from persons responsible. Criminal law and tort law condemn the harmful impact of semen that lands unwanted by the recipient on mucosa. Neither crime nor tort provides full support for this condemnation, as we saw in chapter 1. But here I'm gathering values and stances so widely accepted as to amount to matters of fact. The law about journeys of semen onto mucosa supports this understanding of the veto included here.

The teaching says "get a veto" because rights with respect to semen are negative rather than affirmative. Considerations that steer observers to sympathy and support for other people's desires to obtain the semen they lack (gathered in chapter 6 of this book) express ideals or desiderata, not rights. Semen moved onto mucosa is an experience to which people at both ends of the touching may say no. If you have the ability to ejaculate onto a particular mucosa, you may refuse to do so; if you are in a position to receive semen inside your body, you too may forbid the encounter. When you want to share a transfer of semen with someone else, maybe you'll gain it and maybe you won't. Fulfillment of your desire hinges on whether this someone will cooperate. "Veto" means saying no without having to say why not. Receptors may reject the delivery of semen and ejaculators may decline to supply it; both may nix the transfer for any reason they please and for no reason at all.

How: The National Sex Education Standards curriculum tells teachers that students should be able to "communicate personal boundaries" by the end of fifth grade and, three grades later, "define sexual consent and agency" and also "identify factors (e.g., body image, self-esteem, alcohol and other substances) that can affect the ability to give or perceive consent to sexual activity."[37] The NSES defines an example of sexual consent as "an agreement that occurs between sexual partners about the behaviors they both give permission to engage in during a sexual encounter."[38]

UNESCO standards published in 2018 consider consent central to an effective curriculum: "Teaching young people to acknowledge and respect other people's personal boundaries can help create a society where no one feels ashamed to willingly engage in sexual activity, or to reject it or revoke consent at any point."[39] A learning objective in this book says that children age five to eight should know that everyone "has the right to who can touch their body, where and in what way." Moving to the 12–15 age band, this curriculum envisions "learners" becoming able to express both consent and nonconsent with reference to their "personal boundaries."[40]

What:

[4] Semen can be blocked with a barrier.

[5] Many impacts of semen on mucosa can be undone.

These two go together because both semen teachings are statements about matters of fact and paths for policy to follow in action. They both declare capacities. Semen can be blocked, says [4]. When it isn't blocked from mucosa, makes a landing, and causes an impact, then [5] becomes true and useful: well-established interventions can undo this consequence.

Why: I say "can be undone" to be careful about promising and over-promising. These interventions can fail. Nor do they empower everyone: for example, the decision to terminate a pregnancy belongs to the pregnant person rather than her inseminator. So I don't say that interventions will or would undo; I say they can undo. On many occasions. It's factually correct to tell the public that splash protection from the dangers of semen is available. Note also the importance of not underpromising. Much can be done. Semen brings contact consequences but it also yields to management, as we saw in the previous chapter. Human beings are in charge of this substance.

Saying what human agency can achieve identifies persons who ejaculate and persons who receive semen on their mucosa as agents with choices and power. Actions can overcome adversity. These observations follow a path launched in the first half of my six-item list. The first two announce risks. Number 3 declared the option of a veto. Here, in the fourth and fifth points, semen responds to the nuance present in human will. An individual might welcome contact with semen while wanting it to stay on the other side of a barrier. She might change her mind about contact to which she'd said yes, or in retrospect determine she hadn't really consented. Possessors of mucosa should and can protect themselves.

How: Returning to the National Sex Education Standards, we find more age-and-grade curricular sequences for teaching that semen can be blocked with barriers. By the end of the eighth grade, says the NSES, students should be able to say how to use condoms and dental dams correctly.[41] The end of tenth grade marks a point where students should know the advantages and disadvantages of "contraceptive and disease prevention methods," which include condoms, and be able to apply a decision-making model "to choices about contraceptive use, including abstinence and condoms." When the end of twelfth grade rolls around, students should be able to analyze variables that influence condom use, including "availability, affordability, perception of risk, pleasure."[42] UNESCO has set benchmarks about condom knowledge for three age tranches, the oldest being 15–18 at which point learners are to know about all "modern methods of contraception" including "male and female condoms."[43]

Fact [5], on undoing impacts after they occur, continues the theme of human agency and control over semen. Life goes on after semen lands on mucosa. When this landing delivers an unwanted consequence, several interventions to rid that undesired effect are safe, effective, and feasible.

Outside of official organizations and endorsed curricula, individual teachers have pushed to improve education about how STIs can be treated or cured. For example, a sexual health educator in Kentucky urged "inclusive and non-judgmental" comprehensive sex education. Her message that "anyone can get an STI. Getting an STI is not the end! Most STIs are curable and all are treatable" expressed a valuable view that human beings are more important than Bugs.[44]

Undoing pregnancy, however, is a possibility barely mentioned even in progressive comprehensive sex education materials. UNESCO's 2018 guidelines include a lesson for 15- to 18-year-olds about how local and national laws can impact sexual health, including access to abortion.[45] Additionally, one of the learning objectives under a lesson for students 12 to 15 years old is to teach students how to "assess sources of help and support . . . in order to access quality information and services."[46] Teaching pregnancy and pregnancy prevention to 15- to 18-year-olds includes lessons to make students "understand that unsafe abortions" pose "a serious health risk to women and girls."[47] Weak tea. Do better.

[6] **What**: Semen is a source of pleasure, not just danger.

Why: Semen information for everyone to know includes information about good effects. The most fundamental characteristic of a hazardous substance, as I've remarked, is that it is valuable. "Information," as the element of the Consumer Product Safety Commission guidance that I rendered in bullet points, focuses on information that consumers need and want. As pursuers of happiness, consumers want to know about semen as deliverer of pleasure, not just gloom and concern.

How: There's a lot to be done. Even the progressive federal-government initiative Healthy People 2020 omits pleasure from its list of topics it wants students to learn about sex. Curricula have long equated sex with peril. United States government measurements of sex-ed curricula interpret their communication criterion to cover only risk prevention. Surveys ask educators whether they teach "interpersonal communication skills to avoid or reduce sexual risk behaviors," "how to say no to sex," and "waiting until marriage to have sex."[48] As you know having read this far, I agree about peril. I've filled most of this book with peril.

At the same time, I also insist that both ejaculators and recipients of ejaculate receive instruction about at least two important satisfactions that include semen, the formation of a wanted baby and the sensation of sexual climax associated with ejaculation. These two satisfactions might seem on the surface too obvious to mention. They aren't. How and when semen makes babies is not especially well known even to educated adults, let alone the children I have in mind, and what it feels like to emit semen from one's urethra can for approximately half of us be learned only secondhand.

Like the characteristics of semen covered in chapter 4 that support both sperm and infectious pathogens, the risks and benefits of this substance are connected and interrelated as well as severable. Knowledge about sexual pleasure makes sex safer. For example, researchers have learned about a perception among young people that using condoms and hormonal birth control diminishes pleasure. Education, especially an interactive technique like role play to simulate conversations about birth control methods, could decrease this erroneous belief. Awareness of pleasure also enlarges understanding of what's wrong about coercion, manipulation, and overt sexual assault.

National-level surveys I've mentioned that ask school districts how they cover a list of topics in their sex education curricula could include pleasure. Like everything else I recommend in this chapter, this suggestion is precedented. The United Nations guidance on sex education counts pleasure among its learning objectives; an American counterpart, the set of guidelines published by the Sexuality Information and Education Council of the United States, says here and there that having sex feels good (for example, "couples have varied ways to share sexual pleasure with each other").

Timorous and guarded, I grant, but these official curricula endorse pleasure as a sex education topic, providing a base on which semen education can build. Toward this end, an international nonprofit called The Pleasure Project developed The Pleasure Principles, offered to help the teacher "as a pleasure activist, propagandist or practitioner."[49] Semen information is complete only when it includes joy.

* * *

Even before school curricula end and pupils graduate, unofficial education of every kind influences our children. Our species has always taught and learned outside of schools. Today, continuing the electronic revolution that built our current Internet era, people teach and learn this way more than ever.

Interactivity drives and animates the education that extends beyond school curricula. Today, when we adults learn we typically create dynamic new content. Sometimes without intending or wanting to, for example in the search histories our responses and questions produce, but also on purpose. Billions of people worldwide and millions in the United States participate in social media, defined in a public health paper as "activities, practices, and behaviors among communities of users who gather online to share information, knowledge, and opinions."[50] Participation in this network, and using the internet generally, gives people access to information as consumers and learners but also informants.

In this environment, my statements of fact about semen numbered [1] through [6] above are protean. They won't stand still. You can reach them and make alterations. Play with them, contradict them (type "not" next to a phrase you oppose, paste a disapproving emoji), like them, "like" them with a nonverbal 👍, forward them, publish a post about them, tweet them. Ignore them if you want, but you can't keep them static.

While delivering more information than a learner could ever acquire before daily education came online, the turn to electronic communication also dramatically changed the quality of that delivery. Most of these changes are positive. I'll give thanks for a few. Information is now cheaper to acquire; once acquired it's cheaper and easier to store. It reaches us faster. It can arrive audibly or with its appearance or form modified to accommodate our disabilities; it knows languages that help us learn; it can leap through time and geographic space.

Social media, mentioned just now as a source of bigger quantity, also achieves qualitative change. Again, highly beneficial. Membership in a community connects acquirers of information with peers and fellow travelers. As we learn information, we know we're not alone, on one hand, while asynchronicity and the off switch and the powers to block and quit enable us to keep the community at a distance when we so desire, on the other. This aggregation creates data about tastes, questions, wishes, and needs that can build source material for future research, an agenda pertinent to semen education. We may resent the exploitable trail of facts about ourselves that we generate, but this record of our interests helps to link information to recipients who want it.

The phenomenon of heeding particular individual generators of electronic content strengthens the dissemination of information. Journalists have long regarded social media as central to their work. Creating content and following other creators online supports the accretion, distribution, and revision of factual material that consumers seek. This function unites reporters, the general public, and governments.

Semen education as a flowering, life-improving project necessary to health owes a perverse debt to the Supreme Court's 2022 maneuver that made this substance more dangerous. Dobbs allowed state legislatures to escalate their interferences with pregnancy and the restrictions on abortion they enact in a new post-Roe era. These enlargements of semen's danger generated more demand for information. By taking away the right of a person not to be pregnant, the Supreme Court spurred more seeking of information about semen.

Slightly more women than men use the Internet—one count esti-mates the percentages as 96 versus 93 respectively[51]—and women have for many years outnumbered men among online seekers of informa-tion about health. Searches that women pursue address the well-being of people that these information-seekers care about or look after as well as themselves.[52] This concatenation of interests generates high demand for information about a fluid emitted by male bodies whose health impacts fall with particular significance on female ones.

Seekers motivated to defend the health of themselves or loved ones are searching as we speak. They learn about access to abortion medi-cation, organizations that provide financial support for abortion travel, online communities that unite individuals endangered by pregnancy, and answers to countless questions. Abortion-related queries can be urgent in a physical way, for example *Am I having a miscarriage?* or *water breaking symptoms*, or disconnected from emissions but still compelling to the person at the keyboard, like my efforts to find organizations that provide financial support for abortion travel.

* * *

Semen regulation by information has role models in the regulation of other substances already on the books. These precedents reduce risk and improve the quality of human lives by telling ordinary people what they need to know and can't easily teach themselves. People, even lawyer-people like me, tend to think of regulation as a skein of commands from the government. Do this. Don't do that. Minimums, maximums, check-lists, hoops to jump through, fine print. Comply or risk punishment. Certainly there's truth to this perception, but the bulk of what American regulation commands is the rendering of information.

Mandatory rendering of information rather than mandatory action is the approach to regulation that best unites visions of government across the left-right political spectrum. It aligns most closely with what both consumers and industry can live with. Its vision of human beings as choosers gives regulators work to do while keeping coercion and compulsion to a minimum. Happily for the work of this book, the regulatory strategy that seeks to communicate and stays away from prohibitions or edicts fits well with semen as a source of danger and opportunity. American regulators rarely ban. Good: we're dealing with material that can't be banned. Thinking of semen as an unbannable hazardous substance allows semen policy to learn from current regulations that the public finds acceptable, even popular.

"What do I need to know about this substance to reach good decisions about interacting with it?"—the question that the Consumer Product Safety Commission deems central to hazardous substance regulation—is asked and answered by another federal agency whose mission fits directly with health, the Food and Drug Administration. The FDA's uses of information complement those of the CPSC. Like the Consumer Product Safety Commission, the FDA sets out to protect ordinary lay people even though it doesn't have "consumer" in its name, and it takes a particular interest in substances that touch mucosa. Food and drugs do that. Ditto cosmetics, which the FDA also regulates. Food and some drugs enter our bodies via the mucosal surfaces of our mouth. Cosmetics also reach mucosa. Drugs administered by injection, inhalation, transdermal patch, or placement into the ear or eye or nostril resemble semen in causing impacts when they travel onto human tissue. Drugs designed to be inserted into the vagina or rectum resemble semen even more.

FDA regulations insist on the delivery of information. The F in the agency's name stands for food: let's start with regulations that give us information about what we eat and drink. The public is entitled to an accurate description of food sold for human consumption expressed in weight, numerical count, or a combination of those measurements.[53] Food labels must be legible to ordinary people, a demand that the FDA clarifies by condemning too-small type, insufficient background contrast, obscuring designs or vignettes, and crowding with "other written, printed, or graphic matter."[54] Regulations require sellers to state the food's name, its form (whole or sliced, for example) and whether it's an imitation of another food.[55] If the seller wants to say that the foodstuff has any connection to a disease or health condition, these claims require FDA authorization and also must be "complete, truthful and not misleading."[56] FDA regulations also demand clearly communicated nutrition information.[57]

For drugs, the D of FDA, information demands are heavier. Same mandatory legibility demand we just saw for food labeling.[58] Same insistence on an accurate and clear measurement of quantity.[59] A statement of identity on the drug label.[60] Drugs must come with adequate directions "under which the layman can use a drug safely."[61] Similar information must accompany cosmetics.[62]

Forcing disclosures like these about food, drugs, and cosmetics might seem an obvious move for the government in any wealthy country. Of course consumers should and would receive this information, one might think. But the requirement seems obvious only because it's familiar. Mandates that generate information about risks to mucosa emerged in the twentieth century from human initiative, not nature or anything that sellers volunteered to do. Every American federal-level rule had hurdles to clear before it joined the Code of Federal Regulations.

All the FDA specimens reviewed just now reflect a choice by regulators to demand disclosures that function to make contacts with human mucosa safer. Information about another fluid that travels to the same surfaces with equally significant consequences deserves a comparable degree of attention and energy. Regulation offers precedents in mindfulness that semen regulation can follow.

Agencies whose responsibilities extend further from mucosa give us more role models for the delivery of information that lay people can understand and use. OSHA, whose Bloodborne Pathogens rule covering another hazardous body fluid we met in chapter 7, imposes detailed demands for the appearance and quality of an important source of information, accident precaution signs.[63] The Consumer Product Safety Commission spells out extensive conditions for the labeling of hazards.[64] The CPSC also demands legible labels and extensive factual information from sellers of antennas, both the television and citizen band variety.[65]

Does this talk of labeling bore you? Regulators understand how you feel. Their work supplies you with words but also more than words. This outreach refutes the cliché of regulation as rigid, remote, and speaking to business rather than human beings. Here are a few examples of connection with the lay public supported by federal regulation.

A website with the easy-to-remember domain name of Regulations .gov holds all publicly available materials from nearly 300 federal agencies. Regulations.gov also accepts uploaded comments and applications.[66] Another website called Govinfo publishes rules, proposed rules, and executive orders.[67] Am I still boring you? If you don't need the content on these websites, probably. But when you want a datum of regulation, the point of fact awaits you at your fingertips.

Modern American regulation reaches lay people without making them type words or slog through paragraphs. Elizabeth Porter and Kathryn Watts report that "visual rulemaking," which started with the Obama administration and continues today, generates images, GIFs, and videos about rules.[68] President Obama once narrated a video about his Clean Power Plan that described achievements of environmental regulation, with no jargon. His video didn't even mention the EPA.[69]

Federal regulators also use social media. The Internal Revenue Service, for example, posts lively content—big font, bright colors, dynamic graphics—on platforms that taxpayers can easily find, which as I write includes Facebook, X (sometimes known as Twitter), Instagram, and LinkedIn. The IRS will have moved to a freshly updated list by the time you read this sentence. Other agencies with high visibility on social media include the Consumer Financial Protection Bureau, the Environmental Protection Agency, and the National Highway Traffic Safety Administration. Moving to lay people's screens has improved regulation to a point where, as one expert in administrative law has concluded, all of "modern government" is now more transparent and abler to communicate with the public than ever.[70]

Uniting this twenty-first century approach to communication with an old-school emphasis on words is the federal government's Plain Language Action and Information Network, abbreviated as PLAIN. Staffers in federal agencies who support the Plain Language Act of 2010's mission of clear expression can join the network by volunteering. The mission reminds regulators to focus on what ordinary people can understand.

Guidelines urge agency employees to know their audience, address the user they speak to as an individual person, keep their sentences short, and present their message in an order that people can follow. PLAIN advises regulators to avoid turnoffs: jargon, noun strings, definitions, and abbreviations. Its name violates its own abbreviation rule, I suppose, but vowels in the acronym make it easy to pronounce, and the phrase "plain language information action network" flows without strain. "Write for the web," says PLAIN. Also, understand that users "skim and scan."[71]

The Centers for the Disease Control, which describes itself as "the nation's leading science-based, data-driven, service organization that protects the public's health" has staked out a commitment to accessible communication that pertains closely to the health and safety agenda of this book. The CDC uses research-based criteria in its Clear Communication Index to improve communication about public health.[72] A separate CDC initiative, the Action Plan to Improve Health Literacy, also pushes plain language.[73]

Communicators writing about semen for a busy or distracted "skim and scan" audience might be inspired by work that won the first federally bestowed No Gobbledygook Award.[74] Marthe Kent, holding the title of Director of Regulatory Analysis at OSHA, rewrote a safety rule about a hazardous fluid with wit and brevity. Figure 8.1 shows the old regulation before Kent cured what ailed it.

Your eyes glaze over, I daresay. Mine did. I think someone may have fallen asleep in the middle: "removal form" looks like a misrendering of "removal from." But who can stay alert long enough to tell? As shown in figure 8.2, Marthe Kent felt your pain and ventured a fix.

I invite readers to follow this exemplar and compete on the No Gobbledygook playing field with their own description of semen as a hazardous substance. Spreading the word about this source of

✖ Before

1910 open (94(d) (1) General.

(i) This paragraph applies to all operations involving the immersion of materials in liquids, or in the vapors of such liquids, for the purpose of cleaning or altering the surface or adding to or imparting a finish thereto or changing the character of the materials, and their subsequent removal form the liquid or vapor, draining, and drying. These operations include washing, electroplating, anodizing, pickling, quenching, dyeing, dipping, tanning, dressing, bleaching, degreasing, alkaline cleaning, stripping, rinsing, digestion, and other similar operations

Figure 8.1

✓ **After**

1910.122 When does this rule apply?

1. This rule applies to operations using a dip tank
   containing any liquid other than water:

   - to clean an object
   - to coat an object
   - to alter the surface of an
     object or
   - to change the character of
     an object

2. This rule also applies to drying or draining an
   object after dipping

Figure 8.2

opportunity and danger helps make the best of semen. I leave you with my own response to my invitation. It puts into more adult words the semen school curriculum I argued for a few pages ago, trimmed to fit onto a business card.

- Semen is a hazardous substance.
- The hazards of semen are pregnancy and disease.
- Contact with vaginal, anal, or oral mucosa delivers the hazards of semen.
- Mucosa possessors when offered contact with semen can choose to avoid it or block that contact with a barrier. They can also undo its impacts.
- Semen delivers pleasure when it lands, not just danger. Every hazardous substance has value.

ACKNOWLEDGMENTS

Now that I've written one book about legal controls on female reproductive anatomy followed by this one on a male counterpart, I feel extra indebted to the friends and allies who encouraged my second adventure. Semen as a topic asked more of them. For their thoughtful advice and insights, I thank Sally Bernstein, my sister and wise counselor, along with Lev Raphael, Matt Gallaway, Kelly Kleiman, Larry Fleischer, Jayne Ressler, Evelyn Brody, Jim Huttenhower, Phillip Tommey, Eugene Mazo, Mae Quinn, Lori Andrews, Holt Parker, Ellen Bublick, Heidi Brown, Susan Orlins, Tsachi Keren-Paz, Anna Roberts, and Steven Dean. Ron Krotoszynski strengthened the project at many stages.

Thanks also to workshop participants at Brooklyn Law School, Oxford University, University of Sheffield, University of Edinburgh, and the University of Iowa College of Law for helpful comments and to the receptive audience at University of Western Ontario Faculty of Law, where I talked about semen under the auspices of a distinguished lecture.

Foremost among my colleagues at Brooklyn who made this book possible were Jocelyn Simonson, an inspiring scholar; Kathleen Darvil, exemplary librarian; and Maria Raneri and Joanne Tapia, who typed and formatted parts of the manuscript. Brooklyn students Rachel Roberts, Denna Fraley, David Gonsier, Mackenzie Jacobs, Brendan Ruiz, Katie Fitzgerald, Charles Hennessy, and Beatrice Rubin furnished valuable research assistance, as did Benjamin Smith: Benji also created a visual work depicting my thesis as a journey that helped get this book over the finish line by boosting my morale.

Near that finish line stands my off-and-on hero, Sylvia Zucker Bernstein, who died shortly before I turned in the manuscript. "Why?" she said when I mentioned that my subject seemed to put some people off. "It's perfectly natural." My mother never flinched.

Two law reviews nurtured thinking about semen. Chapter 8 of this book and parts of chapter 5 build on an essay published in the *Columbia*

Journal of Gender and Law; the theme of unmentionability that centers the introduction occupied my article in the *De Paul Law Review* about semen as a product eligible for products liability. My thanks to the organizers of the symposia published in these law reviews, Bridget Crawford and Stephan Landsman respectively, for their generous response when I interpreted their invitation to include an unexpected substance.

NOTES

INTRODUCTION

1 Tim Jewell, Semen Color Chart: What Does Each Color Mean for Overall Sperm Health?, Healthline, July 23, 2023 [https://perma.cc/T9PQ-PZME].

2 Emily Thomas, Aristotle on Making Babies, Aeon, Apr. 4, 2023 [https://perma.cc/FTL4-7GBT].

3 Id.

4 Taber's Medical Dictionary, "Mucosa" [https://perma.cc/R5GA-TWMX].

5 Alex Comfort, The Joy of Sex 56 (1972).

6 Martha Kempner, Why the CDC Stopped Calling Sex Without a Condom "Unprotected Sex," Rewire News Group, Feb. 24, 2014 [https://perma.cc/3V9D-K8KE].

7 Julia L. Marcus & Jonathan M. Snowden, Words Matter: Putting an End to "Unsafe" and "Risky" Sex, 47 Sex. Transm. Dis. 1 (2020).

8 N.Y. Penal Law § 130.00 (current in 2023–24).

9 N.Y. Criminal Jury Instructions § 130.35(1).

1. ANYWHERE IT WANTS TO GO

1 LePage v. Center for Reproductive Medicine, P.C., 408 So.3d 678 (Ala. 2024).

2 Clement of Alexandria: Christ the Educator 170 (Simon P. Wood trans., 1954). The copyright page of this book says "printed with ecclesiastical permission."

3 American College of Obstetricians and Gynecologists, Effectiveness of Birth Control Methods [https://perma.cc/C9PV-WQ3S].

4 Joseph Berger, Moshe Tendler, Authority on Jewish Medical Ethics, Dies at 95, N.Y. Times, Oct. 9, 2021.

5 Judy Mann, Sex and Indifference, Wash. Post, Dec. 10, 1991.

6 Kelly Cue Davis et al., Young Women's Experiences with Coercive and Non-Coercive Condom Use Resistance: Examination of an Understudied Sexual Risk Behavior, 29 Women's Health Issues 231 (2019).

7 Quoted in Alexandra Brodsky, "Rape-Adjacent": Imagining Legal Responses to Nonconsensual Condom Removal, 32 Colum. J. Gender & L. 183, 188 (2017).

8 Jody Lyneé Madeira, Understanding Illicit Insemination and Fertility Fraud, from Patient Experience to Legal Reform, 39 Colum. J. Gender & L. 110, 113 (2019).

9 Alyssa Lukpat, Fertility Doctor Accused of Using His Own Sperm Is Ordered to Pay Millions, N.Y. Times, Apr. 28, 2022.

10 Sydni R. Eibschutz, "Dr., I Don't Want Your Baby!": Why America Needs a Fertility Patient Protection Act, 106 Iowa L. Rev. 905, 921–22 (2021).

11 See Dov Fox et al., Fertility Fraud, Legal Firsts, and Medical Ethics, 134 Obstetrics & Gynecology 918 (2019).

12 Madeira, supra note 8, at 113.

13 Alex Kuczynski, Sweet Chastity, N.Y. Times, Mar. 25, 2007.

14 The Book of Mormon, Making Things Up Again [https://perma.cc/QGL6-JGVT].

15 Alex-Ivar Berglund, Zulu Thought-Patterns and Symbolism 332 (1976).

16 Graeme J. Pitcher & Douglas M. G. Bowley, Infant Rape in South Africa, 359 Lancet 274 (2002).

17 Rachel Jewkes et al., The Virgin Cleansing Myth: Cases of Child Rape Are Not Exotic, 359 Lancet 711 (2002).

18 Nora Ellen Groce & Reshma Trasi, Rape of Individuals with Disability: AIDS and the Folk Belief of Virgin Cleansing, 363 Lancet 1663 (2004).

19 Nancy Tuana, The Weaker Seed: The Sexist Bias of Reproductive Theory, 3 Hypatia 35, 36 (1988).

20 Dignity for Aborted Children Act, S. 293, 117th Congress (2021).

21 Emma Green, State-Mandated Mourning for Aborted Fetuses, Atlantic, May 14, 2016.

22 587 U.S. 490 (2019).

23 Id. at 493.

24 Doe v. Rokita, 54 F.4th 518, 519 (7th Cir. 2022).

25 The Supreme Court said the problem was Planned Parenthood's to figure out. Box v. Planned Parenthood of Indiana & Kentucky, Inc., 587 U.S. 490, 492 (2019) (stating that "on rational basis review, 'the burden is on the one attacking the legislative arrangement to negative every conceivable basis which might support it'").

26 Carolyn M. Fronczak et al., The Insults of Illicit Drug Use on Male Fertility, 33 J. Andrology 15 (2012).

27 Valena E. Beety & Jennifer D. Oliva, Policing Pregnancy "Crimes," 98 N.Y.U. L. Rev. Online 29 (2023).

28 34 Env. Sci. Europe 6 (2012) (authored by Naina Kumar & Amit Kant Singh).

29 Green, supra note 21.

30 Whole Woman's Health v. Smith, 338 F. Supp. 3d 606, 631 (W.D. Tex. 2018), vacated and remanded sub nom. Whole Woman's Health v. Young, 37 F.4th 1098 (5th Cir. 2022).

31 William Blackstone, Commentaries on the Laws of England 130 (1765).

32 Shapiro v. Thompson, 394 U.S. 618, 630 (1969).

33 Saenz v. Roe, 526 U.S. 489, 505 (1999).

34 E.g., Maldonado v. Houstoun, 157 F.3d 179, 188 (3d Cir. 1998); Westenfelder v. Ferguson, 998 F. Supp. 146, 156 (D.R.I. 1998); Mitchell v. Steffen, 504 N.W.2d 198, 203 (Minn. 1993).

35 Zobel v. Williams, 457 U.S. 55, 65 (1982).

36 Roe v. Wade, 410 U.S. 113, 162 (1973).

37 See generally Noah Smith-Drelich, The Constitutional Right to Travel Under Quarantine, 93 S. Cal. L. Rev. 1367 (2022) (surveying travel restrictions in the context of health protection).

2. SEED, THE STARTER

1 Edward Dolnick, The Seeds of Life: From Aristotle to da Vinci, from Sharks' Teeth to Frogs' Pants, the Long and Strange Quest to Discover Where Babies Come from 262 (2017).

2 Martina Johansson et al., Semen Activates the Female Immune Response During Early Pregnancy in Mice, 112 Immunology 290, 291 (2004).

3 John E. Schjenken & Sarah A. Robertson, The Female Response to Seminal Fluid, 100 Physiol. Rev. 1077, 1077 (2020).

4 Laura K. Sirot et al., Sexual Conflict and Seminal Fluid Proteins: A Dynamic Landscape of Sexual Interactions, 7 Cold Spring Harbor Perspectives in Biology 1, 2 (2015).

5 Or so I contend in Anita Bernstein, Formed by Thalidomide: Mass Torts as a False Cure for Toxic Exposure, 97 Colum. L. Rev. 2152 (1997).

6 Abigail Tucker, Mom Genes: Inside the New Science of Our Ancient Maternal Instinct 58 (2021).

7 Id. at 62.

8 Id. at 64, 65.

9 Abigail Tucker, Moms: You Shaped Your Children, but the Reverse Is True, Too—Down to Your Very Cells, Wash. Post, May 6, 2021.

10 Haley Ferise, The Best Protection Is Abstinence (from Funding): The Illegality and Unconstitutionality of Abstinence-Only Sex Education in the United States, 27 U. Pa. J.L. & Soc. Change 19, 30–31 (2023).

11 Meghan Boone, Expecting Violence: Centering the Experience of Violence in Pregnancy, 30 Va. J. Soc. Pol'y & L. 1, 4–5 (2023).

12 Jessica Grose, Women's Health Care Is Underfunded. The Consequences Are Dire, N.Y. Times, Mar. 18, 2023.

13 Francesca Laguardia, Pain That Only She Must Bear: On the Invisibility of Women in Judicial Abortion Rhetoric, 9 J. Law Biosci. 111 (2022).

14 Olivia Campbell, The Curious Case of Motherhood and Longevity, Undark, July 12, 2017 [https://perma.cc/L9J9-9ESX].

15 Cheryl L. Woods-Giscombé et al., The Impact of Miscarriage and Parity on Patterns of Maternal Distress in Pregnancy, 33 Res. Nurs. Health, 316, 317 (2010).

16 Angela L. Ho, Spontaneous Miscarriage Management Experience: A Systematic Review, 14 Cureus 1 (2022).

17 Ferise, supra note 10, at 31.

18 Planned Parenthood, In-Clinic Abortion [https://perma.cc/7CUW-RT98].

19 National Abortion Federation, Violence Against Abortion Providers Continues to Rise Following Roe Reversal, New Report Finds, May 23, 2023 [https://perma.cc/7CUW-RT98].

20 Ferise, supra note 10, at 31; Stephen B. Thacker, Midline Versus Mediolateral Episiotomy, 320 BMJ 1615 (2000).
21 Jakub Pietrzak et al., A Cross-Sectional Survey of Labor Pain Control and Women's Satisfaction. 19 Int'l J. Env'l Res. & Pub. Health 1741 (2022).
22 Boone, supra note 11, at 5.
23 Elizabeth Kukura, Rethinking the Infrastructure of Childbirth, 91 UMKC L. Rev. 497 (2023).
24 Jennifer S. Hendricks, Body and Soul: Equality, Pregnancy, and the Unitary Right to Abortion, 45 Harv. C.R.-C.L. L. Rev. 329, 343 (2010).
25 Stephanie H. Murray, The Pain That Is Unlike All Other Pain, Atlantic, Aug. 12, 2022.
26 Rachael Robertson, Is the U.S. Overcounting Maternal Deaths? New Study Stirs Controversy, MedPage Today, Mar. 14, 2024 [https://perma.cc/HE5E-E6BY].
27 Casey Crump et al., Adverse Pregnancy Outcomes and Long-Term Mortality in Women, 184 JAMA Intern. Med. 631 (2024).
28 Laguardia, supra note 13, at 7–8.
29 Kat Stafford et al., Medical Racism in History Chapter One: Why Do So Many Black Women Die in Pregnancy? One Reason: Doctors Don't Take Them Seriously, Associated Press, May 23, 2023.
30 Maeve E. Wallace, Trends in Pregnancy-Associated Homicide, United States 2020, 112 Am. J. Pub. Health 1333 (2022).
31 Id. at 1334.
32 Cara Murez, Homicide a Leading Cause of Death for Pregnant U.S. Women, U.S. News and World Report, Oct. 20, 2022.
33 Lisa Burden, Adoption Statistics and Legal Trends, FindLaw, July 14, 2023 [https://perma.cc/C99K-L5VS].
34 Aimee Picchi, The Cost of Raising a Child is Almost $240,000—And That's Before College, CBS News, Sept. 14, 2023 [https://perma.cc/4SCS-MWHG].
35 Andrea H. Beller & John W. Graham, Small Change: The Economics of Child Support 165 (1993).
36 S. Katherine Nelson et al., The Pains and Pleasures of Parenting: When, Why, and How Is Parenthood Associated with More or Less Well-Being?, 140 Psychol. Bull. 846, 850 (2014).
37 Id. at 852.
38 Debra Umberson et al., Parenthood, Childlessness, and Well-Being: A Life Course Perspective, 72 J. Marriage & Family 612 (2010).
39 Matthew D. Johnson, Want to Save Your Marriage? Don't Have Kids, Guardian, May 24, 2016.
40 Wei-Hsin Yu & Yuko Hara, Motherhood Penalties and Fatherhood Premiums: Effects of Parenthood on Earnings Growth Within and Across Firms, 58 Demography 247, 249 (2021).
41 Id. at 251.

42 Shelley J. Correll et al., Getting a Job: Is There a Motherhood Penalty?, 112 Am. J. Sociology 1296 (2007); Amy J. C. Cuddy et al., When Professionals Become Mothers, Warmth Doesn't Cut the Ice, 60 J. Soc. Issues 701 (2004).

43 Correll, supra note 42, at 1316–17.

3. PREGNANCY RESTRICTIONS LEVERAGE SEMEN TO CONTROL HUMAN LIVES

1 Amanda Hess, When Motherhood Is a Horror Show, N.Y. Times, May 12, 2022.

2 Justin Weinberg, Philosopher: Missed Class to Get an Abortion? Not Excused, Daily Nous, May 30, 2024 [https://perma.cc/47M3-8JX2].

3 Greer Donley & Caroline M. Kelly, Abortion Disorientation, 74 Duke L.J. 1 (2024).

4 Ben Adams & Cynthia Barmore, Questioning Sincerity, 67 Stan. L. Rev. Online 59, 59 (2014).

5 Burwell v. Hobby Lobby Stores, Inc., 573 U.S. 682 (2014).

6 Dobbs v. Jackson Women's Health Org., 597 U.S. 215, 332 (2022) (Thomas, J., concurring).

7 Lauren Weber, Conservative Attacks on Birth Control Could Threaten Access, Wash. Post, June 5, 2024.

8 Geoffrey Skelley & Holly Fuong, How Americans Feel About Abortion and Contraception, FiveThirtyEight, July 12, 2022 [https://perma.cc/ZH8P-ZDL6].

9 Elizabeth Dias & Lisa Lerer, Trump's Playbook on Abortion Includes This False Charge, N.Y. Times, Sept. 11, 2024.

10 David W. Chen, A New Goal for Abortion Bills: Punish or Protect Doctors, N.Y. Times, Feb. 16, 2023.

11 Selena Simmons-Duffin, Doctors Who Want to Defy Abortion Laws Say It's Too Risky, NPR.org, Nov. 23, 2022.

12 Madeline Fitzgerald, Countries with the Most Restrictive Abortion Bans, U.S. News & World Report, July 13, 2022.

13 Ark. Code Ann. § 5-61-404; S.D. Codified Laws § 22-17-5.1.

14 Sarah Osmundson, All-or-Nothing Abortion Politics Will Leave Women with Nothing, N.Y. Times, Mar. 16, 2023.

15 Dylan Brown, Federal Complaint Denied After Oklahoma Woman Denied Emergency Abortion, KFOR.com, Jan. 21, 2024 [https://perma.cc/954X-QLK5].

16 Amanda Seitz, Emergency Rooms Refused to Treat Pregnant Women, Leaving One to Miscarry in a Lobby Restroom, AP News, Apr. 19, 2024.

17 Mabel Felix et al., A Review of Exceptions in State Abortion Bans: Implications for the Provision of Abortion Services, KFF, May 18, 2023 [https://perma.cc/7R9Y-42W9].

18 Tex. Health & Safety Code Ann. § 170A.002(2)(b)(2).

19 Tracy Smith, Texas Mother Kate Cox on the Outcome of Her Legal Fight for an Abortion: "It Was Crushing," CBS News, Jan. 14, 2024.

20 Eleanor Klibanoff, Texas Supreme Court Temporarily Halts Ruling Allowing Dallas Woman to Get an Abortion, Tex. Trib., Dec. 8, 2023.

21 State v. Zurawski, 690 S.W.3d 644, 671 (Tex. 2024). See Ellen Wright Clayton & Luke A. Gatta, Caught in the Middle: Providing Obstetric Care When Pregnant Women Have Complications, 2024 Utah L. Rev. 823, 829, 831 (quoting from the *Zurawski* record to argue that "physicians should be presumed to be acting in good faith and in accordance with the standard of care").

22 Shefali Luthra, State Abortion Bans Are Preventing Cancer Patients from Getting Chemotherapy, The 19th, Oct. 7, 2022 [https://perma.cc/TA97-MCTL].

23 Callie Cassick, Dayton Woman Denied Life-Saving Chemotherapy Due to Pregnancy, WDTN Evening News, Sept. 15, 2022 [https://perma.cc/C6RZ-3PJ9].

24 Elisabeth Mahase, U.S. Anti-Abortion Laws May Restrict Access to Vital Drug for Autoimmune Diseases, Patient Groups Warn, 378 BMJ 1677 (2022).

25 Katie Shepherd & Frances Stead Sellers, Abortion Bans Complicate Access to Drugs for Cancer, Arthritis, Even Ulcers, Wash. Post, Aug. 8, 2022.

26 Peter Slevin, One of the Last Abortion Doctors in Indiana, New Yorker, Feb. 25, 2024.

27 Sarah Varney, "She Was Gasping for Air": Abortion Fight Shifts to Women Who Suffered Under Strict Bans, L.A. Times, Aug. 8, 2023.

28 Nadine El-Bawab, "I Had to Carry My Baby to Bury My Baby": Woman Says She Was Denied Abortion for Fetus Without Skull, ABC News, Aug. 26, 2022.

29 Eleanor Klibanoff, She Was Told Her Twin Sons Wouldn't Survive. Texas Law Made Her Give Birth Anyway, Tex. Trib., Oct. 11, 2023.

30 Jessica Valenti, Calculated Cruelty, Oct. 19, 2023 [https://perma.cc/9ELJ-NPNT].

31 Angelo B. Hooker et al., Long-Term Complications and Reproductive Outcome After the Management of Retained Products of Conception: A Systematic Review, 105 Fertility & Sterility 156 (2016).

32 Pam Belluck, They Had Miscarriages, and New York Abortion Laws Obstructed Treatment, N.Y. Times, July 17, 2022.

33 AAPLOG Practice Guideline, Concluding Pregnancy Ethically, Evidence-Based Guidelines for Pro-Life Practice, Aug. 2022, at 8 [https://aaplog.org/wp-content/uploads/2023/04/PG-10-Concluding-Pregnancy-Ethically-updated.pdf; https://perma.cc/V8PQ-N63Z].

34 Noesen v. State Dep't Regul. & Licensing, Pharmacy Examining Bd., 751 N.W.2d 385, 389 (Wis. App. 2008).

35 S.D. Codified Laws § 36-11-70; Ark. Code Ann. § 20-16-304(4); Miss. Code Ann. § 41-107-5(1); Miss. Code Ann. § 41-107-3 (b) (including pharmacists among health care providers covered).

36 J. Shoshanna Ehrlich, The Abortion Rights of Teens in the Post-*Dobbs* Era, 30 Cardozo J. Equal Rts. & Soc. Just. 1, 31 (2023).

37 Id. at 39.

38 AAP Committee on Adolescence, The Adolescent's Right to Confidential Care When Considering Abortion, 139 Pediatrics 139 (2017).

39 Hodgson v. Minnesota, 497 U.S. 417, 439 (1990).

40 Bellotti v. Baird, 443 U.S. 622, 640–43 (1979).

41 Lauren Treadwell, Informal Closing of the Bypass: Minors' Petitions to Bypass Parental Consent for Abortion in an Age of Increasing Judicial Recusals, 58 Hastings L.J. 869, 884 (2007).

42 James B. Stewart et al., Jeffrey Epstein Hoped to Seed Human Race with His DNA, N.Y. Times, July 31, 2019.

43 Caroline Davies et al., Prince Andrew Settles Virginia Giuffre Sexual Assault Case in U.S., Guardian, Feb. 15, 2022.

44 Nicholas Liu, "Your Body, MY Choice": Emboldened Far-Right Men Taunt Women on Social Media After Trump Win, Salon, Nov. 8, 2024 [https://perma.cc /K6UX-QAYC].

45 Jon D. Michaels & David L. Noll, Vigilante Federalism, 108 Cornell L. Rev. 1187, 1192 (2023).

46 Moira Donegan & Mark Joseph Stern, Slate, May 4, 2023.

47 Emily Bazelon, Husband Sued over His Ex-Wife's Abortion; Now Her Friends Are Suing Him, N.Y. Times, May 4, 2023.

48 Dobbs v. Jackson Women's Health Org., 597 U.S. 215, 346 (2022) (Kavanaugh, J., concurring).

49 Idaho Code Ann. § 18-623.

50 Alander Rocha, Alabama Attorney General Doubles Down on Threats to Prosecute Out-of-State Abortion Care, Alabama Reflector, Aug. 31, 2023 [https:// perma.cc/58ND-UF9Q].

51 Caroline Kitchener, Texas Highways Are the Next Anti-Abortion Target. One Town is Resisting, Wash. Post, Sept. 1, 2023.

52 Remy Tumin, Ohio Woman Who Miscarried Faces Charge That She Abused Corpse, N.Y. Times, Jan. 3, 2024.

53 Jericka Duncan et al., Brittany Watts, Ohio Woman Charged with Felony After Miscarriage at Home, Describes Shock of Her Arrest, CBS News, Jan. 26, 2024.

54 Laura Huss & Goleen Samari, Self-Care, Criminalized: The Criminalization of Self-Managed Abortion from 2000 to 2010, If/WhenHow: Lawyering for Reproductive Justice (2023) [https://perma.cc/P7UQ-TCLX].

55 Quoted in Maria Sole Campinoti et al., Woman Who Suffered Miscarriage at Home Will Not Be Criminally Charged, Grand Jury Says, CNN.com, Jan. 11, 2024.

56 Sherry F. Colb & Michael C. Dorf, Mandating Nature's Course, 109 Cornell L. Rev. 1655 (2025).

4. "LIKE BUGS"

1 John Hughes, My Penis, National Lampoon, Nov. 1978 [https://perma.cc/2EWK -VZUD].

2 Marianne Willeén et al., The Bacterial Flora of the Genitourinary Tract in Healthy Fertile Men, 30 Scandinavian Journal of Urology and Nephrology (1996).

3 Vivien Marx, The Semen Book 66 (2001).

4 Bilal Chightai et al., A Neglected Gland: A Review of Cowper's Gland, 28 International J. Andrology 74 (2005).

5 L. Priskorn et al., Average Sperm Count Remains Unchanged Despite Reduction in Maternal Smoking: Results from a Large Cross-Sectional Study with Annual Investigations over 21 Years, 36 Hum. Reprod. 998, 1000 (2018).

6 Surabhi Gupta & Anand Kuma, The Human Semen, in Basics of Human Andrology 163, 167 (2017).

7 Jacklyn Johnson et al., The High Content of Fructose in Human Semen Competitively Inhibits Broad and Potent Antivirals That Target High-Mannose Glycans, 94 J. Virol. e01749 (2020).

8 The Global HIV/Aids Epidemic, KFF, July 25, 2024 [https://perma.cc/LUU9 -4TAY].

9 Jessica K. Kafta et al., Endometrial Epithelial Cell Response to Semen from HIV-Infected Men During Different Stages of Infection is Distinct and Can Drive HIV-1-Long Terminal Repeat, 26 AIDS 27 (2012); Johnson, supra note 7.

10 Nikhil Swaminathan, Male Semen Makes HIV More Potent, Sci. Am., Dec. 14, 2007 [https://perma.cc/6WF4-CGY4].

11 Johnson, supra note 7.

12 Samuel K. Lai et al., Human Immunodeficiency Virus Type 1 is Trapped by Acidic but Not by Neutralized Human Cervicovaginal Mucus, 83 J. Virol. 11196 (2009).

13 Amyloid Fibril, Science Direct [https://perma.cc/C7J5-9ZNV].

14 Nadia R. Roan et al., Semen Amyloids Participate in Spermatozoa Selection and Clearance, eLife, Jun. 27, 2017 [https://perma.cc/SG49-LSJ6].

15 Jan Münch et al., Semen-Derived Amyloid Fibrils Drastically Enhance HIV Infection, 131 Cell 1059 1060 (2007).

16 Swaminathan, supra note 10.

17 Sidoniea Lambert-Niclot et al., Detection of HIV-1 RNA in Seminal Plasma Samples from Treated Patients with Undetectable HIV-1 RNA in Blood Plasma on a 2002–2011 Survey, 26 AIDS 971 (2012).

18 Jason Globerman et al., Rapid Response: The Effects of Viral Load and Antiretroviral Medications on Sexual Transmission of HIV, 67 Rapid Review 1, 2 (2013) [https://perma.cc/4VLQ-NDZN].

19 Victor K. Barbiero, Ebola: A Hyperinflated Emergency, 8 Global Health: Science & Practice 178 (2020).

20 Jennifer Kates et al., The U.S. Response to Ebola: Status of the FY2015 Emergency Ebola Appropriation, KFF, Dec. 11, 2015 [https://perma.cc/8H3X-TBF5].

21 Stephen Bart et al., Enhancement of Ebola Virus Infection by Seminal Amyloid Fibrils, 115 PNAS 7410 (2018).

22 U.S. Centers for Disease Control & Prevention, Caring for Ebola Disease Survivors in the U.S. Apr. 25, 2024 [https://perma.cc/M2Y2-UX3C].

23 William A. Fischer II & David A. Wohl, Confronting Ebola as a Sexually Transmitted Infection, 62 Clin. Infect. Dis. 1272 (2016).

24 Bart, supra note 21.

25 Robert Fischer et al., Ebola Virus Persistence in Semen Ex Vivo, 22 Emerg. Infect. Dis. 289 (2016).

26 Centers for Disease Control, Sexually Transmitted Infections Surveillance, Jan. 30, 2024 [https://perma.cc/4EWV-QVB4].

27 Syphilis May Be Transmitted Through Semen, Study Suggests, UW Medicine: Newsroom, Dec. 14, 2018 [https://perma.cc/9YW5-FX8U].

28 Charmie Godornes et al., Treponema pallidum subsp. pallidum DNA and RNA in Semen of a Syphilis Patient Without Genital or Anal Lesions, 46 Sex. Transm. Dis. e62–e64 (2019).

29 Hanen Sellami et al., Molecular Detection of Chlamydia Trachomatis and Other Sexually Transmitted Bacteria in Semen of Male Partners of Infertile Couples in Tunisia: The Effect on Semen Parameters and Spermatozoa Apoptosis Markers, 9 PLoS One e98903 (2014).

30 Mark Anderson, Seminal Plasma Initiates a Neisseria gonorrhoeae Transmission State, 5 mBio e01004–13 (2014).

31 Id.

32 U.S. Centers for Disease Control & Prevention, About Chlamydia, Feb. 20, 2024 [https://perma.cc/RGH4-DQRV].

33 Lavelle Hanna et al., Effect of Seminal Plasma on Chlamydia trachomatis Strain LB-1 in Cell Culture, 32 Infection & Immunity 404 (1981).

34 Christina Muzny, Why Does Trichomonas Vaginalis Continue to be a "Neglected" Sexually Transmitted Infection?, 67 Clin. Infect. Dis. 218 (2018).

35 Camila Braz Menezes et al., Trichomoniasis—Are We Giving the Deserved Attention to the Most Common Non-Viral Sexually Transmitted Disease Worldwide?, 3 Microbial Cell 404 (2016).

36 Alisha Haridasani Gupta, A Third of Women Get This Infection. The Fix: Treat Their Male Partners, N.Y. Times, Mar. 18, 2025.

37 Maria F. Gallo et al., Association Between Semen Exposure and Incident Bacterial Vaginosis, Infectious Diseases in Obstetrics & Gynecology (2011) [https://perma.cc/4M2S-LPSC].

38 Lenka A. Vodstrcil et al., Male-Partner Treatment to Prevent Recurrence of Bacterial Vaginosis, 392 N. Eng. J. Med. 947 (2025).

39 Gallo et al., supra note 37.

40 Credit to Benjamin Smith for this neologism.

41 Archana Bodas LaPollo et al., Researching Black Men Who Have Sex with Men Who Do Not Identify as Gay for HIV Prevention and Services, APHA Annual Meeting, Nov. 2006 [https://perma.cc/YKM3-S9VX]; Fujie Xu et al., Men Who Have Sex with Men in the United States: Demographic and Behavioral Characteristics and Prevalence of HIV and HSV-2 Infection: Results from National Health and Nutrition Examination Survey 2001–2006, 37 Sex. Transm. Dis. 399 (2010).

42 Kyle T. Bernstein et al., Same-Sex Attraction Disclosure to Health Care Providers Among New York City Men Who Have Sex with Men: Implications for HIV Testing Approaches, 168 Arch. Intern. Med. 1458 (2008).

43 Tony J. Silva, Straight Identity and Same-Sex Desire: Conservatism, Homophobia, and Straight Culture, 97 Social Sources 1067 (2018).

44 Preeti Pathela, Discordance between Sexual Behavior and Self-Reported Sexual Identity: A Population-Based Survey of New York City Men, 145 Ann. Intern. Med. 416 (2006); see also Chyvette Williams et al., Differences in Sexual Identity, Risk Practices, and Sex Partners between Bisexual Men and Other Men among a Low-Income Drug-Using Sample, 86 J. Urban Health 93 (2009).

45 Lin Chen et al., Development and Validation of a Risk Score for Predicting Inconsistent Condom Use with Women among Men Who Have Sex with Men and Women, 23 BMC Public Health 734 (2023).

46 Williams, supra note 44.

47 Eileen P. Scully, Sex Differences in HIV Infection, 15 Curr. HIV/AIDS Rep. 136 (2018).

48 Cited in Eshan U. Patel et al., Prevalence and Correlates of *Trichomonas vaginalis* Infection Among Men and Women in the United States, 67 Clin. Infect. Dis. 211, 216 (2018).

49 A. Lennox Thorburn, Alfred Francois Donné, 1801–1878, Discoverer of Trichomonas Vaginalis and of Leukaemia, 50 British J. Venereal Diseases 377 (1974) [https://perma.cc/8EEH-4F79].

50 Patel, supra note 48, at 211.

51 UNC Health News Team, Sickle Cell Disease Continues to Face Underfunding, Lack of Research, UNC School of Medicine, Sept. 11, 2023 [https://perma.cc/ZLY7 -GR7Z].

52 Menezes, supra note 35.

53 J. J. Daly et al., Survival of *Trichomonas vaginalis* in Human Semen, 65 Genitourinary Med. 106 (1989).

54 Menezes, supra note 35.

55 Mohammad K. Parvez & Shama Parveen, Evolution and Emergence of Pathogenic Viruses: Past, Present, and Future, 60 Intervirology 1 (2017).

56 Michael B. A. Oldstone, Viruses, Plagues, and History 8 (2020).

57 Amie J. Eisfeld et al., Pathogenicity and Transmissibility of Bovine H5N1 Influenza Virus, Nature, July 8, 2024.

58 John Cohen, How Long Do Vaccines Last? The Surprising Answers May Help Protect People Longer, Science.org, Apr. 18, 2019 [https://perma.cc/8UEK-PACM].

59 Why Antibiotics Can't Be Used to Treat Viruses, Colds or the Flu, Queensland Gov't: Vaccination & Immunisation Matters, Mar. 29, 2023 [https://perma.cc /HZP5-9XQQ].

60 Antimicrobial Resistance, World Health Organization, Nov. 21, 2023 [https:// perma.cc/Z4T5-2W5G].

61 Mariana Sanches de Mello & Adriana Cristina Oliveira, Overview of the Actions to Combat Bacterial Resistance in Large Hospitals, 29 Rev. Latino-Am. Enfermagem e3407 (2021).

62 Asmat Ali et al., Recent Advancement, Immune Responses, and Mechanism of Action of Various Vaccines Against Intracellular Bacterial Infections, 314 Life Sci. 121332 (2023).

63 Katherine Charlet, The New Killer Pathogens: Countering the Coming Bioweapons Threat, Carnegie Endowment for International Peace, Apr. 17, 2018 [https://perma.cc/P38Y-EQWW].

5. LASTING RELATIONSHIPS

1 Thomas Aquinas, Summa Theologica, Question 81.

2 Aziz Z. Huq & Rebecca Wexler, Digital Privacy for Reproductive Choice in the Post-Roe Era, 98 N.Y.U. L. Rev. 555 (2023).

3 Kashmir Hill, Deleting Your Period Tracker Won't Protect You, N.Y. Times, Jun. 30, 2022.

4 Laura Ceci, Top Global Period Tracker Apps by Downloads 2023, Statista, Mar. 4, 2024 [https://perma.cc/T97G-T4NQ].

5 Danielle Keats Citron, Intimate Privacy in a Post-Roe World, 75 Fla. L. Rev. 1033, 1040 (2023).

6 Kimberly A. Houser & John W. Bagby, Next-Generation Data Governance, 21 Duke L. & Tech. Rev. 61, 63–64 (2024).

7 Catherine Roberts, These Period Tracker Apps Say They Put Privacy First. Here's What We Found, Consumer Reports, May 25, 2022.

8 Citron, supra note 5, at 1042–43.

9 Id. at 1045.

10 Amy Lauren Fairchild et al., Contact Tracing's Long, Turbulent History Holds Lessons for COVID-19, Ohio State News, July 20, 2020 [https://perma.cc/T3UZ -733X].

11 Chamee Yang, Digital Contact Tracing in the Pandemic Cities: Problematizing the Regime of Traceability in South Korea, 9 Big Data & Soc'y 1 (2022).

12 James Gregory, China Deactivates National Covid Tracking App, BBC News, Dec. 12, 2022.

13 Citron, supra note 5, at 1039.

14 Kimya Forouzan et al., The High Toll of U.S. Abortion Bans: Nearly One in Five Patients now Traveling out of State for Abortion Care, Guttmacher, Dec. 7, 2023 [https://perma.cc/662D-TY5T].

15 Huq & Wexler, supra note 2, at 577–78.

16 Matthew Tokson, Government Purchases of Private Data, 59 Wake Forest L. Rev. 269, 274 (2024).

17 Id. at 315.

18 Carolyn Y. Johnson, Even if You've Never Taken a DNA test, a Distant Relative's Could Reveal Your Identity, Wash. Post, Oct. 11, 2018.

19 Herbert B. Dixon Jr., If You Think Your DNA Is Anonymous, Think Again!, 59 Judges' Journal 36, 37 (2020).

20 Caroline Krum & Abhilasha Khatri, Navigating Abortion in Utah: Online Modules, Wait Times and a 72-Hour Hold, Daily Utah Chronicle, May 22, 2024 [https://perma.cc/4ZV7-CE56].

21 Jessica Valenti, Texas is Fabricating Abortion Data, Substack, May 4, 2023 [https://perma.cc/RR8J-7B2W].

22 Lehr v. Robertson, 463 U.S. 248 (1983).

23 Quoted in Margaret Talbot, Amy Coney Barrett's Long Game, New Yorker, Feb. 7, 2002.

24 Shoshanna Ehrlich, Safe Haven Laws Were Never Supposed to Be an Alternative to Abortion, Ms., Aug. 17, 2022; Carol Sanger, Infant Safe Haven Laws: Legislating in the Culture of Life, 106 Colum. L. Rev. 753, 829 (2006); Malinda L. Seymore, Social Costs of Dobbs' Pro-Adoption Agenda, 57 UC Davis L. Rev. 503, 506–7 (2023).

25 Kolby Brock, A Study of Safe Haven Baby Laws in the United States: One Life Saved or Too Many Unknowns to Evaluate? Ohio Wesleyan University (2023) [https://digitalcommons.owu.edu/honors/6].

26 Tonya L. Brito, The Child Support Debt Bubble, 9 UC Irvine L. Rev. 953, 955 (2019).

27 Vincent R. Johnson & Claire G. Hargrove, The Tort Duty of Parents to Protect Minor Children, 51 Vill. L. Rev. 311, 313–14 (2006).

28 Elizabeth G. Porter, Tort Liability in the Age of the Helicopter Parent, 64 Ala. L. Rev. 533, 586 (2013).

29 Seymore, supra note 24, at 510.

30 Id. at 536.

31 Id. at 535–36.

32 David Benatar, Why It Is Better Never to Come into Existence, 34 Am. Phil. Q. 345, 351 (1997).

33 Natalie Morton & Sarah Bell, I Fathered 800 Children, Claims Sperm Donor, BBC .com, Jan. 13, 2016.

34 Natasha Kirtchuk, "The Sperminator": Man Fathers Nearly 140 Kids Through Sperm Donations, i24news.tv, Apr. 10, 2023 [www.i24news.tv/en/news /international/1681157106-the-sperminator-man-fathers-nearly-140-kids-through -sperm-donations].

35 Simon Usborne, "I Thought—Who Will Remember Me?": The Man Who Fathered 200 Children, Guardian, Nov. 24, 2018.

36 Ewan Mowat & Jake Meeus-Jones, Sperm Donor with Dozens of Children Says It's "Charity Work" After Visiting Scottish Brood, Daily Record, Feb. 26, 2024 [https://perma.cc/XT6H-QXD4].

37 Michael J. Higdon, Fatherhood by Conscription: Nonconsensual Insemination and the Duty of Child Support, 46 Ga. L. Rev. 407, 409–11 (2012).

38 S.F. v. State ex rel. T.M., 695 So. 2d 1186, 1187 (Ala. Civ. App. 1996).

39 Cnty. of San Luis Obispo v. Nathaniel J., 57 Cal. Rptr. 2d 843, 843 (Ct. App. 1996).

40 State v. Frisard, 694 So. 2d 1032, 1035 (La. App. 1997).

41 Dubay v. Wells, 442 F. Supp 2d 404, 406 (E.D. Mich, 2006).

42 In re Paternity of M.F., 938 N.E. 2d 1256 (Ind. App. 2010).

43 Samuel L. Dickman et al., Rape-Related Pregnancies in the 14 U.S. States with Total Abortion Bans, 184 JAMA Intern. Med. 330 (2024).

44 Bobbitt v. Eizenga, 715 S.E.2d 613 (N.C. App. 2011); 223 N.C. App. 210 (2012); 238 N.C. App. 362 (2014).

45 Michaela Haas, When Your Rapist Demands Custody, Mother Jones, Sept.–Oct. 2019.

46 Analyn Megison, My Rapist Fought for Custody of My Daughter. States Can't Keep Survivors Tied to Rapists, USA Today, June 20, 2019 [www.usatoday.com /story/opinion/voices/2019/06/19/abortion-laws-bans-rape-parental-rights -column/1432450001/].

47 Daniella Silva, Louisiana Woman Says Her Rapist Was Given Custody of Her Child in Ongoing Court Dispute, NBC News, June 17, 2022.

48 Uniform Parentage Act § 614(b).

49 Eliza Shapiro & Brian M. Rosenthal, In Hasidic Enclaves, Failing Private Schools Flush with Public Money, N.Y. Times, Sept. 12, 2022; Eliza Shapiro, Why Some Hasidic Children Can't Leave Failing Schools, N.Y. Times, June 20, 2023.

50 Julie F. Kay, Prioritizing Children's Educational Interests when One Parent Leaves an Ultra-Orthodox Community, 57 Fam. L.Q. 231, 249–50 (2024).

6. PLEASURES AND SATISFACTIONS OF SEMEN ON MUCOSA

1 Megan Brenan, Americans' Preference for Larger Families Highest Since 1971, Gallup News, Sept. 25, 2023 [https://perma.cc/VF2Y-4R82].

2 Gladys M. Martinez & Kimberly Daniels, Fertility of Men and Women Aged 15–49 in the United States: National Survey of Family Growth, 2015–2019, Jan. 10, 2023 [https://perma.cc/59E6-UW5R].

3 Jenna Grundström et al., Reciprocal Associations Between Parenthood and Mental Well-Being—A Prospective Analysis from Age 16 to 52 Years, 43 Curr. Psychol. 2238, 2244 (2023); Kei M. Nomaguchi & Melissa A. Milkie, Costs and Rewards of Children: The Effects of Becoming a Parent on Adult Lives, 65 J. Marriage & Family 356 (2004).

4 S. Katherine Nelson-Coffey et al., Parenthood Is Associated with Greater Well-Being for Fathers than Mothers, 45 Pers. Soc. Psychol. Bull. 1378 (2019).

5 Harmeet Kaur, Why More Women Are Choosing Not to Have Kids, CNN.com, Sept. 25, 2023 [www.cnn.com/us/childfree-by-choice-women-birth-rate-decline -cec/index.html; https://perma.cc/DJ87-YL43].

6 Lauren Leader, The End of Roe Is Having a Chilling Effect on Pregnancy, Politico, Sept. 13, 2023 [https://perma.cc/CW2N-8E7U].

7 Epicurus, Letters, Principal Doctrines, and Vatican Sayings 56 (Russell M. Geer trans., 1964).

8 American Psychological Association, "Orgasm," Dictionary of Pleasure [https:// perma.cc/W4KF-SSBX].

9 Gert Holstege et al., Brain Activation During Human Male Ejaculation, 23 J. Neurosci. 9185 (2003).

10 My thanks to Mihalis Diamantis for sharing his reflections on this point.

11 Andrea Burri et al., The Importance of Male Ejaculation for Female Sexual Satisfaction and Function, 15 J. Sex. Med. 1600 (2018).

12 Quoted in Tiffany Sostar & Rebecca Sullivan, The Money Shot in Feminist Queer and Mainstream Pornographies, in The Routledge Companion to Global Popular Culture 197, 197 (Toby Miller ed., 2017).

13 Id., see also Chauntelle Anne Tibbals, From the Devil in Miss Jones to DMJ6: Power, Inequality, and Consistency in the Content of U.S. Adult Films, 13 Sexualities 625 (2010).

14 Jesse Bering, Why Is the Penis Shaped Like That? 38 (2012).

15 The studies are published in Rebecca Burch & Gordon G. Gallup Jr., The Psychobiology of Human Semen, in Female Infidelity and Paternal Uncertainty 141 (Steven M. Platek & Todd K. Shackelford eds., 2006) and Gordon G. Gallup Jr. et al., Does Semen Have Antidepressant Properties?, 31 Arch. Sex. Behav. 289, 293 (2002).

16 Jesse Bering, An Ode to the Many Evolved Virtues of Human Semen, Sci. Am., Sept. 23, 2010 [https://perma.cc/NSH7-MGFC].

17 Bering, supra note 14, at 38–39.

18 Jin-Wei Hou et al., Impact of Sexual Intercourse on Frozen-Thawed Embryo Transfer Outcomes: A Randomized Controlled Trial, 8 Contraception and Reproductive Medicine 19 (2023).

19 Frank Nawroth & Michael von Wollf, Seminal Plasma Activity to Improve Implantation in In Vitro Fertilization—How Can It Be Used in Daily Practice?, 9 Front. Endocrinol. 208 (2018).

20 Audrey F. Saftlas et al., Cumulative Exposure to Paternal Seminal Fluid Prior to Conception and Subsequent Risk of Preeclampsia, 101 J. Reprod. Immunol. 104 (2014).

21 Samantha Cole, "Pearl" Necklaces: The People Getting Jewelry Made from Semen, Vice.com, Aug. 30, 2022 [https://perma.cc/63XV-RQVH].

22 Keith Jeffery, MI6: The History of the Secret Intelligence Service 1909–1949 at 66 (2010).

23 See Pew Charitable Trusts, The Long-Term Decline in Fertility—and What It Means for State Budgets, Issue Brief, Dec. 5, 2022, (noting that rating agencies take birth rates into account when evaluating state-level creditworthiness) [https://perma.cc/F564-MZZB].

24 Nellie Bowles, The Sperm Kings Have a Problem: Too Much Demand, N.Y. Times, Jan. 8, 2021.

25 Amanda Smith, I'm a Queer Woman, and I'm Grieving the Ease of Becoming a Parent So Many People Take for Granted, Parents, Oct. 31, 2022 [https://perma.cc/5CCE-SGHE].

26 Abigail Covington, A Good Sperm Donor Is Hard to Find, Esquire, July 14, 2023.

27 Sophie Strosberg, Fertility Treatment Cost Too Much So I Had Sex with a Friend, Parents, Oct. 26, 2023 [https://perma.cc/KN72-E2QN].

28 Amber Ferguson, America Has a Black Sperm Donor Shortage. Black Women are Paying the Price, Wash. Post, Oct. 20, 2022.

29 Id.

30 Amanda Lee Myers & Ariana Triggs, Black Women Looking for Black Sperm Donors Struggle with Harsh Reality of Shortage, USA Today, May 21, 2023.

31 Cynthia R. Greenlee, "I Couldn't Believe This Act of Kindness": How Black Women Trying to Get Pregnant Create Their Own Healthcare Networks, Guardian, Dec. 11, 2023.

32 Id.

33 Vasanti Jadva et al., Why Search for a Sperm Donor Online? The Experiences of Women Searching for and Contacting Sperm Donors on the Internet, 21 Hum. Fertil. 112, 112 (2017).

34 Food and Drug Administration, What You Should Know—Reproductive Tissue Donation, Nov. 5, 2010 [https://perma.cc/DU24-ZQSA].

35 Ercolie Bossema et al., An Inventory of Reasons for Sperm Donation in Formal versus Informal Settings, 17 Hum. Fertil. 21 (2014).

36 Susanna Graham, A Comparison of the Characteristics, Motivations, Preferences and Expectations of Men Donating Sperm Online or Through a Sperm Bank, 34 Hum. Reprod. 2208 (2019).

37 Jacqueline M. Acker, The Case for an Unregulated Private Sperm Donation Market, 20 UCLA Women's L. J. 1, 3 (2012).

38 Naomi Cahn & Sonia Suter, Sperm Donation Is Largely Unregulated, but That Could Soon Change as Lawsuits Multiply, The Conversation, Jan. 18, 2022 [https://perma.cc/6NAJ-2VAK]; April Schweitzer & Alexandra Busto, Increasing Regulation of Reproductive Tissue Banks, Nixon Peabody, May 18, 2023 [https://perma.cc/GX3Q-8KKD].

39 Liz Essley Whyte & Amy Dockser Marcus, FDA to Drop Ban on Sperm Donations from Gay and Bisexual Men, Wall St. J., Apr. 4, 2024.

40 Acker, supra note 37, at 25.

41 Id. at 25–26.

7. WATER MANAGEMENT INFORMS SEMEN MANAGEMENT

1 Anne Sexton, "To a Friend Whose Work Has Come to Triumph," in The Complete Poems 53 (1999).

2 Rachel Bernstein & Anthony Carpi, Properties of Liquids: Intermolecular Forces, Cohesion, Adhesion, and Viscosity, Visionlearning [https://perma.cc/4F5W-VTVL].

3 Trevor Turpin, Dam 19 (2008).

4 Henri Boyé & Michel de Vivo, The Environmental and Social Acceptability of Dams, 14 The Journal of Field Actions: Field Actions Science Reports 32 (2016) [https://perma.cc/783J-ZTVL].

5 Adrienne LaFrance, A Brief History of Levees, Atlantic, Aug 31, 2015.

6 44 C.F.R. § 59.1.

7 Robert Jütte, Contraception: A History 45 (2008).

8 Fahd Khan et al., The Story of the Condom, 29 Indian J. Urol. 12 (2013).

9 Elizabeth Boskey, Polyisoprene Condoms for People with Latex Allergies, VeryWellHealth, June 19, 2024 [www.verywellhealth.com/polyisoprene-condoms -for-people-with-latex-allergies-3132698].

10 Mildred S. Dresselhaus & Paulo T. Araujo, Perspectives on the 2010 Nobel Prize in Physics for Graphene, 4 ACS Nano 6297 (2010).

11 Y. S. Marfatia et al., Condoms: Past, Present, and Future, 36 Indian J. Sex. Transm. Dis. AIDS 133, 137–38 (2015).

12 Aine Collier, The Humble Little Condom: A History 9 (2007).

13 Nicholas Pinter, The Problem with Levees, Sci. Am. Blog, Aug. 1, 2019.

14 Louis P. Cain, Raising and Watering a City: Ellis Sylvester Chesbrough and Chicago's First Sanitation System, 13 Tech. & Culture 363 (1972).

15 Lauren Nowacki, 8 Ideas to Drain Water away from Your House, Rocket Homes blog, Dec. 28, 2023 [www.rockethomes.com/blog/homeowner-tips/how-to-divert -water-away-from-your-home].

16 Rachel K. Jones et al., Better than Nothing or Savvy Risk Reduction Practice? The Importance of Withdrawal, 79 Contraception 407 (2009).

17 Matthew Roberts & Keith Jarvi, Steps in the Investigation and Management of Low Semen Volume in the Infertile Man, 3 J. Can. Urol. Assoc. 479, 479 (2009).

18 Jan Gerris, Methods of Semen Collection Not Based on Masturbation or Surgical Sperm Retrieval, 5 Hum. Reprod. Update 211, 212 (1999).

19 Dua for Rain, My Islam [https://perma.cc/MSJ4-EGDC]; A Prayer for Rain, Catholic Rural Life, June 20, 2023 [https://catholicrurallife.org/a-prayer-for-rain /#:~:text=Look%20on%20our%20dry%20hills,Amen; https://perma.cc/S4C4 -UYBJ].

20 Emilio Morenatti, Pray for Rain: Spanish Farmers Hold Unique Mass Amid Drought, AP News, Mar. 26, 2023.

21 Janet Pelly, Does Cloud Seeding Really work?, Chemical & Engineering News, May 30, 2016 [https://perma.cc/M46C-P462].

22 Chelsea Harvey, Eight States Are Seeding Clouts to Overcome Megadrought, Sci. Am. Blog, Mar. 16, 2021 [www.scientificamerican.com/article/eight-states-are -seeding-clouds-to-overcome-megadrought/].

23 Alejandra Borunda, Wildfire Smoke Is Transforming Clouds, Making Rainfall Less Likely, National Geographic, Aug. 23, 2021 [https://perma.cc/4MU7-FTTA].

24 NASA Earth Observatory, The Impact of Urban Pollution on Rain, Dec. 11, 2006 [https://perma.cc/43FN-NPRX].

25 Kelly McSweeney, Making It Rain: The Science of Weather Manipulation, Now, Aug. 14, 2020 [https://perma.cc/LLF8-YNEF].

26 Yann Arthus-Bertrand, On Water, European Investment Bank, Sept. 6, 2019 [https://perma.cc/9WBS-KSHZ].

27 R. J. Forbes, Short History of the Art of Distillation 14 (1970) (quoting Aristotle, Meterologica).

28 Maryam Zafer et al., Effectiveness of Semen Washing to Prevent Human Immunodeficiency Virus (HIV) Transmission and Assist Pregnancy in HIV-Discordant Couples: A Systematic Review and Meta-Analysis, 105 Fertility & Sterility 645 (2016).

29 Sedigheh Ahmadi et al., Antioxidant Supplements and Semen Parameters: An Evidence Based Review, 14 Int. J. Reprod. BioMed. 729 (2016).

30 National Oceanic and Atmospheric Administration, Point vs. Non-Point Water Pollution: What's the Difference?, Nov. 15, 2016 [https://perma.cc/6XA2-SJ2C].

31 33 U.S.C. § 1362(6).

32 Laura H. Bachmann et al., CDC Clinical Guidelines on the Use of Doxycycline Postexposure Prophylaxis for Bacterial Sexually Transmitted Infection Prevention, 73 Morb. Mortal. Wkly. Rep. No. 2, June 6, 2024, at 3 [https://perma.cc/MY44-UELV].

33 Laura López González, Don't Take Chances: Why Doxycycline is a Great Bet Against STIs, UCSF News, July 13, 2023 [https://perma.cc/U5R7-V98Y].

8. REGULATING SEMEN

1 Ashlee Valentine, Car Ownership Statistics 2024, Forbes, Mar. 28, 2024 [www.forbes.com/advisor/car-insurance/car-ownership-statistics/]; Ronald Montoya, What Is the Percentage of Electric Cars in the U.S.?, Edmunds, Jan. 12, 2024 [www.edmunds.com/electric-car/articles/percentage-of-electric-cars-in-us.html].

2 15 U.S.C. § 1261(f)(1)(A).

3 15 U.S.C. § 1261(g).

4 Available at Federal Hazardous Substances Act (FHSA) Requirements [https://perma.cc/DT73-AXGQ].

5 U.S. Food & Drug Administration, Personal Protective Equipment for Infection Control, Feb. 10, 2020 [https://perma.cc/D23X-CF2Z].

6 29 C.F.R. § 1910.133(a).

7 29 C.F.R. § 1926.95(a).

8 40 C.F.R. § 260.10.

9 CP Lab Safety, Secondary Containment and Container Regulations [https://perma.cc/YH42-CPVK].

10 Id.

11 John Stover & Yu Teng, The Impact of Condom Use on the HIV Epidemic, Gates Open Research, Mar. 18, 2022 [https://perma.cc/HNE5-W7YK].

12 Id.

13 Diane B. Francis et al., Perceptions of a Campus-Wide Condom Distribution Scheme: An Exploratory Study, 75 Health Educ. J. 998 (2016).

14 Where Can I Get Free Condoms in My State?, GoodRx, July 23, 2024 [https://perma.cc/E2Y5-WQCK].

15 Pam Belluck, Condom Contest Produces 812 Ideas for Improvement, N.Y. Times, Nov. 20, 2013.

16 Sarah K. Calabrese et al., HIV Preexposure Prophylaxis and Condomless Sex: Disentangling Personal Values from Public Health Priorities, 107 Am. J. Pub. Health 1572, 1572 (2017).

17 40 C.F.R. § 264.175.

18 Does Secondary Containment Have Your Head Spinning, New Pig [https://perma.cc/9CB8-CZF7].

19 29 C.F.R. § 1910.1030.

20 29 C.F.R. § 1910.1450.

21 40 C.F.R. § 170.160.

22 Richard C. Dart et al., Expert Consensus Guidelines for Stocking of Antidotes in Hospitals That Provide Emergency Care, 71 Ann. Emerg. Med. 314, 318–19 (2018).

23 Quoted in Philippe Grandjean, Paracelsus Revisited: The Dose Concept in a Complex World, 119 Basic Clin. Pharmacol Toxicol. 126, 126 (2016).

24 PrEP vs. PEP, National Institutes of Health [https://perma.cc/2HBH-9QZ5].

25 Guneet Kaur et al., "The Difference Between Plan B and ella®? They're Basically the Same Thing": Results from a Mystery Client Study, 8 Pharmacy (Basel) 77 (2020).

26 18 U.S.C. § 1461.

27 Tina Smith, I Hope to Repeal an Arcane Law That Could Be Misused to Ban Abortion Nationwide, N.Y. Times, Apr. 2, 2024.

28 Elizabeth Nash & Isabel Guarnieri, Eight Ways State Policymakers Can Protect and Expand Abortion Rights and Access in 2023, Guttmacher Institute, Jan. 2023 [https://perma.cc/5DDF-59FP].

29 Jon King, Whitmer Talks Economic Proposals, Abortion Rights and Trump at Detroit Conference, Mich. Advance, June 13, 2024 [https://perma.cc/BW2U-32PX].

30 Nash & Guarnieri, supra note 28.

31 See Richard B. Katskee, Paying for Praying: What's Wrong with the Faith-Based Initiative?, Human Rights, Summer 2006, at 4.

32 United States v. Kennerley, 209 F. 119, 120–21 (S.D.N.Y. 1913).

33 Centers for Disease Control, Incidence, Prevalence, and Cost of Sexually Transmitted Infections in the United States: Fact Sheet, Mar. 8, 2024 [https://perma.cc/34LC-GLSB].

34 Brooke D'Amore Bradley, Sex Education After Dobbs: A Case for Comprehensive Sex Education, 39 Berkeley J. Gender L. & Justice 121, 132–34 (2024).

35 World Health Organization, School Health Education to Prevent AIDS and STD: A Resource Package for Curriculum Planners: Teachers' Guide 38 (1994) (hereinafter Resource Package).

36 Id. at 23, 24.

37 Id. at 52, 24.

38 Id. at 61.

39 United Nations Educational, Scientific, and Cultural Organization, International Technical Guidance on Sexuality Education: An Evidence-Informed Approach 91 (rev. ed. 2018) (hereinafter International Technical Guidance).

40 Id. at 56.

41 Resource Package, supra note 35, at 26, 32.

42 Id. at 52–53.

43 International Technical Guidance, supra note 39, at 22–23, 72, 75.

44 Kayla Lowe, STIs, Stay Education Ready, AllaccessEKY.org, Sept. 29, 2020 [www .allacceseky.org/blog/2020/9/29/stis-stay-education-ready; https://perma.cc /5K4E-C7L2].

45 International Technical Guidance, supra note 39, at 47.

46 Id. at 63.

47 Id. at 75.

48 Leslie M. Kantor & Laura Lindberg, Pleasure and Sex Education: The Need for Broadening Both Content and Measurement, 110 Am. J. Pub. Health 145–48 (2020).

49 The Pleasure Principles, The Pleasure Project [https://thepleasureproject.org/the -pleasure-principles/].

50 Michael Stellefson et al., Evolving Role of Social Media in Health Promotion: Updated Responsibilities for Health Education Specialists, 17 Int. J. Environ. Res. Public Health 1153 (2020).

51 Ani Petrosyan, Adult Internet Usage Penetration in the United States from 2000 to 2023, by Gender, Statista, Mar. 1, 2024 [https://perma.cc/manage/create?folder =182975].

52 Casey Dluhos-Sebesto et al., Women's Health Information Survey: Common Health Concerns and Trusted Sources of Health Information Among Different Populations of Female Patients, 2 Women's Health Reports (New Rochelle, N.Y.) 173 (2021) [https://perma.cc/VPL8-MNMK].

53 21 C.F.R. § 101.7.

54 21 C.F.R. § 101.15 (a) (b).

55 21 C.F.R. § 101.3.

56 21 C.F.R. § 101.14.

57 21 C.F.R. § 101.9.

58 21 C.F.R. § 201.15.

59 21 C.F.R. § 201.51.

60 21 C.F.R. § 201.50.

61 21 C.F.R. § 201.5.

62 21 C.F.R. § 701.12 (location of manufacturer); 21 C.F.R. § 701.3 (ingredients).

63 29 C.F.R. § 1910.145.

64 16 C.F.R. § 1500.121.

65 16 C.F.R. § 1402.4.

66 Frequently Asked Questions, Regulations.gov [https://perma.cc/MW3G-7E4B].

67 U.S. Gov't Publ'n Off., Federal Register, GovInfo [https://perma.cc/manage/create ?folder=182975].

68 Elizabeth G. Porter & Kathryn A. Watts, Visual Rulemaking, 91 N.Y.U. L. Rev.
    1183 (2016); Elizabeth Porter & Kathryn Watts, Visual Regulation—and Visual
    Deregulation, Yale J. Regul.: Notice & Comment, Jan. 29, 2018 [https://perma.cc
    /QU3M-C5S4].

69 See id. (referencing the Obama White House, President Obama on Amer-
    ica's Clean Power Plan, YouTube, Aug. 2, 2015 [www.youtube.com/watch?v
    =uYXyYFzP4Lc]).

70 Michael Herz, Administrative Braggadocio, Yale J. Regul.: Notice & Comment,
    Jan. 30, 2018 [https://perma.cc/manage/create?folder=182975].

71 Plain Language Action and Information Network, Plain Language Guidelines
    [https://perma.cc/MH3F-2CNC].

72 The CDC Clear Communication Index: Clear Communication Index User Guide,
    Nov. 19, 2020 [https://perma.cc/86QV-8GTW].

73 Centers for Disease Control, National Action Plan to Improve Health Literacy
    [https://perma.cc/C67C-BKRZ].

74 Office of the Vice President, No Gobbledygook Award 1 [https://perma.cc/784W
    -WKHF].

INDEX

ABOUT THE AUTHOR

ANITA BERNSTEIN is Anita and Stuart Subotnick Professor of Law at Brooklyn Law School. Her books include *The Common Law Inside the Female Body*, *Marriage Proposals: Questioning a Legal Status*, and multiple editions of *Questions and Answers: Torts*.